Truth in Aquinas

A wide-ranging and unusually accurate account of Aquinas on truth, human understanding and ontology that responds to current philosophical and theological concerns . . . .
John Inglis, Associate Professor of Philosophy, University of Dayton

In this book, Milbank and Pickstock present a wholesale re-evaluation of the thought of Thomas Aquinas. They claim, against many received readings, that Aquinas's philosophical account of truth is also an entirely theological one. His understanding of truth as *adequatio* is shown to be inseparable from his metaphysical and doctrinal treatment of the participation of creatures in God as *esse*; from his theory of the convertibility of the transcendentals as mediated by the transcendental 'beauty'; and from his Christology and theology of the Eucharist. This vision is remote from the assumptions undergirding modern accounts of truth as correspondence or coherence or redundancy. Since these accounts are all in crisis, Milbank and Pickstock ask whether Aquinas's theological framework is not essential to the affirmation of the reality of truth as such.

Compelling and challenging, *Truth in Aquinas* develops further the innovative theological project heralded by the publication of the seminal *Radical Orthodoxy* (Routledge, 1999).

John Milbank is the Frances Myers Ball Professor of Philosophical Theology at the University of Virginia. His previous publications include *Theology and Social Theory* and *The Word Made Strange*. **Catherine Pickstock** is a Lecturer in Philosophy of Religion at the University of Cambridge, and a Fellow of Emmanuel College, Cambridge. Her previous publications include *After Writing: On the Liturgical Consummation of Philosophy*. They are the editors, with Graham Ward, of Routledge's *Radical Orthodoxy* series.

Truth in Aquinas

John Milbank and Catherine Pickstock

London and New York

First published 2001
by Routledge
11 New Fetter Lane, London EC4P 4EE

Simultaneously published in the USA and Canada
by Routledge
29 West 35th Street, New York, NY 10001

Routledge is an imprint of the Taylor & Francis Group

© 2001 John Milbank and Catherine Pickstock

Typeset in Times by Exe Valley Dataset Ltd, Exeter
Printed and bound in Great Britain by
Clays Ltd, St Ives plc

British Library Cataloguing in Publication Data
A catalogue record for this book is available
from the British Library

Library of Congress Cataloging in Publication Data
A catalogue record for this book has been requested

ISBN 0–415–23334–8 (hbk)
ISBN 0–415–23335–6 (pbk)

For Fergus Kerr O.P.

Truth the ancient types fulfilling

St Thomas Aquinas
Ecce! Panis Angelorum

Contents

Preface

One can detect four main attitudes toward truth in contemporary thought. The first is a doubt as to the possibility of truth altogether; the second is a confinement of truth to practice rather than theory; the third, a confinement of truth to theory rather than practice, but a theory so esoteric that only a tiny minority is privy to it; the fourth promotes, in the face of the first attitude, a fideistic affirmation of some religious truth or other.

In the case of the denial of the possibility of truth, this can take many different forms. Sometimes truth is regarded as an unnecessary term because it is held to denote simply an affirmation of what is the case. But if this 'what is the case' is not held to be true, then it reduces to what appears to be the case, or is held to be the case for certain practical purposes. Sometimes, again, truth is regarded as strictly relative to a certain set of cultural assumptions, and where the latter is regarded as arbitrary, then relativism or conventionalism ensues, with the consequence that there is no truth in any absolute sense. Finally, the same approach can receive an ontological extension, in such a way that even natural arrangements in time are regarded as aleatory. There may be temporary truths of fact, in the sense of contingent events of relation between things, including a relation to human understanding, but these facts do not arise according to truth in the sense of a coherent logic. For this position, the only truth that remains is the truth of the aleatory itself, which is enthroned as a positive value.

For this first position, then, either truth is inaccessible, or else reality itself is not amenable to notions of truth. In the latter case, one has a full theoretical nihilism, whilst in the former case, one has a kind of practical nihilism.

The second position is an elaboration upon one version of the first. It holds that if truth as correspondence to reality is either unavailable or meaningless, then this is no cause for despair, because truth belongs much more naturally to practical rather than theoretical activity. Sufficient truth for human purposes is available in the successful attainment of humanly sought ends. Such attainment discloses to us a certain reality outside of which lies only vain speculation. However, this attitude drains truth of its connotations of the indefeasible, and of its sense of value. The first consequence follows, because if human achievement provides us no clue as to what is ultimately the case, then it is no more than a fleeting and contingent set of contrived circumstances. Such circumstances may be true for a time, as truths of factual occurrence, but can in the end prove not true at all. For while, certainly, human access to truth can only be time-bound, if truth has no connotations of the eternal and abiding, then it is hard to see why it is called truth at all.

The second consequence follows because if the only measure of the truth of a practice is its success, then anything that works is regarded as just as good as anything else, so long as it works also, without regard for any judgement as to the inherent desirability of what has been constructed. In this fashion, truth becomes detached from the good. Furthermore, the criterion of success ushers in a bad infinite, for when is one to decree that a process has reached its ripeness? The boundaries of truth so understood perpetually recede, and can only halt by dint of the imposition of an arbitrary assertion of will. So here again a truth confined to time proves elusive within time.

The third position, by contrast, possesses an unbounded confidence not just in the truth of natural science, but in its ability to provide a true ontology rather than merely a very limited disclosure of certain aspects of reality lending themselves to manipulation and prediction (as the present authors would rather assume). Here the truth of science resides not merely in the success of its operations, as for the second position above, but rather in what those operations are held to reveal. In this way, truth is here an entirely theoretical matter and this is all the more the case because truth as a property of the way things are is seen to be entirely indifferent to the goodness of things and to their beauty and value for human beings.

It is characteristic of modern natural science that it will hold something to be true which is extremely counter-intuitive and often remote from what people think to be the case, and indeed from what they are capable of understanding. This imposes a gulf between the everyday world and the ironic gaze of the scientific sage from the height of his privileged insight. Truth, therefore, of the most ultimate kind has here become the property of an élite, by the same token that it is freed from its traditional convertibility with the good and the beautiful. Increasingly, this cold truth is regarded as the only truth, and society, to the detriment of democracy, allows its guardians to take vital decisions which the rest of us can scarcely comprehend.

The fourth position can be regarded as essentially reactive. In the face of secular scepticism, pragmatism and positivism, many religious people tend to take refuge in the notion that there is nonetheless another source of truth enshrined in certain texts, practices and traditions. Ironically, for these texts, practices and traditions to acquire absolute authority outside the workings of human reason, they have to be regarded positivistically, in a fashion which mimics scientific positivism itself. The irrational strangely colludes with the most vigorously reduced rationalism, and often one finds that various funda-mentalisms and fideisms are able happily to coexist with, and even to re-inforce, the technoscientific capitalism of our day.

Against the background of the above delineated crisis of truth, the present authors have undertaken a new reading of Aquinas's understanding of truth. We have turned to Aquinas because, in his writings, one can discover an entirely different approach to truth which allows one, first of all, to recover correspondence without a sense of redundancy; secondly, to regard truth as at once theoretical and practical; thirdly, to demonstrate that all truth is a matter of faith as well as reason, and vice versa; and, fourthly, to indicate that truth is immediately accessible to the simplest apprehension, and yet amenable to profound learned elaboration.

The first chapter, 'Truth and correspondence', seeks to show that the notion of truth as correspondence is in crisis only because it is taken in an epistemological rather than ontological sense. Usually Aquinas himself has been read anachronistically according to the canons of epistemology, and read this way, he has nothing to offer contemporary thought. However, we seek to show that in Aquinas, correspondence indicates a real ontological proportion between being and intelligence in a perspective where these are regarded as transcendentally convertible. For Aquinas, within the human modus, there is a distinction between intelligence and being, and yet also an unfathomable link between them which we dimly discern according to an act of aesthetic judgement. This perspective ensures that truth does not simply reduce to our mode of apprehension of what is the case, as is bound to occur on the epistemological model for which the intellect is accorded no necessary ontological dignity, but is merely supposed to mirror a reality itself indifferent to being comprehended. This possibility of retrieving truth as correspondence, and therefore truth itself in a strong sense, is however indissociably linked with Aquinas's theology and metaphysics of participation.

In the second chapter, it will be shown how Aquinas's general theory of truth applies both to his understanding of the operation of reason and to the operation of faith. We will argue that, contrary to usual readings, reason and faith in Aquinas represent only different degrees of intensity of participation in the divine light of illumination and different measures of absolute vision. And, furthermore, that reason itself requires faith because it already presupposes the operation of grace, while, inversely, faith still demands discursive argumentation and is only higher than reason because it enjoys a deeper participation in the divine reason which is direct intuition or pure intellectual vision. In this way, Aquinas offers no support to those who claim that there can be a philosophical approach to God independent of theology, but neither, on the other hand, does he offer support to those who demand a confinement to Biblical revelation independent of the Greek legacy of metaphysical reflection. Rather, it will be shown that, for Aquinas, revealed theology supplements metaphysics with history and requires a completion of the theoretical ascent to truth with a meeting of the divine descent in liturgical practice.

The commencement of this descent is at the Incarnation. In the third chapter, it will be shown not only how, for Aquinas, truth is only restored for fallen men by the hypostatic union, but also how this restoration involves certain ontological revisions in excess of their occasion: namely the conjoining of an ontic event with *esse ipsum* and a kenotic elevation of the sensory over the intellectual, and more specifically the sensory as touch. In Christ, this new sensorial access to truth is something one both contemplates and reproduces through the enactment of the sacraments.

This double relation to Christ corresponds to the way in which, for Aquinas, truth in God is both something envisaged and something actively performed by the Father in the Logos. Because we participate in this truth, for us also it is something that we see as a reflection of the invisible in the visible, and, at same time, something that we construct, as it were unwittingly, through our artistic and liturgical attempts to praise the divine. Seeing and making are combined in the mutuality of *touch* which is most intensely taste; and the Eucharist, as foretaste of our beatitude, newly discloses to us that this supreme intuition is itself also a 'touching'.

In the fourth chapter, the nature of this liturgical completion of truth is elaborated. Here it will be shown how we have a certain anticipation of the beatific vision in this life because God descends in the Incarnation and its perpetuation in the Eucharist to our immediate sensory awareness, wherein alone we enjoy intuitive understanding. In this fashion, it is the lower reason which is required to educate our higher reason, although this new priority of the sensory is accompanied by a linguistic and emotional play between presence and absence. For Aquinas's Catholic position, the most abstruse intellectual reflection on truth passes into the more profound and ineffable apprehension of truth in the Eucharist. In this way, there is no gulf for him between the most elite and the most common.

Many people have contributed to the formation of this book, but we would like in particular to thank Fergus Kerr O.P., John Montag S.J., and the Revd Simon Oliver. We gratefully acknowledge permission given to reprint earlier versions of its chapters. The first chapter, by Catherine Pickstock, was delivered as the Annual Aquinas Lecture 1999 in Blackfriars, Oxford, and was first published as 'Imitating God: The Truth of Things According to Thomas Aquinas' in *New Blackfriars* (July 2000). The authors thank Fergus Kerr O.P. for permission granted. The second chapter, by John Milbank, was first published as 'Intensities', in *Modern Theology* (October 1999). The third chapter is by both authors, and is hitherto unpublished. The fourth chapter, by Catherine Pickstock, was first delivered at the Homeland conference on the Eucharist held at Duke University 1998, and was published as 'Thomas Aquinas and the Quest for the Eucharist' in *Modern Theology* (April 1999). The authors thank the editors of that journal. There are five institutions to which the authors owe their gratitude: the Department of Religious Studies at the University of Virginia, the Faculty of Divinity, Cambridge University, Peterhouse, Cambridge, Emmanuel College, Cambridge, and the British Academy which awarded Catherine Pickstock a postdoctoral fellowship.

A.J.M. and C.J.C.P.

1   Truth and correspondence

I

How should one respond to the death of realism, the death of the idea that thoughts in our minds can represent to us the way things actually are in the world? For such a death is widely proclaimed by contemporary philosophers.

In summary, they argue that since we only have access to the world via knowledge, it is impossible to check knowledge against the world in order to see if it corresponds with it. This is a powerful and perhaps unanswerable contention, and yet if we accept it, it seems to follow that there can be no such thing as truth at all.

In what follows, however, we wish to argue that one need not accept these essentially secular conclusions. Rather, we want to suggest that a reconsideration of Aquinas can help us to meet the problems arising from the seeming insupportability of a correspondence theory of truth. This might appear to be an inquiry doomed from the outset, since Aquinas is himself a proponent of just such a theory. However, we will try to show why he is not quite the correspondence theorist he is sometimes taken to be, but rather something much more interesting: a theological theorist of truth who challenges in advance the assumptions of modern epistemologists at a level they do not even imagine.

First, however, let us see what sorts of difficulties arise if one rejects correspondence altogether. Bruce Marshall has argued that one need not fear suspicion of correspondence, for, first of all, the death of realism need not mean an out-and-out embrace of anti-realism, and, secondly, theology introduces a specifically Christological mode of correspondence according to which, Christ the God-man is true in his imitation of the life of the eternal Trinity.[1] In the first case, according to Marshall, there is in fact an alternative to anti-realism which does not make appeal to correspondence. Marshall furnishes us with a variety of reasons why, for the purposes of one's day-to-day existence, one should turn to a 'disquotational' theory of truth, which is not anti-realist, although it involves no notion of correspondence, as espoused by Alfred Tarski and later Donald Davidson. This, he claims, is the best available philosophical – though not theological –

account of what truth is.[2] Why is it such a good theory of truth? The main reason, supposedly, is that it is not really a theory of truth, properly speaking, since for disquotationalism, truth reduces to being, or to 'what is the case', and so avoids any ill-conceived comparisons of being and thought altogether. So, when one says 'It is true that one is in Oxford', one might as well dispense with the 'It is true that' and simply say 'one is in Oxford'. Since there is here no freight of correspondence between truth and reality, this theory has no need of recourse to realism. Instead it is ontologically neutral. This means, as Marshall argues, that for all practical and linguistic purposes, the world simply 'is' as it presents itself to us, or as we pragmatically take it to be.[3]

Having established this, Marshall nonetheless argues, in the second place, that there *is* an instance when correspondence must re-surface. For the Christian, he says, what one most seeks is to imitate Christ, who 'is' the Truth.[4] So, here, invoking Aquinas's account of the incarnate Christ's embodiment of eternal truth and our participation in this by imitation of Christ, Marshall allows for a mirroring of thought and reality in a realm quite remote from the busy commerce of everyday where disquotationalism exerts its minimalist rule.

Now, there are various reasons why one might wish to be critical of Marshall's defence of the Tarski–Davidson theory of truth. Put briefly, one might suggest the following. First, the 'disquotational' theory of truth does not necessarily point us beyond what is conventionally taken to be true, and fails to offer any reasons why it might or might not be justified to make a particular assertion; and so, after all, one might say (despite Davidson's disclaimers, which appeal implicitly to a scientistic naturalism ungrounded by his own primary philosophy), that this seems tantamount to a return to relativism.

It is true that Davidson, and Marshall in his wake, seek to evade a pure deflation of truth, and also relativism, through an espousal of 'holism' as to meaning. The possibility of mutual understanding is held to require the assumption that all basic human concepts are identical in all cultures and all cohere with each other. However, this disputable claim is itself compatible with a kind of naturalistic apriorism; 'truth' here may be merely the bias of the human species. As John McDowell and Hilary Putnam point out, it seems that, for Davidson, sensory information from the world cannot impinge as 'meaningful' within the conceptual space of human beliefs and cogitations. Davidson only establishes an emphatic realism when he affirms that the external world determines through material causality the workings of our brain, which he takes as equivalent to mental events in terms of a matching of neural effects to instances of thought, item by item. Despite this matching, Davidson obscurely allows no complete reduction of the psychic to the neural. He remains, therefore, with an unsustainable dualism which must collapse either into a thoroughgoing physicalism, which would hand the determination of truth entirely over to natural science, or else into a species-relativism in such a way that the one 'coherence' we are locked into, perhaps discloses nothing whatsoever concerning the world and is itself radically inexplicable.

Secondly, Marshall fails to mention that this purely secular account of truth runs into a number of aporias or contradictions. Indeed, the most obvious of these is that 'disquotationalism' does not negotiate the one most crucial instance where one really cannot get rid of the word 'true', namely, in the sentence presumably very close to disquotationalist hearts: 'It is true that all instances of the word true are redundant'.[5] One might think that one could also reduce this sentence to 'all instances of the word "true" are redundant'. However, this is not the case, because in this meta-statement, whether formulated in the version explicitly including the word 'true' or not, one is saying that the world is such that one can only approach it pragmatically or conventionally or phenomenalistically, and if that claim is made, then this is tantamount to asserting that treating the world in this way in fact corresponds to the way the world is. Even though such a correspondence is unverifiable, it is still *assumed*, in such a way that one does indeed treat the world and knowledge as two different realms, and then claims that knowledge matches the world when knowledge is taken as conventional or pragmatic. 'Truth' here, therefore, cannot be disquoted and is not redundant, because one has made a meta-assertion about the relation of knowing to being, and that is precisely the domain in which the notion of truth retains an indispensable operativity.

To put this another way: one cannot avoid this meta-assertion of truth to undergird disquotationalism, because otherwise there is no alternative way of ruling out the strong realist idea that one can have insight into what truly is the case for the depth of things according to their essential reality. Indeed, not only is such a view a plausible alternative to a conventionalist or pragmatist one; one could even argue that to reject it is counter-intuitive. For if one insists that truth is simply the way things appear to us to be, thus denying any correspondence between our mind and the way things are in themselves, then things must really be lying to us, because the way things appear to us must be concealing the way things are in themselves, or else concealing an underlying emptiness which is the real truth of things. In the latter case, if one were to say 'There is nothing', one would in fact be corresponding to reality.

The problem, then, is that if one asserts that one cannot get beyond the succession of the way things appear to us to be, then what is it that makes that state of affairs itself appear to us to be the case? One must here make appeal to a meta-phenomenon which would be the horizon of disclosure for all specific phenomena, but it is at this point that something like a correspondence theory of truth reappears at the heart of the very theory which claims to have done away with correspondence.[6]

In the third place, what is perhaps more worrying about Marshall's argument, is that he founds his exaltation of Tarski and Davidson upon a partially unsatisfactory construal of Aquinas's theory of truth. As we shall see, if Marshall had espoused more wholeheartedly Aquinas's concept of truth, there would be no need for him to promote a dualism between the secular realm, where the redundancy of truth can reign unchallenged, and the theological realm, where correspondence is possible through Christ.[7] For it will be shown that Aquinas's fundamental theory of truth is as theological as it is philosophical, and is only a correspondence theory in a sense which depends entirely upon the metaphysical notion of participation in the divine Being. Hence, while, indeed, Aquinas thinks that the way to fulfil truth for fallen man is by imitation of the God-man (as will be discussed in Chapter Three), more generally he supposes that any truth whatsoever is a participation in the eternally uttered Logos. Now, Marshall does observe that Christological truth can inform all our apprehension of the world, so that we see it as created and participating in God and come to realize that, theologically speaking, to be in the truth is 'to correspond' to God in whom we participate. However, he underestimates the extent to which Aquinas's more mundanely philosophical account of human knowing of material things through correspondence as such involves participation, since it is predicated on a view of the world as created. In this way, it is not simply Aristotle's account. Thus just to the same measure that Marshall espouses a dualistic account of truth and insinuates a gap between Aquinas's general theory of truth and his Christology, so also his theological view of truth is overweighted to Christology and does not sufficiently begin with the doctrine of Creation.

We will now therefore try to show that Marshall to a degree misconstrues Aquinas's theory of truth as correspondence. One problem, from an historical point of view, is that he attributes a post-Fregean approach to Aquinas. (While one can perhaps see the beginnings of something anticipating Frege in the later Middle Ages, this is more to be allied with anti-Thomistic developments.)[8] Marshall claims that Aquinas has two theories of truth, the first being a thoroughgoing Aristotelian correspondence of mind to reality, and the second, a grammatical or semantic theory in which truth is borne and brought about by sentences, and no 'metaphysics of knowledge' is necessarily assumed.[9]

One might perhaps concede momentarily that Aquinas attends to the question of whether something is true by attending to what it means, and this could be seen as a semantic approach. But for Aquinas, grammar is grounded in ontology, because the criterion for making sense, or deciding which word can be conjoined with which other words and in what way, is what *belongs together* or *could belong together* in ontological reality, either in things outside the mind, or in the mind's mode of understanding those things.[10] In the latter case, this criterion is logical as well as ontological only in the very 'unmodern' sense that there is a logical way of being, a way of things existing in the mind, which for Aquinas is as real as their extramental, material existence. By contrast, to separate Aquinas's semantic interest from his metaphysics of knowledge is to treat the former in terms of post-Bolzanian and post-Fregean logical 'realities' rather than ontological actualities (one might say here that it is to approach Aquinas as if he were Duns Scotus or even William of Ockham).[11]

For Marshall, this second, 'semantic' approach to truth in Aquinas allows one to assimilate his approach to modern disquotationalist theories, while shifting his affirmation of correspondence into a more purely fideistic register, for which the consequences of doctrine appear unanticipated by philosophy. By contrast, Marshall considers that earlier modern rationalist and empiricist philosophies have directly inherited Aquinas's first approach to truth, which emphatically affirms correspondence, even if they weaken the metaphysical ground for this approach by abandoning the Aristotelian idea of a literal migration of form from embodied thing to the understanding mind. (Marshall himself, unlike the present authors, considers this Aristotelian notion to be unsustainable.) But this assertion misses the point that modern theories of correspondence are grounded in epistemology rather than ontology, and that it is variants of a 'semantic' approach in the late Middle Ages (wrongly attributed to Aquinas by Marshall) which mediated this shift. Today such approaches may indeed have discovered that 'correspondence' is non-sustainable within a merely epistemological purview, but initially they encouraged the quest for a truth prior to, or independent of, being.

By regarding Aquinas's notion of correspondence as in continuity with modern notions, Marshall appears to over-assimilate Aquinas's philosophical account of human knowing to recent correspondence theories which falsely imagine a raw aconceptual apprehension of the world as a basis upon which the comparison that correspondence appears to require between knowing and being can be founded.[12] This supposedly raw aconceptual apprehension is then 'compared' with an equally raw purely semantic internal grasp of meaning. However, for Aquinas, the real is identified in the meaningful, just as the semantic is identified in the ontological. Thus, as we shall see, correspondence or adequation for Aquinas is not a matter of mirroring things in the world or passively registering them on an epistemological level, in a way that leaves the things themselves untouched. Rather, adequating is an event which realizes or fulfils the being of things known, just as much as it fulfils truth in the knower's mind. Correspondence here is a kind of real relation or occult sympathy – a proportion or harmony or *convenientia* – between being and knowledge, which can be assumed or even intuited, but not surveyed by a measuring gaze. For Aquinas, crucially, being is analogically like knowing and knowing like being. This is what makes Aquinas's theory of truth – unlike modern theories – an ontological rather than epistemological one. Indeed, the conformity or proportion which pertains between knowing and the known introduces an aesthetic dimension to knowledge utterly alien to most modern considerations.[13] And, in addition, truth for Aquinas has a teleological and a practical dimension, as well as a theoretical one – that is to say, the truth of a thing is taken as that thing fulfilling the way it ought to be, being the way it must be in order to be true.[14] These two dimensions of truth, as the way a thing is and the way it ought to be, come together, because for Aquinas they coincide in the Mind of God. So whereas for modern correspondence theories and some other theories such as coherence theory and diagonalization, one first has a theory of truth and then might or might not apply it to theology, for Aquinas, truth is theological without remainder.[15]

After examining exactly in what sense Aquinas is a correspondence theorist, one therefore discovers a defence of a realist theory of truth of a very extreme kind (for here one's mind corresponds to the ways things are at the very deepest level), against claims that truth reduces to whatever is the case according to convention or pragmatic motivation or phenomenal appearances. It follows that if Aquinas is to help us overcome the problems of correspondence, three things must be attended to: first, the idea that one can only have correspondence at all if one has God; secondly, the consequently entailed notion that a correspondence theory of truth is equally to be seen as a coherence theory of truth – that is, a theory of truth in which things are seen as true if they cohere or hold together – since here the ultimate true being of things is their supreme intelligibility in the divine Mind; and, thirdly, the implication that neither correspondence nor coherence applies in quite the way one might think according to secular canons.

II

This difference between Aquinas's and later correspondence theories of truth is perhaps nowhere more apparent than in the first article of *De Veritate* which opens with a consideration of the relation of truth to being.[16] Such a starting-point would make no sense at all for contemporary theories of truth which would tend to start epistemologically with a question such as 'How do we know a thing?' From the very outset, then, Aquinas shows us that he does not intend to *refer* truth to being, as if it were at a kind of static speculative epistemological remove from being. Rather, he is asking about truth as a *mode of existence*. This is not, however, to suggest that truth is a particular *kind* of being, but rather that it is convertible with Being as such in the entirety of both terms.[17] Such a view is, of course, fundamental to the mediaeval tradition of Aristotelianized neoplatonic convertibility of the transcendentals which assumes that Being, which is the focal transcendental, beyond all hierarchical qualifications, is equally close to every level of the metaphysical hierarchy; equally close, that is, to genus, species, substance and accident – an accident, for example, may be less self-standing than a substance, but it just as much exists as does a substance.[18] So when one says that Truth is convertible with Being, one is saying that Truth is also a transcendental; that Truth, like Being, shatters the usual hierarchy of categorical priorities in such a way that the humblest creature equally shines with the one light of Truth as the most exalted, and is just as essentially disclosive of it.

However, if Truth is convertible with Being in this way, why do we need to *add* Truth to Being? Why do we give them different names? There are several reasons for this, all relating to the way we see things from our perspective of situatedness and diversity.[19] Because of our finite modus of understanding, we see Being under different aspects. Under one of these aspects of Being (that described by the term 'Being' itself), the things we see seem to us to be discrete and to reside in themselves. For Being's equal proximity to everything, whether genus or species and so forth, seems to indicate a maieutic or private closeness of Being to each thing, and hence of that thing to itself, so that under this aspect, all things appear to remain in quietude, distinct from one another and in some sense rather self-absorbed.[20]

But this distinctness-of-things is not phenomenologically exhaustive, for one does not tend to experience things as existing only in an esoteric or hidden way. Things, according to our modus, also appear to *relate* to one another. This appearance of relating is twofold. First of all, beings relate to each other by moving outwards from themselves towards one another and towards their ends. This aspect is especially realized in Life, and concerns the Good (or teleological ends) of those things.[21] Secondly, there is an aspect by which things are *inside* each other, or are assimilated to one another. This is the formal immanence of other things in oneself that constitutes Knowledge, and is, like the orientation to the Good, a relationship of *convenientia*, of fitting and appropriate belonging-together, or of analogy.[22] Every being is in this way related to knowledge, but some beings only insofar as they are known and not as themselves knowing. Just as outer relation is especially realized in living creatures, so inner relation is most realized in the living creatures who can understand. Now, for Aquinas, one must refer these three Augustinian determinations of Being – Being, Life and Knowledge – to one another, for together they form a circle. As a being, a thing remains in itself; as living, it opens itself through the operations of life towards others; and as known or knowing it returns from others to itself.[23]

In these three stages or aspects of our modus, we see the interpenetrations of Being and Truth. But, more mysteriously still, one might say that this circle traces the mediations of a further transcendental, namely, Beauty, which seems to bestow itself obliquely on each of these three stations. Beauty, because it is to do with harmony, fittingness and proportion, including that between being and knowing, is at once invisible and hyper-visible for Aquinas; it is oblique and yet omnipresent. But how does Beauty mediate? First of all, insofar as Being is something which resides in itself by a kind of integrity, Beauty is apparent as the measure of that integrity;[24] secondly, insofar as Beauty is involved in the manifestation of things in their integrity, without which there could be no visibility, it is fundamental to knowledge; and thirdly, insofar as Beauty is linked with desire (Beauty being defined by Thomas as that which pleases the sight), it is crucial to the outgoings or ecstases of the will and the Good. This role of Beauty, although little explicitly averred to by Aquinas, is actually essential to grasping the character of his theory of understanding. For when he speaks of a *proportio* between Being, knowledge and willing (of the Good), and not mathematical *proportionalitas* which would denote a measurable visible ratio, it is clear that Aquinas alludes to the ineffable harmony between the transcendentals, whereby in the finite world they coincide and yet are distinguished.[25] Thus Beauty shows Goodness through itself and the Good leads to the True, yet we could never look at these relations as at a measurable distance. And this sense of something immanently disclosed through something else in an unmeasurable way, but in a fashion experienced as harmonious, is precisely something *aesthetic*. Every judgement of truth for Aquinas is an aesthetic judgement.

This aesthetic circling of mediations and analogical outgoings and returns which links everything together, is an aspect of Being which exists *in the Soul* (and supremely in the divine Soul).[26] This does not mean that the Soul arrives in the manner of an afterthought, as it were, once the private closeness of Being to distinct things has been established. For these aspects of Being do not unfold successively. It is rather the case that distinct things simply would not *be* without the Soul's knowing of them. Therefore Soul, as a further refraction of Being, does not primarily mirror phenomena, but is itself a primordial mode of Being. So, assimilation or adequation here, though obviously including crucial elements of a realist concept of truth, has an idealist dimension as well, which suggests that this is by no means an ordinary kind of correspondence. Being is not prior to knowing, so if Being measures knowledge, knowledge equally measures Being. One might call this 'ideal realism'. For, indeed, because Truth and Being are convertible, one with another, there is a continuity between the way things are in the external material world and the way things are in our mind.

But this 'continuity' is not to be taken lightly. It is not for Aquinas a continuity in the sense of a mirroring or reflecting, of our thoughts simply being 'true to the facts'. Rather, there is a sort of parallel or analogy between the way things are in material or separated angelic substance and the way things are in our minds. It involves a real relation, whereby our thought occasions a teleological realization of the formality of things, and, in doing so, is itself *brought to fruition*. This realization of things is manifold and complicated (we will say more about this later), but for now let us note that it pertains to the way in which the *thinking* of things actually brings them to their telos. This happens, because, for Aquinas, truth is less properly in things than in mind – it is usually, as it were, a dormant power until it comes to be known, at which point the power of its truth is awakened.[27]

This awakening suggests to us a further way in which Aquinas's concept of truth differs from later models. For whereas the latter might be inclined to treat of being as a mere inclusive genus of that which is simply 'there', with indifference as to quality and perfection, and which one's mind can know or represent, for Aquinas, knowledge is just as much a mode of being as the existence of material or otherwise self-standing substance. Indeed, Aquinas speaks elsewhere of *esse intelligibile* – of thought as intentional existence – building upon Augustine's idea of thought as a 'higher kind of life'.[28] Intellection, then, is not an indifferent speculation; it is rather a beautiful ratio which is instantiated between things and the mind which leaves neither things nor mind unchanged. This means that one must think of knowing-a-thing as an act of generosity, or salvific compensation for the exclusivity and discreteness of things.[29] Indeed, as we have already seen, in intellection, the Soul mediates things: 'The Soul is in a manner all things' as Aristotle declared in the *De Anima*.[30] It is a *corrective or remedy*, according to Aquinas in *De Veritate*, for the isolation of substantive beings.[31] If, for example, one were to know a willow tree overhanging the Cherwell, our knowing of it would be just as much an event in the life of the form 'tree' as the tree in its willowness and in its growing. An idea of a tree, therefore, is not in any way a mere representation or fictional figment, as it later became for Duns Scotus and William of Ockham.[32] Its truth is not, as modern realism assumes, ever tested by a speculative comparison with the thing itself. Indeed, the very notion of a 'thing itself' is radically otherwise, for it is only 'itself' in its being conformed to the intellect of the knower, in its being ordered to a beautiful ratio or proportion. The thing-itself is only itself by being assimilated to the knower, and by its form entering into the mind of the knower.[33] Truth is not 'tested' in any way, but sounds itself or shines outwards in beauty.

So far, we have seen that, for Aquinas, truth is neither epistemological nor primarily a property of statements. We have seen more positively that it is convertible with Being, that it is a mode of existence and that it is related to a particular aspect of Being, which, according to our modus, is received as a kind of analogical or beautiful assimilation between things. If it is convertible with Being and is a manner of assimilation between things, it seems that truth is *disappointingly elusive*, and a realist might feel dissatisfied not to know exactly where truth is to be found. Where, indeed, are we to find truth? For Aquinas the place of truth is manifold and hierarchical, and one finds it gradually by means of an ascending scale. One might begin by saying that truth is a property of things, that a thing is true if it fulfils itself and holds itself together according to its character and goal.[34] Thus, one can say 'This is true rain' if it is raining very hard. A philosopher might scowl at such a usage and say that it is a sloppy metaphorical instance of the word 'true'; but for Aquinas, this would be an entirely proper use, as it would here refer to the most ideal rain, that is, rain fulfilling its operations of life, realizing its 'second act' of relations to others and to its telos, by which in exceeding itself apparently accidentally (inasmuch as it might otherwise remain in its substance just up in the clouds), it actually becomes *more* itself super-substantially. Indeed, a thing is deemed 'less true' if it is impeded in some way from its ordinary operations, whether by poison or sickness.[35]

But what is happening when a thing is fulfilling its telos? A thing is fulfilling its telos when it is *copying God in its own manner,* and tending to existence as knowledge in the divine Mind: so a tree copies God by being true to its treeness, rain by being rainy, and so on.[36] If a thing is truest when it is teleologically directed, and that means when a thing is copying God, this would suggest, as Aquinas indeed affirms, that truth is primarily in the Mind of God and only secondarily in things as copying the Mind of God. Any suggestion, therefore, that Aquinas's realist theory of truth is a simple correspondence of mind to thing is here qualified by this subordination of all things to the divine intellect.

In addition, one can note as an aside, that whilst it is the case that some variants of correspondence theory might claim an unmediated aconceptual apprehension of things, Aquinas seems to suggest that when one knows a thing, one does not know that thing as it is by itself, but only insofar as one meaningfully grasps it as imitating God. How very odd this seems, for one would normally regard imitation as a secondary and therefore less authentic operation of life, but here it becomes the highest form of authenticity attainable for material things.[37] However, the placing of imitation ahead of autonomy suggests that, for Aquinas, borrowing is the highest authenticity which can be attained. One must copy in order to be, and one continues only as a copy, never in one's own right.[38]

But if all things are subordinated to the divine intellect in this way, does this mean likewise that Aquinas's concept of truth is after all an idealist theory which has no essential recourse to an encounter with the way things actually are? Certainly there is an idealist *aspect* here; however, the very referral to the divine intellect reveals a concept of understanding not as the unfolding of *a priori* truths, but as an orientation towards the ideal as embodied in actuality. Why? Because, as Aquinas explains, truth is in the Mind of God in the same way that an idea resides in the mind of a craftsman.[39] Hence, truth as an idea expresses divine desire – and this is desire for the Good, which brings into our discussion a further trans-cendental (besides Being and Truth). Like Truth, the Good also concerns Being in its relational aspect. But whereas Truth discloses the relations between things to the intellect – all their combinations and separations – the Good discloses their relations to desire (we have already seen how this disclosure is made manifest by beauty which shows us the relations between things as desirable). Such a suggestion that *desire* is disclosive of the real, that desire just as much as knowledge corresponds to Being, suggests an additional way in which Thomist *adequatio* differs from modern corres-pondence theories, since these would be unable to encompass, and indeed would regard as outlandish, any notion that we register the way things *are* in terms of the way they *ought* to be.

Let us pause a moment to assess the foregoing conclusions about the nature and whereabouts of truth.

First of all, we have seen that truth *in God and in the world* is, on the one hand, an ideal although actual reality, because it expresses desire for the Good; and, on the other hand, it is real because it is convertible with Being. But as concerned with the coherence and beauty of being which realizes desire, as well as concerned with being in its fundamental psychic – which means relationally co-inhering – aspect, truth is present primarily in the act of intellect.

Secondly, we have seen that truth is also *a property of all finite modes of being* insofar as they participate in God. These modes include both individual material substances (such as a stone, a tree, a cricket bat) and also intellectual existences (such as human and angelic minds). This means that truth is in individual material substances and intellectual existences, not in the sense that one might point to them and say that they 'are the case', as for modern theories, but because they imitate God in their appointed modes and aim for their appointed ends. And in performing their various tasks, they analogically show us something of God.

We have seen, in the third place, *that truth is in the human intellect*. It is there in two ways: first, following Augustine, by means of divine illumination,[40] and, secondly, following Aristotle, by receiving forms as species from individual material substances.

III

It is this *third* aspect of truth's being in the human intellect which returns us to what we have described as the 'aesthetic moment' in Aquinas's theory of knowledge. For when the human intellect receives into itself the species of the material substances it knows, it does not know them in the manner of an arraignment of inert facts. Rather, it must always *judge* or *discern* whether they are true to themselves.[41] This means that even corresponding to finite objects is really only a corresponding to the Mind of God. In the first place, the mind must judge whether, for example, a tree is being true to itself, according to the mind's divine inner light of illumination. By doing this, the mind discerns or grasps an analogical proportion of things to God, and finds here a manifestation of the invisible in the visible. Thus, what it finds here is beauty which 'pleases' the sight, and delights the judgement.[42] Here again, as with the ethical dimension of truth, one finds something very strange to the modern mind; for where the latter thinks of knowledge as an abasement of subjectivity before the inertly objective, Aquinas sustains, in knowing, a delicate balance between the objective and the subjective. If one requires a beautiful appearance in order to manifest the truth, then while it is indeed the objective that is registered, this registration is only made by the subjectively informed power of rightly desiring sight and judgement. There is, indeed, a certain 'what' which pleases, but this 'what' is only acknowledged as 'pleasing'. Likewise, the invisible really does shine through the visible, and yet this is only apparent for a subtle power of discernment; it is obviously not present in the manner of a 'fact'.

In the second place, one asks, what is it that we are knowing when we discern the treeness of a tree? For to know such a thing is not to know an isolatable fact or proposition; it seems more to be the knowing of a kind of manner or operation of life. But in knowing the treeness of a tree, we are knowing a great deal more besides. Since the tree only transmits treeness – indeed, only exists at all – as imitating the divine, what we receive in truth is a participation in the divine. To put this another way, in knowing a tree, we are catching it on its way back to God.[43] One could even say, given the foregoing, that for Aquinas, as he indeed affirms, knowledge is God's perpetual return to Himself. This is not a movement in the sense of a discursive passage from known to unknown, but a kind of encircling, a movement out of Himself and returning to Himself, always already completed from the beginning of eternity. For God, in knowing His own essence, also knows other things in which He sees a likeness of Himself, since He grasps Himself as participable, and so He here returns to His essence.[44]

To say that things are only really true in God would suggest that Aquinas is in this instance modifying Aristotle in the direction of Augustine and neoplatonism. However, Aquinas combines Aristotle with neoplatonism in an entirely new way. Following Aristotle, he sees even the human soul as fundamentally an animal soul, or a 'form of forms' which holds together a living material organism. He regards intellect as merely a *power* of the soul, rather than its essence.[45] It would seem then that in the most daring fashion, Aquinas sees the power of the mind as in some way 'accidental' to us, in the manner of an 'oxymoronic' proper accident (a category deployed by Aquinas and not Aristotle). Such a proper accident is an example of the second act of operation already referred to, which is beyond the first act of subsistence. Here again a seemingly semi-accidental second act can rise ontologically above the first act and even come to define a thing's essence beyond its essence, in a super-essential way. Hence the human animal need not 'think', but only when it does so is it human, and the more it exercises intellect the more it is human.[46]

And yet this suggestion that intellection is as it were a borrowed power might seem to downgrade the mind. But, if anything, the reverse is the case. For Aquinas here deploys the neoplatonic legacy and the metaphysics of participation to show that he regards our capacity for thought not as a ruefully humiliated endeavour, but as a partial receiving of divine intellection. Just as we only exist for Aquinas by participating in Being – which is also 'accidental' to our essence, since we do not 'have' to be, and yet super-essential, since Being alone gives us our determinate essence – so also we only exist humanly, that is, according to a higher kind of life, exercising our intellects, by participating in Knowledge. Thus it seems that what is extra to us most defines us; here one must observe that intellection is akin to grace, because the most important part of us is in fact not part of our animal essence at all, but is super-added to us, properly and yet accidentally.

Thus, despite appearances to the contrary, Aquinas's theory of human knowledge does not make intellection an illusory or humiliated enterprise. Nonetheless, it seems there is a very great difference between our relation to knowledge and that of God, who knows by His very essence. Following Pseudo-Dionysius and Augustine, Aquinas surpasses pagan neoplatonists who thought that the One and the Good lay beyond the subjective and psychic, ineffably above *nous*. For these thinkers, since the ultimate transcended mind, our mind could not analogically predicate anything concerning it. Aquinas, by contrast, incorporates Aristotle's idea of the Prime Mover as *nous*, but, unlike Aristotle, for whom *nous* was simply self-identical thought thinking itself, introduces a certain note of relationality and difference into God, even before elaborating a Trinitarian theology. Thus he speaks of God's knowledge of all the modes in which He can be participated (in this way, God knows the creation), something of which Aristotle does not speak. God knows things fully in knowing their ends, their perfection, which includes all that they are.

And yet, peculiarly, it is precisely this difference between God's manner of knowing and our own, which makes our manner of understanding, in a strange and entirely humble way, God-like. For God, as cause of knowing, is in Himself superabundantly knowing, and not simply an wholly inscrutable and unknown cause of our knowledge.[47] For this reason, we can know something – albeit very remotely – of God's knowing of Himself. That is to say, we can analogically predicate knowledge of God. Although our own imitations of God's knowledge are always marked by imperfection and diversity, even here what seems a deficiency in our modus in fact betokens its own remedy.[48] One might think, for example, that God's perfect knowledge of Himself would be in no way diverse, but would be oneness personified, as in the neoplatonic tradition upon which Aquinas draws when he characterizes God as Unity itself, One, and simple. Yet even God's Oneness contains within itself a superabundant plenitude which our very diversity – or very difference from God – seeks to express, albeit analogically. And it is paradoxically from within the idea of God's utterly unified and simple understanding of Himself, that one is pointed towards a kind of diversity. This is demonstrated by the question of whether there can be a perfect copy of God. Such a copy would, like God, have to be One.[49] Aquinas cites Pseudo-Dionysius to the effect that there can be such a perfect copy, even though, or even because, God is One, namely, the person of the Son who contains within himself all principles of diversity, since, for Aquinas, unlike later mediaeval theologians, God creates *ad extra* in and through the generation of the Son *ad intra*. Precisely because God is One, no otherness lies outside Him, and since this oneness cannot ever be diminished, it can be entirely shared amongst all this variety. Thus from the very idea of God's understanding Himself in a self-sufficient and unified act, one is directed towards the Trinitarian diversity.

IV

But there still remains the question of God's knowledge of singulars; this, surely, radically differentiates our manner of knowing from that of God.[50]

For although God is pure Mind without remainder, and therefore a more spiritual kind of knower than human beings, nevertheless His knowledge is more concrete than ours. This is because when we know a thing, we cannot directly apprehend its material individuation, since, for Aquinas, following Aristotle, matter cannot enter the human intellect. The limits of one's intellect, as we know from Augustine's famous topos in the *Confessions* that to make is to know, keep pace with one's capacity to produce.[51] So, just as we can produce a form in things, like a craftsman, so we can know forms (while, inversely, forms literally arrive in our minds as abstracted species). However, we cannot produce matter with our intellect, and so we cannot *know* matter, and hence cannot know singulars.[52]

By contrast, Aquinas suggests that God is much more of a country bumpkin (*rusticus*) capable of a brutal direct unreflective intuition of cloddish earth, bleared and smeared with toil.[53] For God's mind, although immaterial, is (in a mysterious way) commensurate with matter, since God creates matter. Because he can *make* matter, so also he can *know* it. This does not mean that He receives matter into Himself; He does not receive forms or species either. Rather, He knows by the one species which is His essence, and knows things outside Himself entirely by His productive capacity – form and matter alike – for both are more fundamentally existence. At this point, one might note how very far Aquinas has moved from Aristotle.

It seems, then, that despite the graceful accident of our capacity to know beyond our natures, yet we cannot aspire to the noble estate of bumpkinhood where singulars can be espied and known in all their singularity – albeit in a mode beyond our finite contrast of singular with universal. Or can we? It seems that a token bumpkinhood is not denied us. Aquinas develops an account of how we do in a certain measure participate in the divine knowledge of singulars. God, as we have seen, knows singulars in time precisely because he is timelessly outside them and brings them to be from nothing. However, by stressing the nature of human knowledge as a ceaseless movement and a dynamic interaction between soul and body, Aquinas finds an adequation or approximation to the divine manner of knowing. He elaborates, beyond Aristotle, an account of knowledge as a relay system of signification. To explain this better, one must explicate the 'Aristotelian', 'Augustinian' and 'Thomist' phases in Aquinas's account of understanding.

In the 'Aristotelian' phase, the form departs from individual material substance, the hylomorphic form/matter compound, and enters on the path of abstraction. As it travels further along this path, the form becomes 'species' and is further abstracted as it passes through the 'senses' of the human observer, then into the imagination, to arrive at the ultimate Aristotelian destination of the Mind.

Here the species is received initially by the passive intellect, but then is articulated or expressed by the active intellect, the *intellectus agens*. Following Augustine, Aquinas describes the product of this expression as *verbum*, the inner word.[54]

Here, in articulating the 'Augustinian' phase, Aquinas suggests, beyond Aristotle, that a concept does not just leave matter behind. For this reason he is *less* idealist than Aristotle and moreover his greater realism draws on Platonic resources. The fundamental reason for this is theological. For Aristotle, the material element was simply inimical to understanding – it was still to do with irrational formless chaos. But for Aquinas (as for all post-Biblical monotheisms and 'almost' for the neoplatonists), matter is created by God, and therefore itself fully proceeds from Mind. Thus if our mind in order to understand must abstract from matter, this is a deficiency of understanding.

However, the Augustinian dimension compensates somewhat for this deficiency, because here the concept, as inner word, is like a sign. A sign points away from itself by means of its nonetheless essential mediation, back to what it represents. Thus Aquinas, like Augustine, speaks of all knowledge as intentional, as returning to concrete things that we cannot fully grasp. This concurs with the fusion of intellect as *intention* with desire, which returns us to things, encouraging us to learn more of them, since to intend something is also to desire to know more of the truth of the thing – this goal being regarded as a good. Thus in Aquinas, there is much more sense than with Aristotle, of knowledge as a never completed project.[55]

The 'Augustinian' phase still does not explain, however, how we can have any inkling of singulars. For however much the sign points us back to the form/matter compound, we still cannot be sure that it exists, since matter cannot enter into the mind. Here Aquinas develops – perhaps in a very new way – a theory of the imagination, long before Kant. Just like Kant, in fact, he thinks that whenever we sense, we also *imagine* something, because imagination is the mysterious point of fusion of sense and intellect.

Nevertheless, there is an important difference between sense and imagination. We are aware of sensing. But we are not normally aware of imagining, and even when we imagine something absent, we look through the transparency of this image towards the thing invoked, as if, says Aquinas, looking in a mirror.

Now because matter cannot get inside the mind, senses cannot provide the mind with awareness of singulars – rather, the senses have to be mediated by the imagination. Thus imaginary images of things here become an oblique mediating principle which provides a mysterious echo of material sensing in the intellect (or somewhere halfway between sense and intellect) and in this fashion we receive a notion of the singular and hence some awareness of the form/matter compound. Moreover, by virtue of the transparency of mediation, its presence in our intellect is mysteriously more than a fiction or figment. Because for Aquinas truth 'corresponds' not by copying but by a new analogical realization of something in the mind in an inscrutable 'proportion' to how it is in reality, the imagination can act creatively without fictional betrayal. Indeed, it *must* act creatively if it is to be 'true'.

However, because we simply look through the imagination as if through a mirror and abstract the species from the imagination as from the senses in order to know, we can only be aware of the singular image via a reflexive return to the imagination; as when looking at something in a mirror one becomes aware of the mediating principle – the glass surface of the mirror itself. Here one looks through the image at the species, but reflexively one is aware of the image. This is not exactly a self-conscious reflection, because it accompanies *all* knowing. Hence, very oddly for us, Aquinas associates the concrete aspect of understanding with a reflexive operation. He also stresses that although our mind cannot know singulars, we know not just as mind but as a person and as a mind/body composite – and as such we *do*, in a way, know singulars. Of course, as a proper bumpkin, God does not need to be subject to such complex phases, for He does not know discursively or by syllogism or dialectic.

All the same, we have seen that the act of intellection is accidental to us and yet defines our nature as human beings. And this has led us to investigate the possibility that our nature as human beings is paradoxically by definition *to exceed* our nature and enjoy further 'accidental' participations in the divine. We have seen, moreover, that this seems to be the case in several ways, but particularly in the exercise of our imagination which is the ecstatic principle by which our mind mysteriously overcomes the limits of its capacity to produce and hence know material singulars. In other ways, too, we have seen that those features which most differentiate us from God – such as our diversity – furnish us with the means by which we might analogically penetrate that difference. Thus here also, where it might seem that Aquinas stresses the difference and distance of human knowing, it turns out that we know by participation in divine knowledge; and moreover that this relation to the above is mediated by our turning to the material world below.

V

In conclusion to this chapter, we would like to consider one more aspect of God's knowledge – as a self-expressive creative act – to see whether any further parity can be drawn even here with Aquinas's presentation of human knowledge. For in the foregoing, there have been several intimations that human knowledge has a self-expressive or creative dimension; not only have we seen that knowledge involves an 'aesthetic' moment whereby one must judge the beauty of a particular proportion, but also that the practice of *imitation* or mimesis and the exercise of *imagination* is not merely a passive receiving, but rather one which gathers up images and modifies them.

But there is a third principle, namely, the dynamic movement or displacement of energy involved in knowledge (which contrasts to a more modern concept of knowledge as a static gaze or mirroring). Here Aquinas notes that Plato, and sometimes even Aristotle, was prepared to see knowledge as a kind of motion, and he cautiously concurs. Indeed, Aquinas gives several examples of a real procession in the mind: conclusions, he says, really proceed from principles; an actual conception really proceeds from habitual knowledge; our ideas about the essences of subordinate things proceed from ideas about the essences of higher things.[56] Even when the mind understands itself, it thinks of an expression, and not directly or reflexively of the mind. When the mind understands itself, it must proceed from itself, express itself, in an intellectual word. Moreover, this emanative expression, in contrast to Aristotle, transitively proceeds, and in some ways can be seen as craft-like, as a construction or internal operation of art, insofar as the procession of the word involves a development of thought that is originally constitutive of thought, in such a way that there is no original thought without such an expressive elaboration.[57]

It is no accident, indeed, that the final and efficient cause – both end and archetype – of external expressions, described in *De Veritate* as the *verbum cordis*, should be seen not as a static ideal, but as akin to the interior shaping form of *ars* involved in all exterior artistic expression. Such an *ars* or *verbum* must itself come into being, by a kind of anterior creative supplementation. This suggests that in some way all human knowing is to be seen as an artistic production, which again emphasizes that truth is regarded in ontological rather than epistemological terms, since it is in this way construed as an event rather than as a mirroring.[58]

Moreover, this paradigm of knowledge as co-originally self-expressive, immediately points us to the Trinity, as Aquinas indicates, thereby suggesting a certain 'natural' intimation of this reality in God, despite his explicit confinement of the Trinity to revealed truth. This occurs in two ways: first, in the obvious sense of begetting a word in and through its own essential realization; and, secondly, in terms of the manner of emanation involved. This should be conceived in terms of the hierarchy of emanations described in the *Summa Contra Gentiles*, where the higher the level of emanation, the more the procession or production is inwardly contained, in such a way that God, as the most perfect being, can emanate from Himself without leaving Himself.[59] Such a containment of emanation, one would think, would be reserved for God alone. And yet it seems that Aquinas's idea of the inner word in the human intellect in a certain way remotely approximates in its manner of procession to the inward emanation within God. For the mind can produce a word that is distinct from itself, and yet remains within itself; the mind *is* not these concepts (the inner words) and yet cannot *be* mind without its concepts.

What all this suggests is that correspondence in Aquinas's theory of knowledge means something far more nuanced than a mere mirroring of reality in thought. Rather, as we have seen, there is an intrinsic *proportio* or analogy between the mind's intrinsic drive towards truth, and the way things manifest themselves, which is their mode of being true. This *proportio* is assumed and experienced, but cannot be observed or empirically confirmed. It is assumed, because mind and things are both taken as proceeding from the divine creative mind, in such a way that the very source of things is dimly echoed in our minds which generate understanding. Yet it is also *experienced*, because the harmony between mind and things pre-established by God, is not a Leibnizian pre-establishment where no *real* relation between mind and things taken as windowless monads pertains. Rather, the proportion creatively ordered by God between mind and things really and dynamically flows between them, and in receiving this proportion, and actualizing it, we come to know.

If there can be correspondence of thought to beings, this is only because, more fundamentally, both beings and minds correspond to the divine *esse* and *mens* or intellect. Therefore correspondence, for Aquinas, is of what we know according to our finite modus, to God who is intrinsically far more knowable, and yet for us in His essence, utterly unknown. This means that rather than correspondence being guaranteed in its measuring of the given, as for modern notions of correspondence, it is guaranteed by its conformation to the divine source of the given. While to advance to this source is of course to advance in unknowing, it is only in terms of this unknowing, increased through faith, that we confirm even our ordinary knowing of finite things.

Moreover, this conformation to the unknown divine mind is far more emphatic in its claim than simply an analogical drawing-near or resemblance. It is an assimilation, an ontological impress which moulds or contrives the very forms of things; and all this happens, as it were, without our knowing it, without our contriving it, in the modern more pejorative sense of the word as 'forcing a shape', deceitful practice, invention or dissembling. One could perhaps say that correspondence in the modern sense of the word fits far better these later meanings of contrivance, for it lays claim to grasp phenomena as they are in themselves, and not as they are insofar as they imitate God. So, in fact, what the mind corresponds to here is things *divided* from themselves, from their real ground in divine *esse*, and so to things forced to dissemble.[60] But what is 'contrived' or brought to pass according to Aquinas's notion of fashioning or making-well, occurs transparently; as with the invisible mediations of beauty, we look through this 'making' without seeing it, even as we know beyond ourselves by means of it; we forget that *what* we know is *more* than we can possibly know. And, moreover, even when we are knowing ordinary temporal things, straining to be like bumpkins apprehending a lunar eclipse, even then, at such a moment of lowly endeavour, the motions of our intellect and of our will vastly exceed their capacity, and mould themselves into the idiom of the procession of the eternal Word from the Father, and that of the Holy Spirit from the Father and the Son. Thus, just as for Aquinas, to correspond in knowing is to be conformed to the infinite unknown, so likewise our knowing of anything at all – however local – is in some measure an advance sight of the beatific vision, and union with the personal interplay of the Trinity.[61]

2   Truth and vision

I

If truth, for Aquinas, as we have seen, is inherently theological, then is the theology involved, an affair of reason or of faith? Or is it first an affair of reason, and later an affair of faith?

In the most usual interpretations, Aquinas is seen as espousing a sharp distinction between reason and faith, and concomitantly between philosophy and theology. Furthermore, this distinction is viewed as both benign and beneficial: on the one hand, it safeguards the mystery and integrity of faith; on the other hand, it allows a space for modern secular autonomy, while discouraging the growth of political theocracy and hierocratic control of knowledge.

The present chapter will, however, argue that this dualistic reading of Aquinas is false. Dualism concerning reason and faith emerges not from Thomas, but rather from intellectual and practical tendencies within the late mediaeval and early modern periods (even if they were somewhat enabled already by the Gregorian reforms with their sharper divide of the lay from the clerical). Moreover, its consequence was not benign, but instead itself encouraged, with and not against early modernity, a theocratic and hierocratic authoritarianism.

For the more science and politics were confined to immanent and autonomous secular realms, then the more faith appealed to an arational positivity of authority invested with a right to rule, and sometimes to overrule, science and secular politics, whose claimed autonomy, being construable as pure only in formalistic terms, was by the very same token open to substantive breaching. Theocracy required the 'other' realm of the secular in order to have something over which to exert its sway: thus the most theocratic construals of papal authority emerged only in the later Middle Ages, as physicalist theories of the rights of a finite power legitimated by absolute power over lesser powers enjoying, intrinsically, only a limited sway. Quite shortly afterwards, similarly theocratic theories were deployed by absolute monarchs, and the resulting blend of theological voluntarism and physicalist theory of the rights of *de facto* power is not without echo in the later articulation of totalitarian philosophies.[1]

Moreover, the nineteenth- and twentieth-century neo-Thomistic promotion of papal power, was likewise predicated upon gnoseological dualism, not monism. In order to combat the sway of idealism and positivism, nineteenth-century Catholic thinkers such as Joseph Kleutgen argued, inaccurately, that mediaeval Christian thinkers had developed a purely autonomous philosophy, more rationally sound than the philosophies of modernity, whose conclusions were nonetheless in strict harmony with those of faith.[2] The outcome of this new reading of the Middle Ages was to lend the Roman Catholic hierarchy a double support; on the one hand, it received the supposedly neutral acclaim of reason (underwriting its authority in the educational and scientific sphere), but, on the other hand, its claims to speak in the name of something beyond reason were thereby rendered more plausible. Moreover, just as a supposedly 'Thomistic' reason was often in fact contaminated by empiricism and positivism (in over-reaction to idealism), so likewise a faith regarded as entirely other to reason was grounded on revealed 'facts' and literalistic decrees of appointed authority. Here again, the strong concessions to reason only led to a final and unquestionable trumping of reason by faith. And if, so often, theological 'liberals' ascribe to something like this framework, then they need to be aware of just this genealogy.

However, if the dualistic legacy of neo-Thomism is in this way sinister in its consequences and implications, can one really dissociate it from the teachings of Aquinas himself? How is one to deny, in Thomas, first of all, the presence of his clearly stated view that we can know many things in God's Creation by rational attention to it, without the assistance of faith? And how is one to deny, in the second place, the role in his work of a purely philosophical theology, as opposed to that of *sacra doctrina,* which appeals to revelation?

Let it be said straightaway that it is possible to cite passages in Aquinas which appear incontrovertibly to support these positions. Thus he does indeed say that we can know many things by the light of natural reason without appeal to faith.[3] And he does indeed say that the theology pursued by philosophy, is able, by the natural light of reason alone, to know God as first cause, which is to say as creator, if nothing more.[4]

However, exegesis is easy; it is interpretation that is difficult. And Aquinas, more than most thinkers, requires interpretation. Some thinkers, like Heidegger, appear on the surface to be obscure and deep, but on analysis are revealed as offering all too clear and readily statable positions. But as Rudi te Velde very well intimates, with Aquinas the opposite pertains.[5] Only superficially is he clear, but on analysis one discovers that he does not at all offer us a decently confined 'Anglo-Saxon' lucidity, but rather the intense light of Naples and Paris which is ultimately invisible in its very radiance – rendering the wisest of us, for Aquinas after Aristotle, like owls blinking in the noonday.[6] Of course it is true that Aquinas does indeed refute shaky positions with supreme economy, simplicity and clarity of argumentation, but the *arcanum* of his teaching lies not here. It resides rather in the positions he does affirm, often briefly and like a kind of residue, akin to Sherlock Holmes's last remaining solution, which must be accepted in all its implausibility, when other solutions have been shown to be simply impossible. Often this conceptual residue is prefaced by a revealing *quoddamodo* and we are left contemplating, not a discursive chain, but a bare single word such as *proportio, convenienter, claritas* or *ordo*, and must attempt to fathom its conceptual depths in relation to other 'remaining' concepts and locutions. At the heart of Aquinas's thought, commentators discover highly problematic notions – the real distinction of *esse* and *essentia* in creatures, the primacy of act over possibility, the intrinsic perfection of *esse*, 'proper accidents', 'active potential', 'real relations', 'intelligible being', the distinction of 'first' from 'second act', the nature of *ens commune* as distinct from *esse,* and the relation of participation to substance in his overall ontology – all of which exhibit a certain profound obscurity which resists easy interpretation or analysis.

Bearing these general procedural remarks in mind, our claim in the present case is that Aquinas's apparently clear avowal of an autonomous reason and philosophical theology cannot be rendered consistent with certain other crucial passages in his writings and therefore must be re-interpreted. In the light of other passages, we shall argue, the distinctions between reason and faith, on the one hand, and 'philosophical' theology (*divina scientia*) and *sacra doctrina*, on the other, can only be considered as relative contrasts within a more fundamental gnoseological situation embracing the two poles, in either case. For both instances (reason/faith; philosophical theology/*sacra doctrina*) we will make this claim in two stages. First of all, we will establish that the distinguished approaches can at the very most be thought of only as distinct phases within a single gnoseological extension exhibiting the same qualities throughout. Then we will further establish that even the phases are not clearly bounded in terms of what can or cannot be achieved. To the contrary, it will turn out that the single extension has an equally single 'intension' stretched between its beginning and end and accessible at any point along the continuum, although in different degrees of concentration – giving varying 'intensities'. Having established these points concerning Aquinas's method, we shall then show how his 'rational' treatment of Creation is informed by faith, while his exposition of the revealed Trinity is in fact highly demonstrative. Throughout we hope to show how a 'radically orthodox' position (primarily characterized by a more persistent refusal of distinct 'natural' and 'supernatural' phases and a consequent assault upon an autonomous naturalism as 'nihilistic'), can indeed be rendered as an attentive reading of Aquinas.

II

There can be no doubt that Aquinas distinguishes between faith and reason. The difficult issue, though, is just how. For it is equally clear that they are but phases within a single extension.

Thus Aquinas declares that both the natural powers of thought and the superadded powers given in grace and glory both operate through participation in the uncreated and intelligible light of the divine intellect.[7] In the case of the former, natural powers, the *intellectus* or 'higher reason' enjoys a certain very remote approximation to the divine intuition, or immediate intellectual vision, which operates without recourse to discursive unfolding.[8] Hence it enjoys some vision of the pure divine form without matter only known to our *modus cognoscendi* as the diverse transcendentals of Being, Unity, Truth, Goodness and Beauty. By way of this vision it permits the 'lower reason' in its higher scientific aspect (as identified by Aristotle) to discern by judgement in some measure the 'simple essences' of finite substances as (literally) conveyed into the human mind by way of the senses. Concerning those essences it cannot be deceived, in such a way that here it partakes infallibly of the divine power of intuitive recognition. (John Jenkins has recently refuted Lonergan's denial of this aspect of intellectual vision in Aquinas.)[9] However, since in concrete reality no simple essences subsist (else they would rival God in their simplicity),[10] no pure scientific cognition is ever exercised by us without discursive mediation: no cognitive 'sight' without cognitive 'language'. And in the case of the higher reason's partial grasp of undivided transcendental principles, it is all the more the case that this arises through and after our comprehension of material divided things. Moreover, even in perceiving the contingent combinations of finite essences, we can, indeed, unlike God, be deceived, and must always exercise judgement by questioning just what we do see, and in allowing for deceptive appearances.[11] Here the subordinate discursive aspect of the lower reason comes particularly into play.

This discursive aspect of the lower reason, while assuming certain scientific principles that are in turn judged in the light of the higher reason's gaze upon the eternal, itself calls again upon the higher light of judgement (by way of analysis), to make its specific intentional pronouncements upon evidence and probable coherencies. In such a circular fashion, *ratio* and *intellectus,* while distinguished, nonetheless operate as a single power.

Thus, when making pronouncements about the truths of external things and in further realizing these truths within itself (since Aquinas holds that truth resides primarily within the intellect, but secondarily within things),[12] the mind continues to be informed by the intellective vision of truth, goodness and beauty. This is essential because Aquinas holds, as we described in Chapter One, that the truth residing in things is not simply their ontological manifestness (though this is crucial, and rules out any epistemological approach to truth, since what if it were universally the case that all beings absolutely hide themselves?) but also a truth to themselves or degree of realization of their own perfection, or own goodness.[13]

In this way, as we saw in Chapter One, a thing is 'true' to the degree that it participates in the divine standard for its own realization. Hence in pronouncing on and manifesting the truth of a thing, the human intellect itself assesses it in the light of this standard, and its sense of how manifest a thing is, or how manifest ('true') the intellect can make it, is inseparable from its sense of its perfection or appropriate goodness. Moreover, as we further concluded, this assessment is itself a registering of the inscrutable 'proportion' that pertains between the being of things and the human intellect – an analogical proportion which Aquinas specifically identifies as a participation in transcendental beauty.[14]

In contrast to many presentations, therefore, it can be seen that Aquinas's entire treatment of truth must be brought within the domain of his philosophical theology. It is not the case, for Aquinas, that one can be sufficiently assured of some specific truth merely by attending to a feature of the divine Creation, without necessarily recognizing it as created. On the contrary, for Aquinas, one can pronounce no judgement of truth without assessing a degree of appropriate participation in the transcendental attributes proper to divinity (though this is not to say that such an assessment need always be carried out with full reflexive consciousness of the *proportio* between creature and creator). Were one to attempt to comprehend a finite reality not as created, that is to say, not in relation to God, then no truth for Aquinas could ensue, since finite realities are of themselves nothing and only what is can be true.

If *intellectus* offers a certain measure of direct cognitive vision – though never, for now, apart from the discursiveness of *ratio* – then the 'light of faith' is for Aquinas simply a strengthening of the *intellectus* by a further degree of participation in the divine light. This strengthening shifts the balance of thought slightly away from discursivity and further towards the divine pure intuition – since an increase of 'light' means an increase in the relative immediacy of understanding.[15] In the case of the operation of reason, we have seen in the first chapter that Aquinas's continued Augustinian and neoplatonic construal of truth as inner *illuminatio* can nonetheless incorporate (as it could already in Augustine, Proclus, and Dionysius, if not Plotinus) an essential Aristotelian detour through the truth embodied in finite creatures and conveyed to us only via the senses. And while faith involves an intensification of participation in divine intellectual intuition, the same fusion of inner and outer is sustained in the knowledge accessible by faith (although it is just this fusion which is undone in later neoscholastic accounts of revelation).[16] Here, also, for faith as for reason, the passive intellect marries the infallible witness of intellectual light to the infallible intuition of the senses (infallible so long as nothing contrary to the ordinary run of nature, such as a mirage, intervenes to distort their deliverances). Thus the paradigmatic scene of revelation, for Aquinas, is represented by the instance of prophecy. Here a supernatural supplement of infused cognitive light is inseparably conjoined with some extraordinary sensory vision, miraculous event, or at least novel historical occurrence.[17] Since all these latter three may only, as finite instances, mediate the divine in the shape of enigma, the visions which they offer are partial and can be disclosed in their meaning – and so fully seen – only through acts of interpretation (beginning with the prophet himself), as essential for faith as for reason. Thus while an approach to pure vision is strengthened by faith, it still does not constitute a moment isolatable from discursive mediation.

It follows that, for Aquinas, revelation offers the extraordinary only in a very qualified fashion. Even the miraculous must be apprehended by the senses in the normal way, and is in continuity with the usual operation of nature insofar as what ultimately matters about both is the meanings they convey, not the equally limited realities which they instantiate. And the extraordinary is indeed confined to the manner or means of disclosure of meaning, since the meaning disclosed is simply divine reality. Thus if reason leads us up to a God unknowable in this life, faith leads us to the same destination, and with the same restriction. It is only in post-Baroque conceptions of revelation that faith appears to answer to something 'more' – to new disclosures of information about God and about what God has done. Paradoxically, such newness can appear to throw into relief and to substantiate the pure autonomy of reason. But where, as with Aquinas, 'revelation' denotes simply God's self-disclosure, then no new domain other than that of reason is opened up, since, as we have seen, we are only able to think at all within the arena of the divine self-disclosure and our partial grasp of the divine *reditio ad seipsum* in which he substantially consists. Thus instead of reason's autonomy being thrown into relief by faith, reason itself, and the goals of reason, are further fulfilled by faith.

It follows that reason and faith are at the very least construed by Aquinas as successive phases of a single extension always qualitatively the same. That is to say, always conjoining inner illumination of the active intellect by God with formation of the passive intellect by species received from creatures, whose being, equally with our intellect, is formed and measured by participation in the divine understanding.

III

There can equally be no doubt that Aquinas distinguishes between the theology that pertains to philosophy, on the one hand, and *sacra doctrina*, on the other. But again the difficult issue concerns exactly in what manner.

In this case, however, there would seem on the face of things to be a clearly made distinction. Breaking with Aristotle's alternations and *aporias,* Aquinas declares that the prime subject of metaphysics is being and not the first cause.[18] By 'being' as subject-matter, Aquinas means here its transcendental properties such as 'substance', which need not inhere in matter (rendering them meta-physical) and excludes the 'causes of being' (only secondarily dealt with), which are its first principles, including the first cause: these cannot inhere in matter. One is tempted to say that with this development metaphysics has become a fundamental ontology; however, this transformation was yet to come (with Scotus). In Aquinas's case the subject-matter of metaphysics is not being in its entirety, but *ens commune,* that being which is 'common' to finite creatures and distinguished from their natures or essences; being which is entirely secondary and created. God only enters into consideration for this newly restricted metaphysics insofar as it is obliged, like any science, as part of its procedure, to inquire into the causes of its subject-matter.[19] Again, as with any science, however, this inquiry must be very incomplete since (for Aquinas's set of Platonic/Aristotelian assumptions), the cause of a subject-matter must necessarily transcend it, and so be 'higher' than the effect it produces. By this token, the cause invoked necessarily belongs to the domain of a higher science, above the one being pursued. Hence, in the present instance, metaphysics is able barely to indicate the cause of *ens commune,* to pronounce it 'God', and to indicate negatively the properties of inconceivable absolute and simple power and undividedness it must possess in order to be able to bring forth actuality.

But concerning God as he is in himself, his 'whatness', it must remain silent. Such matters are the concern (according to the exposition in the opening question of the *Summa Theologiae*) of a higher science, above metaphysics. However, this higher science, uniquely, is beyond the capacities of human reason, since it concerns the spiritual and infinite, and human reason is attuned only to material finite things, not even to disembodied intelligence and still less to infinite reality. Therefore, in this case uniquely, there is a science that can be possessed properly only by that which it is the science of – God, who, being simple, is of course absolutely identical with his own self-understanding.[20] The only possible mode of access for human beings to this final science is in consequence by divine self-disclosure, upon which *sacra doctrina* is based. Like other restricted sciences, *sacra doctrina* borrows its assumptions and first principles from a higher science, but here this is the absolute science possessed by God and the blessed alone.[21]

The new Thomist restriction of metaphysics and consequent confinement of metaphysical knowledge of God to the *an est,* reserving to *sacra doctrina* the exposition of the *quid est* [22] (insofar as some remote intimation of this has been revealed to us), opens, of course, a tempting possibility for mediation between Barth and Aquinas on a post-Kantian basis.[23] For if one suggests, as one validly can, that the metaphysical knowledge of God as first cause in Aquinas is both thin and tentative, then the way lies open to stress that for him, as for Barth, all certainty regarding God derives from scripture. Now this stress is by no means false, but it can tend to ignore the fact that, for Aquinas, in an unBarthian fashion, scripture records the event of the augmentation of human intellect through a deepened participating in the divine simplicity. Thus, for Aquinas, it is less that metaphysics is abandoned by reflection on scripture, and much more that it is fulfilled in its intention, but beyond its own understanding of this intention. It is both suspended and subsumed. And we shall soon see that this continued deployment of metaphysics by *sacra doctrina* in fact calls into question the neat division of

cognitive range between *an est* and *quid est.* The post-Kantian mediation
between Thomas and Barth will turn out to be false, because the weak
analogical recourses of metaphysics which reason to God only as first cause
are in fact the only terms in which *sacra doctrina* can receive and
comprehend the revelation of God as he is in himself. Since metaphysics can
in this way be elevated, its limitations for Aquinas do not amount to the
drastic ones perceived by Kant.

However, in terms of the apparently sharp *an est/quid est* division, it
would seem that Aquinas authorizes, if not a fusion of Kantian philosophy
and Barthian theology, then at least a clear division of theological subject-
matter between a doctrine of Creation accessible for metaphysics, on the one
hand, and the rest of the credal teaching – supremely the doctrine of Trinity
– accessible only for *sacra doctrina,* on the other.

But were matters as simple as this, then one would expect Aquinas to have
divided up his substantive teaching accordingly. However, he does not do so.
Specifically, it is by no means clear that he ever engages in 'metaphysics' in
his own right, as opposed to commenting on metaphysical treatises in a
context which virtually equates metaphysics with 'pagan teaching'.[24] The
nearest he comes to this might be the explicitly apologetic *Summa Contra
Gentiles,* wherein he does indeed treat of God in relation to creatures by way
of rational 'ascent' in the first three books, and then of God in himself by
way of revelatory 'descent' in the fourth book, which includes an account of
the Trinity.[25] This is not, however, necessarily regarded by Aquinas as an
ideal scheme according to the intrinsic demands of the subject-matter, and
since the scheme is abandoned in the *Summa Theologiae,* there is every
reason to assume (as Aquinas indeed indicates)[26] that it is adopted for
reasons of apologetic strategy. Of course, that it can be so adopted is highly
significant, and might seem to betoken the clear-standing independence of a
metaphysical approach to God. However, throughout the first three parts
scripture is cited (if with discrimination) and, more decisively, the doctrines
of the beatific vision and of grace are dealt with, despite their (fully
acknowledged by Aquinas) Christological and Trinitarian presuppositions.
It is as if Aquinas's approach to apologetics was in fact highly pragmatic, in
such a way that in the 'broadly monotheist' first three parts, he included not
only metaphysical considerations, but also doctrinal matter that might not
appear so immediately alien to Muslims and Jews.

However, the *Summa Theologiae* should be taken as a more realistic guide
at once to Aquinas's purely theological and to his most mature understanding (especially if it is intended for 'beginners' only in the sense of standing at
the commencement of the most advanced stage of theological learning).[27]
Here the treatment of the triune God is inserted after the exposition of
divine unity (so concluding a single continuous treatment of God at the
outset) and before a later reverting to more 'philosophical' topics (for
example, concerning ethics). Moreover, in the *Summa Theologiae* it is clearer
than with the *Summa Contra Gentiles,* that the work throughout belongs to

sacra doctrina. If God's unity and perfection are 'demonstrated', they are nonetheless also treated as revealed by scripture and testified to by tradition[28] (while, inversely, merely probable arguments are offered for the Trinity). Moreover, scripture primarily, and Christian tradition secondarily, are seen as contributing far more compelling evidence for the intellect (that is to say, as providing, much stronger, because immediately apparent *reasons*) than the even more weakly intuitive deliberations of philosophy.

Michel Corbin has pointed out another crucial difference from the *Summa Contra Gentiles*.[29] In the latter work, metaphysics operates within *ratio* and *scientia,* while the province of *sacra doctrina* tends to be that of *similitudo* – an imagined likeness of the divine intellect scarcely amounting to science. Correlatively, metaphysics here offers through all its *rationes* a mere *similitudo* of *sacra doctrina*.[30] However, in the *Summa Theologiae*, both metaphysical theology and *sacra doctrina* are brought firmly within the domain of *scientia*.[31] This is not at all, as Corbin rightly insists, merely in terms of a structural isomorphism. The latter was, indeed, all that was involved in Aquinas's initial understanding of *sacra doctrina* as *scientia* in the *Commentary on the Sentences:* here it meant simply that theology, also, makes deductions from first principles. Now, however, theology participates in the divine science, the mind of God, which includes in immediate indivision both 'principle' and 'derived conclusion', these being only distinguished according to our *modus significandi.* This is the new theory of *sacra doctrina* as a 'subalternate' science, borrowing from the conclusions of a higher science somewhat as music borrows from mathematics[32] – though the analogy can be, for Aquinas, only a remote one, since mathematics does not 'pre-contain' music, nor in principle swallow it up without remainder, as the *Scientia Dei* so subsumes *sacra doctrina* in both instances.

If, however, in the *Summa Theologiae*, there is a much more integral relation between divine self-understanding and sacred theology, there is also a much more integral relation between sacred theology and metaphysics. The 'preliminary' role of metaphysics on its own as establishing God as first cause is now barely gestured towards,[33] and instead the focus is upon the need for *sacra doctrina* itself to deploy philosophical arguments.[34] Moreover, no longer does metaphysics offer vague similitudes of theological similitudes (in a fashion which tends to suggest more of a cleavage between discursive reason and the positive authority of faith). Instead, theology has direct recourse to metaphysical *scientia* – its unarguable principled insights and its discursive arguments – because it is in itself simply the deepening and strengthening of science. This recourse is not at all necessary because of any innate deficiency on the part of *sacra doctrina*, since, in principle, as the grasp of divine self-knowledge, it is not cognitively deficient in any respect whatsoever – not in relation to philosophy as metaphysics ('first' philosophy), nor in relation to philosophy as the various liberal arts. Rather, it is necessary on account of the innate deficiency of human reason, which cannot, short of the final vision of glory, grasp what is in itself most intelligible, but must explicate this in terms of reasonings clearer to humanity, but in themselves less clear, which is to say, less *rational*.

Thus, as Corbin establishes, in the *Summa Theologiae*, philosophical theology figures much less as an independent phase with procedures and assumptions other than those of *sacra doctrina* (its role being now that of *manuductio*). To the contrary, it seems that within the scope of a single consideration (whether of, for example, the divine truth, or the persons of the Trinity), one passes imperceptibly from the relatively discursive to the relatively intuitive, as we more nearly approach the pure divine insight. Therefore, it is not at all here the case that reason offers certainty, and faith a clinging to uncertainties. Instead, there is one continuous passage of reason/faith from illusory relative certainty to obscurely envisaged absolute certainty. In addition, one can point out that in the realm of metaphysics, even the relative certainty proffered by reason is very weak. For scientific demonstration proper depends, for Aquinas after Aristotle, on a univocity of terms answering to a univocity between causes and effects. For Aquinas, this contention disallowed a transgeneric 'science' in the strictest sense, since the community of being (which Aquinas terms 'analogical'), permits no clear conception of a distinct operating substance (what *is* being outside its community?), nor of specific differentiation which constitutes scientific definitions (as nothing can be added to being, and it is no more nor less being in all its categorical and individualized manifestations).[35] Since, however, Aristotle placed the first mover within the genus of substance as the 'highest genus' that is 'immutable substance', and even saw it in its underived self-standing as paradigmatic of a substantive being, he was able to speak scientifically of 'God'.[36] Aquinas, however, by identifying God with non-generic *esse*, and by specifically excluding God from genus and from substance in the sense either of distinct essence or self-standing individual (though not in the sense of self-subsistent),[37] also ensures that there can only be an analogical and not strictly scientific approach to the divine. Hence, for example, his 'demonstrations' of God's existence can only be meant to offer weakly probable modes of argument and very attenuated 'showings'.

It is here significant that, despite Aquinas's supposedly more *a posteriori* and cosmological bent, he does deploy, almost as much as Anselm, an Augustinian 'logic of perfection'. Indeed, after the consideration of divine simplicity and being in the *Summa Theologiae*, the consideration of divine perfection and goodness immediately follows.[38] This is required, since a projection of what must belong to the perfect, alone allows one to establish God's further attributes, given that he is radically unknown (and indeed it is actually presupposed by Aquinas even for simplicity and being). This primacy of perfection in Aquinas cannot simply be a matter of his empirically observing that in nature the relatively perfect precedes the relatively imperfect, since there is no available sensory information that will confirm this pattern in the most sublime height. Here, indeed, it *might* seem that we only know the most perfect (or absolute good) 'to be' because we respond to a certain pre-ontological insistence of the ideal (Plato's Sun of the Good beyond Being which itself discloses Being).

Thus *a posteriori* demonstration from creatures plays a weak role in Aquinas, and there is in fact much more Augustinian *a priori* (so to speak) argument – in terms of 'what must' belong to perfection – than is usually allowed. It is even the case that we only know God to be the fullness of *esse* without particular essential limitation, or restriction to this or that possibility of unrealized actuality, because we also know all finite beings under the aspect of *bonum*, or their always more or less desirability, and therefore cannot conceive of any bare 'fact' that does not incite some sort of assessment. (The idea that something 'either exists or not', without degrees of intensity of existing, is impossible for Aquinas, as it must still be for theology, since it implies a neutral, inert, meaningless and uncreated existing as belonging to a thing in its own right.) While, for Aquinas, in terms of substance, a thing primarily is said 'to be', and secondarily is said 'to be good' (since mere existence is also good), in terms of its operation it is primarily regarded as 'good' (since operation involves teleology) and secondarily as 'existing'. Yet (as we shall see) the 'second act' of operation is, for Aquinas, itself a superadded degree of *esse* that is more hyperessential than the 'original' given substance. This suggests strongly that we only grasp *esse* in its most intense aspect of superaddition to original substance (and essence) under the aspect of goodness (although of course the apprehensions of *esse* and *bonum* are only distinct for finite understanding).[39] Nonetheless, it suggests equally that, for Aquinas, the guiding apprehension of perfection is *not* after all of a pre-ontological formal possibility (as it soon became for Duns Scotus) but rather is a dim and remote perception of a plenitude of infinite actuality. The insistence of the ideal is, after all, as much ontological as pre-ontological.

Therefore Aquinas does not really have recourse to an *a priori* vision of the Good in the sense of a Kantian epistemological reflection on the structures of finite understanding, but to a Platonic and Augustinian ontological recollection of something real and eternal. If this recourse indicates the limits of Aristotelian cosmological aspirations in Aquinas, it is equally the case that, like Augustine, he refuses (as he thinks, against Anselm) any purely *a priori* philosophical theology, or argument from the conception of the highest perfection to the necessity of its existence. On the contrary, Aquinas does not regard perfection as self-evident when reduced to bare possibility, and therefore is able to entertain (apparently) equally a nihilistic possibility: although the highest good would have to *be*, there need not be a highest good.[40] Hence, after all, the only thing that authenticates perfection (and indeed, the only thing that defines it), must be some sort of experience of its actuality. And this is indeed implied by Aquinas's repeated insistence on God's partial communication of his good to creatures, in such a way that their goods can only be understood as good in their pointing away from themselves to the perfection they hint at (their own partial perfection consisting in just this hint).[41] That which clinches his exposition of the divine attributes is neither the ascent from effect to first cause nor the *a priori* grasp of the latter, but rather the (Dionysian) reading of the divine signs and symbols as disclosed in the hierarchies of participating creatures.[42] Such an hermeneutic space is, in metaphysical terms, highly elusive and unstable, since it is grounded neither in firm *a posteriori* evidences, nor in solid *a priori* necessities. Given this conclusion, it is not surprising that in the *Summa Theologiae* Aquinas asserts the tentative character of all philosophic deliverance about God in the face of revelation, and claims that even philosophic 'certainties' are either confirmed more strongly, or can even be overruled by, *sacra doctrina*.[43]

If metaphysical theology is so uncertain that it enjoys, at best, a weak autonomy, this is not at all to say that, for Aquinas, by contrast, *sacra doctrina* is triumphantly disclosive. Here, instead, we discover that the contrast of the two theologies now further breaks down, but this time from the opposite direction. For while it is said of metaphysical theology that it can only know that God is (as first cause), what he is not, and by no means what he is, exactly the same restrictions are placed on *sacra doctrina*.[44] It is, therefore, after all not the case that for Aquinas philosophy knows God barely to be, while theology proper declares his nature. To the contrary, it seems that both can do the former, and neither can do the latter. So what does *sacra doctrina* add, and why are there two theologies?

At this point another temptation arises, and one somewhat succumbed to by those, in the wake of Henri Trouillard, wishing to slant Aquinas in a henological rather than ontological direction.[45] This is to suppose that what revelation discloses is an absolute degree of divine unknowability, a *deus absconditus* at a 'distance' absolutely removed even from the causal apex of being arrived at by philosophy, and so from intellection, actuality, unified mind and personality. One problem with this position is that it seems to leave the finite symbolic and historical vehicles of revelation stranded in a pure positivity, just as the gulf which it imposes between infinite and finite must tend to a quasi-manichean refusal of finitude.[46]

Such a second temptation – a radicalization of the first Kantian one, since it renders the beyond-limits an empty sublime – should also be resisted. For in his *Commentary on Boethius's De Trinitate,* Aquinas explicitly follows Gregory the Great's as it were 'Hegelian' deconstruction of a 'Kantian' distinction between the *an est*, taken as a bare acknowledgement that there exists an ultimate noumenon (to speak in Kantian terms), and the *quod est,* taken as knowledge of God 'in himself'.[47] Aquinas, after Gregory, insists that one cannot know that a thing is without having some dim inkling of what it is, since nothing is ever manifest or judged as manifest in entirely neutral anonymity. This applies, one might interpolate, even in this extreme limit situation, since to glimpse any boundary, even an absolute boundary, must be to see, however inchoately, beyond that boundary, else one's gaze would pass right through it and one would register no boundary after all.

One can also point out the crucial but unstated and merely implicit coherence here with Aquinas's refusal of the ontological argument, as detailed above. For one might indeed be able to acknowledge a bare absolute cause without content were such a possibility existentially self-authenticating, but if this is not the case, then indeed one will only affirm such a cause if in some manner (it is very difficult to say how) its reality is manifest to us and we know incoherently what it is. (This is an actual theoretical presence of course deemed impossible by Kant, but on the basis of a non-problematization of limits which Aquinas had already surpassed. Also one can note here that the Kantian 'practical' postulation of God runs from 'ought' to 'can' to 'is', and so, in effect, is the ontological argument denied in theoretical reason. And since, for Kant, only practical reason observes fully the priority of the possible, and is thus for his rationalism much more rational than theoretical reason, which is taken to be too much in slavery to actuality, the ontological argument is, in Kantian terms, much more properly 'practical'.)[48] Thus Jacques Maritain (however much he has been sneered at) was absolutely right as against Gilson and others to claim that there is some inchoate temporal knowledge of the divine essence in Aquinas.[49] And two other considerations support this conclusion. First of all, philosophical reason for Aquinas concludes to God (the ground of causation) as *esse ipsum,* but since God's essence is 'to be', to arrive in this fashion at an apparently bare existential affirmation is, uniquely in the case of God, to arrive also at some recognition of essence, albeit with the strict proviso that we no more comprehend what it is simply 'to be' in the infinitive (without tensed, pronomical or other mode of inflection), than we comprehend the divine *essentia.* However, the recent scholarship of Rudi te Velde and others has insisted that form and essence do not collapse into *esse* in God for Aquinas, but rather *esse* and *essentia* absolutely coincide in God, in such a way that God is superformal, 'most formal of all' and infinitely determined (not emptily existential). This reinforces the view that to encounter – in some fashion – God as *esse,* is to encounter him in some small degree as he in himself.[50]

The second consideration concerns Aquinas's view of causality. Aquinas consistently takes a neoplatonic view according to which an effect is like its cause, indeed pre-eminently exists in its cause. As Jean-Luc Marion astutely suggests, this causal origin is really for Aquinas less Aristotelian 'cause' than the Dionysian 'requisite' (*aitia*), or attribution to the original source of the 'gift' of the effect in its whole entirety as effect.[51] For this view (which entirely circumvents David Hume's correct critique of the metaphysics and physics of causality), a cause does not really 'precede' an effect, since it only becomes cause in realizing itself as the event of the giving of the effect. Thus, for Aquinas, in the case of divine causality, the decision to create and the 'eminent' reality of creatures are included in the eternal uttering of the *Logos.*[52] Inversely, an effect does not really come after a cause, since only the effect realizes the causal operation and defines it. In other words, there is always a Humean surplus of pure inexplicable 'succession' which is the apparently random surplus of a new event over the event which precedes it, unless a cause is more than a cause, but rather the entire gift of the effect and the emanation of the effect, which itself defines the cause as cause. (One can see how the Trinity perfects this conception.) Hence the doctrine that effects resemble their causes is not an embarrassing metaphysical residue in Aquinas, but an intrinsic part of an essentially non-metaphysical (!) trans-mutation of cause, since metaphysics tends to view cause as straight-forwardly prior to, and independent of, its effects. As Marion indicates, a reduction of causality to efficient causality fulfils the metaphysical aspir-ation, and does not withdraw from it, as is usually thought. Given this understanding of causality in terms of requisition and participation, to know God as cause – as supreme form, as supreme goal, as the supreme being, perfection and manifestedness of things – must mean to enter more deeply into effects, in such a fashion that one starts to know more of them also in their source and origin.

Thus instead of insisting that, for Aquinas, not even *sacra doctrina* knows the divine essence in this life (though this is largely true), it is much more important to insist that even philosophical theology knows something of this essence (and one can note that, for Aquinas, even knowledge of finite essences is merely partial).[53] The question is, how can this be, without idolatrous impiety, and this will be answered in the next section. For now what is clear is that the *an est/quid est* contrast entirely fails to distinguish the two theologies. Corbin is quite correct to note that interest in any such distinction fades away in the *Summa Theologiae*.

Moreover, when one brings into juxtaposition (as Aquinas explicitly does not), the presentation of 'metaphysics' in the *Commentary on Aristotle's Metaphysics*, and the presentation of *sacra doctrina* in the *Summa Theologiae*, then one is struck by the fact that both are subordinated, albeit in different manners, to an inaccessible *Scientia Dei*. As we have seen, the subject-matter of metaphysics for Aquinas is unequivocally being (whereas for Aristotle it was aporetically and ontotheologically either being-in-general or the first-being [God], in such a way that in a circular fashion God is an instance of being in general and yet being in general is paradigmatically defined in terms of the perfect substance which is God).[54] However, the ultimate goal of investigation of a subject-matter, according to Aquinas, is discovery of its cause, and hence God as cause of *ens commune* is a secondary concern of metaphysics. Here, though, one might ask, what is the relation between concluding to a cause which is the subject of a higher science (God's own) in metaphysics, and deriving the first principles of one's science from a higher science (God's own) in *sacra doctrina*? For are not, for Aquinas, as for Aristotle (as not for post-Kantian philosophy), epistemological principles identical with ontological causes? Is not the end here also the beginning? To be sure this does not necessarily mean that higher causes/principles are always adequate grounds of effects/consequences – this constitutes the

'Humean' deficiency already alluded to. Hence the realities of mathematics (abstractable from specific matter, not from any matter) are certainly principles and causes of physical realities (only present in specified matter) and yet they do not 'account for' physical motion (the heart of physics after Aristotle), any more than mathematics fully 'accounts for' music. However, Aquinas speaks of the need for a science fully to account for the genus of its subject-matter, citing the physical investigation of 'natural bodies'.[55] Now physics, for Aquinas, fully accounts for motion, the heart of such realities, in terms of an appeal to the first mover, God. And this pushes us nearer to a cause not simply 'prior' (certainly not temporally, but also in a certain sense already described, not even ontologically), a cause which can alone be adequate, fulfilling the 'requisite'.

The 'first mover' emerges as the conclusion of a consideration of the subject-matter of 'moving things'. But as Aquinas's arguments for a first mover (*all* the five ways, taken together) show, they only work because motion is understood from the outset as being undergone with a purpose, or for a reason, and on account of a goal in accord with a nature. Therefore, if all these motions are themselves unmoved, their very motions – which is to say their purposes, reasons, goals, and natures – are themselves illusory.[56] In knowing motions, therefore, which are all aims towards perfections (while the latter are only knowable as participations of the supreme end, the supreme good), the first mover is really radically presupposed. The conclusion to a cause only works because of an initial dim apprehension of the cause as principle.

So must not something similar apply in the case of metaphysics? Are not its argued-to causes also secretly initially-presupposed principles? One could, however, argue here that Aristotle, unlike Plato, discovers principles purely immanent to finitude in the shape of real abstract universals not situated at a distance from the particulars from which they are abstracted: specifically the principles of substantive form (uneasily and aporetically poised between concrete individual and general essence). One could further argue that Aquinas renders those principles more independent (compared with Aristotle) of any paradigmatic appeal to the unmoved first mover. On this understanding (which has some plausibility), Aquinas would have moved half-way towards a Scotist pure ontology independent of theology, by allowing for a complete prior knowledge of finite essence and substance innocent of later queries as to origins. However, such a position would assume, like Scotus, that finite things univocally 'are' as much as the infinite, whereas Aquinas affirms that they only 'are' in a derived, approximate, analogical sense. Since he also takes pure being, *esse,* to be alone absolutely self-subsistent (in such a way that its individuating 'is' is its general nature and vice-versa, as if Socrates 'were' humanity – although God is neither 'individual' nor 'general'), it follows that finite things are also only substantive in a derived sense. Hence Aquinas speaks of metaphysics as concerned with *passiones entis* or the 'proper accidents' of being (*ens commune*) which are the several predicaments, *including* substance.[57] The point here is that finite being is not on its own account subsistently anything, but is only granted to be in various ways, although these include the mode of finite necessity, and the mode of (relative) substance. Moreover, these accidents are 'proper', since finite 'common' being can only *be* through these characteristic modes, and only these accidents paradoxically grant it the various things proper to itself which essentially define it.

Nothing, therefore, for Aquinas, in the finite realm properly 'is' of itself, nor is 'subsistent' of itself, nor is essentially formed of itself. If it is true (as commentators all acknowledge), that being is an *adveniens extra* which is 'superadded' to essence or form as an 'accident' (a locution Aquinas never altogether abandons),[58] then it is equally true that, since Aquinas holds that *forma dat esse*,[59] form or essence are also superadded, and essence cannot be a kind of independent receiving finite 'base'. (Erich Przywara worried about this in Aquinas, but almost needlessly, although essence/form never, for Aquinas, quite holds parity with *esse*.) As Rudi te Velde points out, were this so, then essence would appear to be an element positively proper to finitude and outside participating emanation, whereas Aquinas affirms that all finite being emerges from nothing only as, and through, its likeness to the divine. In keeping with this perspective, he holds that the higher in the scale of being things are (advancing, after Augustine, as we saw in the first chapter, from being through life to intelligence), the more they are defined in their essence not through their 'first act' of subsistent existence such as the 'burning' of fire, but rather through their properly accidental 'second act' (or second perfection) of effective operation (which is also a more intense existing, so that second act is more to be characterized as *esse*, first act more as *essentia*) – such as the heating and drying and liquefying caused by fire.[60] At the *telos* of this operation, things are also defined through a 'third perfection' which is the ecstatic attaining to 'something else' that is yet one's goal, one's rest. Supremely, under this scheme, as we described in the first chapter, thought is not the substantive essence of soul, since soul is the form of an animal, and its thinking power in humanity may be dormant, but rather a mere 'power' of the soul, even if – as a proper accident – it is 'consequent' upon the essence of the soul. And yet the 'actively potential', and properly accidental emanation of this power, is nonetheless what most defines the human animal.[61] With his effortless cunning (although it is the cunning of Proclean neoplatonism itself), Aquinas fuses Aristotelian naturalism with neoplatonic participation – this non-essential, mere thinking-tool owned by an animal is nonetheless the superadded descending *palladium* which renders us superessentially as we are, more than we are.

If *esse* and *essentia* are superadded, then so is subsistence. It is true that existentially 'to be' and essentially 'to be something' and substantively 'to be something in this' (e.g. human only by being Socrates or whomsoever), are only distinguished in finite creatures and therefore in one sense (as affirmed by Jean-Luc Marion in the case of being),[62] it is only creatures who are, or have natures or substances. However, in another equally or even more crucial sense, 'something' cannot fully be except by being absolutely all realized possibilities (for in this way it cannot not be and it cannot be more than it is); nor can something be fully defined except through an infinite operation; nor can something fully subsist unless it combines the self-standing of an individual with the self-determination of an essence and the repletion of unqualified *esse*.[63] Thus while God is beyond substance as given foundation, individual or universal, it is also the case that in none of these three finite modes (there being for Aquinas no original matter to supply a pure foundation) is true subsistence to be found, as it is in God. Creatures, for Aquinas, beneath the level of patterns of granted relative necessity and subsistence, are radically accidental. But not thereby, of course, accidents of the divine substance; rather they subsist by participation in this substance.

Nevertheless, Aquinas proclaims that metaphysics most of all treats of substance.[64] What can this mean, if metaphysics is now primarily about *ens commune*, not God, and yet subsistence is alienated to God? Is it that Aquinas's metaphysics moves in an ontotheological circle after all? No: it is rather that to look for the cause of *ens commune* (or *esse commune*, as sometimes phrased), finite essence, and finite substance, is to re-comprehend this 'subject-matter' in its own fundamental depth of origin from *esse* identical with *essentia* and *subsistentia*. In this causal referral, no surplus of integral effect remains, unlike the case of physical motion in relation to mathematics and geometry, or music to mathematics. But, at the same time, one must be referring all to a cause already dimly grasped as principle, since *ens commune*, finite essence and finite substance are only comprehensible as faint adumbrations of the one divine formal archetype. This is theoontology, not ontotheology, for in order to comprehend this archetype, it did not need first to be situated in a 'general discourse' about being, essence and substance, indifferent to finite and infinite, as later articulated by Scotus.[65] Therefore, in referring its subject-matter to a higher cause and a higher science, metaphysics must for Aquinas be moving (unlike physics or music) towards its own abolition. This is not, of course, because he espouses a theological arrogance, but merely because nothing can be added to the divine knowledge or divine power. Any philosophical additions which continue to be required are a consequence of our continued (but potentially ever-diminishing) imperfection, not of a kind of divinely-decreed division of intellectual labour.

But the more radical implication of the above analysis is that the meta-physical argument from subject-matter to alien higher cause is structurally indistinguishable from *sacra doctrina*'s derivation from alien higher principles. It seems, then, that metaphysics as self-abolishing and self-evacuating (in order to fulfil itself), is already, in some weak sense, *sacra doctrina*: indeed Aquinas explicitly affirms that all speculative sciences participate in and anticipate the light of glory – an assertion which is equivalent to such a claim, since what constitutes *sacra doctrina* is precisely this participation and anticipation.[66] And, after all, how can metaphysics remain as 'the architectonic science', if there is a still higher, more architectonic science, which is nonetheless radically unknown? This being the case, in order to fulfil its architectonic role, metaphysics must seek revealed guidance from above, thereby becoming merely artisanal, subordinate and no longer metaphysical.

Inversely, therefore, *sacra doctrina* now articulates the real metaphysics, the real ontology, theology, gnoseology, and so forth. And just as the causes found by metaphysics at the end were really the principles known at the beginning, so, counterwise, the principles revealed to *sacra doctrina* at the outset are really the causes sought at its conclusion. For *sacra doctrina* does not add consequences drawn by human science to principles derived from divine science, as music might infer harmonies from mathematical ratios. On the contrary, since the divine principles include immediately in all their simplicity all the 'consequences', or rather, since here there are only principles,[67] *sacra doctrina* seeks to penetrate more and more the consequential effectiveness or causal potency of the divine principles of knowledge which are equally the divine principles of action (since in God theory and practice are identical). Just like metaphysics, only with more intensity, it begins improperly with created effects and refers them in their entirety – removing them from their own nullity to their divine letting-be – to the divine cause, which exceeds *sacra doctrina*'s powers of comprehension. Thus, as with faith and reason, the difference between the two theologies in Aquinas is at most one of degree and of different phases within a single extension.

IV

However, in the case of both pairs, even this distinction of phases is not so clear. First of all, let us return to the issue of faith and reason.

In the first question of the *Summa Theologiae*, Aquinas asks why, if God can be naturally known, he has to be discursively inferred, and is not immediately apparent. In reply, however, he affirms that there is, indeed, an inchoate ordering of all human reasoning to the beatific vision, the final intellectual intuition of God.[68] Thus beneath the distinction of *fides* and *ratio* along our temporal ways, lies the much more fundamental contrast between *in patria* and *in via*. According to this contrast, both faith and reason are dim anticipations of the final vision of glory. One here finds confirmed the view that, for Aquinas, since *a priori* reasonings to God are refused, and straightforward *a posteriori* inductions are equally impossible, discursive reasoning about God must presuppose a disclosure of God to our *intellectus*, which enjoys a very remote participation in the divine immediacy of vision. In the passage cited, Aquinas compares this remote glimpse to a first sight of 'Peter' in the distance before we know that it is, indeed, Peter who approaches. It is therefore clear that Aquinas, like Augustine before him, associates our continuous approach to the beatific vision with 'the Meno problematic', or the need already to know something before one can possibly come to know it – for how else will one in the first place seek to know it at all? And the same problematic (with the added example of the child first addressing all men vaguely as 'father') is alluded to in the passage in the *Commentary on Boethius's de Trinitate* already discussed, where it is directly associated with the assertion that we must in some way already know the divine essence in order to affirm God's existence.[69]

From Augustine and Anselm, therefore, Aquinas has inherited a deep identification of the Platonic problematic of knowledge with Christian eschatological tension. For the first two thinkers, reason itself is faith seeking understanding, since for thought to get going it must not only trust its first sight of a man in the distance, but must first believe the reports of others that this is to be called 'man'. And if, for all these thinkers, reason for now can only be faith, then, inversely, faith for now can only develop its insights rationally and discursively, while finally it is destined to be pure *intellectus*, when we shall see as we are seen (though not enjoy any Hegelian 'comprehension' of the absolute). Once freed from our bodily carapace, the contrast between object seen and medium-seen-by disappears (here Aquinas is Aristotelian and neoplatonic since he refuses an alleged Platonic 'polytheistic' diversity of many forms 'illumined' by the sun of the Good), and we see only what we see by, the uncreated light, though we receive it still only in part, and also as created.[70]

However, Aquinas introduces a yet more dramatic association of knowledge in general with eschatological vision. In the middle of part one of the *Summa Theologiae*, he executes the most extraordinary *chiasmus*. For in expounding the divine attributes, one might expect Aquinas to proceed, after his treatment of being, simplicity and perfection (goodness), quite shortly to transcendental truth and intellection. Instead, before anything has been said of divine intellect or will (approaching 'personhood'), Aquinas details God's presence to creatures, under the heading of divine substance.[71] This drastically indicates that God's omnipresence simply is God himself, and that there cannot really be any being 'other' than God. Such omnipresence is seen as the direct effect of divine goodness, and elsewhere Thomas cites Dionysius's 'daring to say' that God on account of his goodness exists 'as it were outside of himself'.[72] For only this impossible self-exteriorization will explain how there can be something other to God participating in God, when God is in himself the repletion of being. This impossible conjecture is the most that can be said. In part one of the *Summa Theologiae*, however, it is added that God is especially and uniquely present to intellect, where 'he dwells as if in his own temple'; also it is made clear that intellect simply is this more intense presence, and that this presence is only by grace.[73] Thus at the heart of the chiasmic reversal – Creation and humanity dealt with under divine substance – grace appears for the first time, and in the midst of what some have taken to be an exercise in purely rational theology. One could interpret this to mean that, for Aquinas (and here we press perhaps beyond the *nouvelle théologie*), all creatures subsist by grace in the sense that they only subsist in their constant 'return' to full divine self-presence, while intellect simply is the consciousness of this return.[74] Thus not only is the intellect grace; it is in a sense simply the site of manifestation of the creature, and so of grace. Because we are mind, humans specifically are destined to be deified.

It is only after this description of mind as the event of divine kenotic descent, that Aquinas re-describes it as also the event of eschatological ascent: in other words, his account of the beatific vision is deliberately placed quite shortly after his account of divine omnipresence. In this account, as de Lubac pointed out (thus continuing and recommencing the real theological revolution of the twentieth century),[75] Aquinas argues that reason has a natural urge to *see* the divine essence, since science is unsatisfied till it knows the nature of a cause. And since nature cannot be frustrated, he further argues that this urge must be capable of fulfilment.[76] On the other hand, he equally affirms that such a supernatural fulfilment surpasses the capacity of human nature, in such a way that reason can only fulfil its aspiration by grace.[77] Today, Catholic conservatives like J.-H. Nicolas, who wish to back away from de Lubac's revolution, try to claim that only the fulfilment is granted by grace, while the impulse to the beatific vision is purely natural.[78] Yet this cannot be the case, because a nature is fulfilable as a nature; it demands as of right fulfilment, and hence if we are naturally orientated to the supernatural, this can only be because our original and 'most proper' nature is a paradoxically superadded nature (a supreme instance of 'second act'), giving us more than our due as our due, and pulling us naturally beyond our nature in an *ecstasis* at the outset.

But since our mind cannot fulfil its own rationality, except through knowing the divine essence, and since otherwise it would not 'see' that the highest imaginable perfection 'is', whereas it might not be, rendering the world without order or meaning (and imagination mere fiction), there simply would be no 'reason' whatsoever, outside the orientation to beatitude. Mind is the continuing event of this orientation, suspended between the already of a pre-discursive glimpse of the final vision of God, and the not yet of the full realization.

It might, however, be contended that these passages which seem to render reason as faith (and whose drastic implications are still resisted by much conservative and liberal Catholic theology within their shared assumptions), are confusing aberrations, not hermeneutically decisive. But in reply one can point to the cruciality of the context of the passage on orientation to beatitude: namely the chiasmic *interruptus* (also present in a different way in the *Summa Contra Gentiles*),[79] of the treatment of divine substance. The chiasmic reversal is completed when, after the treatment of the creation and finite mind under divine substance, Aquinas proceeds to treat divine truth and intellect under divine operation. Thus to the elevation of our being into the divine substance, answers God's foreshadowing, within himself, of a proceeding beyond himself. And surely this chiasmic structure implies that

Aquinas is advancing from an 'impersonal' knowledge of God as One and Good, shared with pagans like Proclus, to a more Christian apprehension of God as intentional mind and will and so as personal. Also, that while the first knowledge may be relatively a matter of rational ascent, the second is only granted through the radical descent of grace (even if Aristotle was able to anticipate fully-divine *nous*). Moreover, intellection as a more intense presence of God, already suggests that God must first be disclosed if he is to be desired, and thus that in us, as in God, *logos* must precede will (in God the Holy Spirit) – while only a gracious right-willing and desiring allows us to recognize what appears as a horizon of aspiration.

Thus it would appear that reason is not even a 'phase' distinct from faith – though it may offer a lesser degree of intensity – since it is situated in the same 'intense' suspension between time and eternity, and Aquinas affirms, as has been said, that all speculative sciences participate obscurely in the beatific vision. And this interpretation is confirmed by Aquinas's treatment of the historical perspective. Before the fall, reason was perfected by an original grace and righteousness which included an anticipation of the Incarnation in its aspect of glory (as Bruce Marshall has rightly insisted).[80] From this we can see that the beatific orientation is always, also, a Christological one. After the Fall, humans lost this original righteousness, and became incapable of obeying the natural law: Aquinas is quite clear, we cannot do any genuinely 'natural' good.[81] Equally, as Bruce Marshall has also pointed out, Aquinas declares that the 'partial' knowledge of God enjoyed by the pagans is no knowledge at all, since, given the divine simplicity, to know only some of the divine attributes is not to know any of them properly (and we shall see later, that the exposition of the Trinity completes the account of divine simplicity).[82] However, as Eugene Rogers has stressed, since God's creative action is not to be thwarted, the original righteousness becomes, after the fall, immediately available again as redeeming grace, already present in natural and historical typological anticipations of Christ.[83] For Aquinas, indeed, 'the invisible things of God' in Romans always made visible everywhere, suggested precisely a manifestation of the divine essence, which can only be made available by grace.

V

If faith and reason are not distinct phases, then neither are the two theologies. In fact, this has already been more or less demonstrated in section III, since there it was seen that metaphysics self-collapses into *sacra doctrina*, while the latter, as *in via*, must remain in the unsatisfactory transitional state which is 'metaphysical'.

Now, however, we wish to underline Aquinas's transmutation of the idea of an architectonic science, and his undermining of metaphysics' independent architecture. The vital issue here is the handling of the transcendentals, and, in particular, Being.

Can metaphysics, for Aquinas, really sustain a treatment of being as transgeneric? And is *ens commune* (the subject of metaphysics) like *esse* (a divine attribute) genuinely transgeneric? Commentators tend to dismiss Aquinas's occasional description of *ens commune* as a genus as a vague locution, but this may be too hasty.[84] For when discussing whether God enjoys knowledge of particulars, unlike our abstracting mind, Aquinas refuses one Arabic position according to which God only knows creatures under their 'being in general'.[85] This does, indeed, suggest that *ens commune*, since it is really distinct from creaturely *essentia* (for creatures might not be), is a kind of abstracted, 'bare' existential. (Here one might note that, for Aquinas, 'being' does not coincide with 'real', since for him 'real' stands in contrast with 'intellectual' or 'formal', not with nullity: hence mathematical entities 'are', but are not 'real'; reality denotes a more intense degree of being.)[86] It would follow that if metaphysics examines the accidental predicaments of *ens commune*, it cannot properly deal with *esse*, which as transgeneric, is just as fully instantiated in the concrete individual as the universal essence, or in an accident as in a substance. So what may be unstated by Aquinas, and is yet everywhere implicit, is that there is a radical inconsistency between Aristotle's claim, on the one hand, that metaphysics is the science of being which is transgeneric, and his claim, on the other, that as an architectonic science it only lays down an abstract ground plan, leaving the details of intellectual treatment to other sciences whose narrower scope is yet beyond its own competence. For if metaphysics deals with being, then surely it should deal with all there is. Surely it should be as variously artisanal as it is architectonic? At this juncture a formal/material distinction becomes deconstructible: the most general categories which we must presuppose – being, unity, truth, goodness, etc. – can only be formally defined through the endless empirical task of material description and re-description of an infinite number of particulars: metaphysics here becomes also history.

God's self-knowledge, as simple, is at once formal and material, and therefore exceeds the metaphysical as the ground of the historical. For whereas the self-thinking of the Aristotelian first mover is abstract, and does not extend to material particulars and so is 'metaphysical', the self-thinking of God, for Aquinas, includes all the exact details of every way in which he can be participated.[87] Therefore it is only architectonic to the degree that it is also artisanal, and only lays down the formal ground plan as the ideal comprehensive *esse* of the entire construction: since God's *theoria* is also practice, his 'preceding' idea is only realized with the completed 'work' of his emanating *verbum*.[88] Thus even for God, a pure seeing is also an immediate judging articulation. And since God is *esse*, he does indeed immediately contain in a unified expression which is also a single intuition (in such a way that, as we saw in Chapter One, God is a 'country bumpkin' as much as he is an artisan, and not at all a logician nor a politician),[89] an infinitude of participated knowledge. In this way God's science corresponds to the transgeneric status of *esse* – the impossibility of hierarchically dividing it, or

of qualifying it by addition – in a way that metaphysics as merely foundational and preliminary simply cannot. (This also shows that Aquinas,
by rendering God's science equally and ecstatically present to the lower
as to the higher, breaks with Aristotle's psycho-political paradigm for
metaphysics – referred to by Aquinas in his *Proemium* to his commentary
on the Metaphysics – which appeals to the need for self-government, or
rule of lower parts of a whole by a higher.) It is in consequence clear
that, as Marion now rightly declares, Aquinas entirely alienates *esse* to
God.[90] But in that case, since the divine essence which is *esse* is only
disclosed to *sacra doctrina*, he also alienates *esse in toto* to *sacra doctrina*
(and likewise subsistence, form and essence, since these also, as shown in
section III, belong properly to God alone and are superadded along with
esse).

Now it may seem that this Platonic and theoontological reading of
Aquinas is at variance with his Aristotelian recognition of a level of
abstraction of universal form which does not involve elevation and separation. Aquinas makes this recognition because he accepts Aristotle's
argument that forms situated eternally apart from finite things cannot really
be the substantial forms of those things, or in other terms do not account for
their separate subsistent existence.[91]

However, Aquinas's Aristotelian criticisms of Plato with respect to theology (for example in the *Commentary on the de Causis*)[92] again and again
involve: (1) the refusal of many forms as inconsistent with monotheism; (2)
the refusal of forms prior to the intellect as inconsistent with a personal God;
and (3) the refusal of matter as privative as inconsistent with Creation. In
other words, the Aristotelian critique of Platonic theology (as Aquinas
supposed it to be), is basically a bolstering of a Christian critique. And the
same thing can even be said of his defense of Aristotelian finite substance,
since this secures the independent reality and goodness of the Creation.
However, in his early *Commentary on Boethius's de Hebdomadibus*, Aquinas,
after Boethius, faced a dilemma: if created substances are only good as
receiving good from God, that is, by participation, then how can they be said
to be good at all, good in themselves, good in their substance?[93] Solving this
dilemma in part motivates Aquinas's switch of emphasis from *bonum* to *esse*:
for he argues that it is subsistent existence, as a participant in *esse*, that is
itself the most fundamentally participatory thing. Hence, a thing can be good
of itself, and yet also good only by borrowing, since its very own being is
the most borrowed thing of all. But, at the same time, and inversely, that
which is lent by God, granted to be participated in, is primarily the gift of
relative self-standing, in accord with the Dionysian idea that God's goodness
is his 'standing outside of himself'. Both these notions reconstrue participation as grace and kenosis, but they do not *add* grace and kenosis to
participation.

However, since relative individual self-subsistence, always open to the
super-essential addition of second act, is now itself radically participatory,

Platonism trumps Aristotelianism in Aquinas, in such a way that instead of the most general and abstract being removed from material things, it is rather individual material things which are paradoxically removed from themselves – referred beyond themselves in order to be recognized as themselves (and this may well be the real Plato, as Aquinas could not have known).[94] But this concrete material unity which is thus referred upwards, is also equally a general formal unity and being, in such a way that the transcendentals, unlike *genera*, are fully present in each one of their instantiations. Therefore, the upward referral of unities in their trans-cendental unity, which is not that of diverse species, is not in danger of diversifying the divine in a 'polytheist' fashion.

It follows that there can indeed be no secure, immanent, Aristotelian consideration of either being or substance for Aquinas, since metaphysics will not answer to the transgeneric manifestness of being (nor even of substance taken in a fully transcendental sense, according to which even an accident must have a certain secure integrity: for Aquinas accidents 'are' through substance).[95] Only God's own science, and then *sacra doctrina*, can so answer. Thus *sacra doctrina* as meta-architectonic is really only archi-tectonic as also artisanal and bumpkin-like. It does not, declares Aquinas, in apparent deficit of metaphysics, supply any principles to subordinate sciences; however, in excess of metaphysics, it can judge the conclusions of all subordinate sciences.[96] This must follow, since *sacra doctrina* is the true transgeneric science of *esse* and can in principle further illuminate being in all its instantiations. Thus although it deals with the real under the aspect of *revelabile* (as sight with reality under the aspect of colour), when anything discloses God it must, since it has its entire being from God, disclose itself more intensely and without remainder. God knows all things in their eminent reality – therefore it is clear that a disclosure of this science does not, in principle, require supplementation by other sciences, and can, in principle, as Aquinas insists, revise all their conclusions. However, this is not a programme for the extermination of other faculties, since for now theology continues to be mediated by metaphysics, and even more by the philo-sophical liberal arts, as those disciplines concern concrete specificities to which theology proper (*sacra doctrina*), unlike metaphysics, extends. One could even say that theology only exists in its infusing inflection of the arts and not somehow 'in itself'. Philosophy as metaphysics, however, because of its inadequate response to its own subject-matter, as detailed above, does have a tendency to be 'evacuated' by *sacra doctrina*.[97] (For this process, Aquinas offers military as well as chemical comparisons.)[98]

But why, if *sacra doctrina* judges even conclusions, does it offer no principles? The answer is astutely offered by Corbin: it is because theology as science in Aquinas redefines the very idea of science, away from discursivity and towards pure intuition, on its way to the beatific vision.[99] Thus to receive, obscurely, the first principles of divine science from God, is also to receive obscurely all the conclusions of divine science, which *are* the principles, since

God only sees (although he sees through making, and through making sees). So, as Corbin argues, even though *sacra doctrina* is now conceived as more 'scientific' than previously, this now implies that it receives divine principles/consequences with a greater non-discursive immediacy. But since we, as embodied creatures, can only enjoy an intense intuition via the senses, we now aspire higher only by attending more closely to the lower sensory realm to which God condescends. As metaphysics is now for *sacra doctrina* history, our reasoning must occur much more through images, narratives, and liturgical offerings. Above all, it is *sacra scriptura* as read, manifested, and performed (for it was not yet a discrete, foundational and merely written text), which now shows us science at its most scientific.[100]

Metaphysical theology and *sacra doctrina* are not then discrete phases, since for Aquinas there is only one never-fully-realized temporal passage from metaphysical discursivity with its incapacities fully to think the transgeneric (or to comprehend the formal as the material and vice versa), to the perfect vision of the divine self-understanding. But the mark of progress along this *via* is increasingly to see such historical development as itself the cognitive goal – itself the continuous manifestation of the transcendental. This is to look in history for the complete divine descent which can alone correct our wilfully wayward vision (which cannot see the invisible which is fully manifest in the visible) – a descent always presupposed as the only possible sustaining of original righteousness, but a descent which, much more emphatically, we are always yet to arrive at, even *anno domini,* as our final conclusion.

VI

Is it not the case, however, that Aquinas considers that natural reason can know God as one, and as creator, whereas faith is required to know God's inner life as triune? The first half of this contention must be considered false; first, because we have seen that the understanding of God as intellectual and willing, and so as creative, presupposes grace; and, secondly, because creatures are causally referred to the divine *esse*, which as transgeneric and inclusive of all reality is revealed as a divine name, not infallibly inferred.

In addition, it has been seen how not only Creation as a whole is a gift for Aquinas, but each creature is ceaselessly re-constituted through supplementation, in such a way that the 'more' and 'later' is taken paradoxically to define it. These instances of proper accidents arising through the second act of operation, also involve the constitution of 'real relations' (as, for example, between thing causing and thing caused), in such a way that relations entered into in time can nonetheless be included in the definition of what a thing essentially is.[101] Here also, one can see how the transcendentally non-generic character of the most fundamental predicaments extends now for Aquinas to event. And it is within the field of relation that the transcendentals 'Good' and 'True', along with willing and knowing, are instantiated. For the Good concerns the intrinsic proportionate ordering of one thing to another, a real relation, while the True concerns the presence of one thing in another: a merely one-sided relation *secundum dici* with respect to the thing known, but a real relation with respect to the knowing power and its expression of its knowledge of the other.[102]

It is surely clear that this new theological ontology of constitutive supernatural supplementation and ecstatic relationality reveals a cosmos already in a sense graced, and in such a fashion that the supplement of grace will not seem in discontinuity with existing principles of ontological constitution.

However, such ontological revision, undertaken by theology, would appear to be ruled out if one takes it to be the case (ignoring the *aporias* of the transgeneric), that one can draw up a list of categorical presuppositions once and for all, since their 'formality' is uncontaminated by material 'event'. This, however, is claimed by many Catholic theologians and philosophers. Nicholas Lash, for example, insists that metaphysics has gone wrong when it has mistakenly supposed categories like 'being' to be substantive, while those thinkers from Aristotle to Wittgenstein who insist on the formality of the categorical are all saying essentially the same thing.[103] But, surely, the realization that the categories we must presuppose in order to think or speak at all are not 'things', in the sense of ordinary 'objects', is more the beginning of perplexity than it is the dissolution of an illusion? For if they are not entities, then are they merely convenient and unavoidable fictions, as for nominalism? Or else, are they somehow universally real and entitative, yet not in the normal thing-like mode of entities, existing primarily in the mind but also somewhat in specified individuals (as for Aquinas)? Or are they psychological biases (Hume, Nietzsche)? Or else subjective yet necessary pre-conditions for the display of phenomena (Kant)? Or alternatively preconditions enshrined in an objective logical universe (Bolzano, Frege)? Or, yet again, are they embodied in a hard-to-disentangle mixture of animal and cultural ritual behaviour (Wittgenstein)? None of these construals crudely hypostasize the categorical, but they are all very different, and are ultimately perhaps rooted in different visions of the world, beyond the reach of argumentation. But in such a situation it is surely valid to imagine that a theological vision will have its own interpretation of the need for, and presentation of, categorical presuppositions.

Indeed, the consequence of theology not doing so is likely to be idolatry, as witnessed by the case of the late medieval and early modern scholastics. Since they on the whole came to regard transcendental being in purely philosophical terms as an empty, univocal category of mere existentiality, and no longer as an attribute of perfection, they could make no real sense of God as hypostasized *esse*.[104] And in consequence of this inability to grasp a subtle sort of hypostasisization, they were indeed forced to reduce the divine *esse* to the status of a thing, since the only conceptual resource left open to their theology was to conceive God as 'a' being, however supreme.

The empty univocal concept of being which became the groundwork of modern metaphysics arises from elevating the logical grasp of being – a thing simply 'is' or 'is not' – over the ontological grasp, for which all actuality manifests more or less intense existence according to its innate perfection. The prior logical or formal grasp is then permitted to structure ontology in such a fashion that this is really an ontology of the *virtually* real, and no true ontology at all. Too often in the twentieth century such a strategy has been read back into Aquinas, in order to secure a dimension of pure metaphysics in his writing which will be compatible with the modern metaphysical edifice – always erected, ever since Suarez at least, on a logical/formalist and later transcendentalist base.

Thus Bernard Lonergan contended that, for Aquinas, a metaphysician is simply a sort of more powerful logician. Actually, in the context cited, what Aquinas said is that metaphysics is more powerful than logic, since the latter deals with the predicaments only as intellectual entities, beings of reason, whose truth is merely probable – since their degree of ontological subsistence is rather weak – while the former deals with real actualities and as a result possesses a greater certainty.[105] This entirely ontological conception of logical reality is clearly at variance with any mode of semantic access to phenomena after Bolzano and Frege, since for Aquinas logical possibility is only a faint version of real substantive actuality. It is designed to 'intend' this actuality, and guaranteed only by this actuality. For example, the 'logical' identification of Socrates with white in the mind in the phrase 'Socrates is white' – which taken literally identifies one genus with another – is only designed to disclose the inherence of the accident 'white' in Socrates's substantial being (if this is indeed the case in actuality).[106] Otherwise, logic would be trapped inside a nonsense world where Socrates really was identical with whiteness, given that we have to see how an accident inheres in a substance, and logic of its own capacity cannot conceive this. Therefore, were the metaphysician merely a more powerful logician, we would for Aquinas be ushered into a mad universe where everything could be identified with everything else.

The primacy granted to logic in the structuring of ontology by Lonergan, correlates with his hostility to any notion of intellect as vision, or to intellectual intuition in the sense of encounter with the real presence of the ideal, which we have shown to be fundamental for Aquinas. Lonergan subscribed to something akin to a Neo-Kantian/phenomenological notion of the *a priori*, as not once and for all accessible, but rather as continuously unfolding in the presence of phenomena, and in its open horizon somehow pre-assuming an orientation to the divine (but not as encounter with participated divine light, as for Aquinas). However, he insisted that this unfolding discursivity involves 'explanation' beyond Husserl's mere description, and this seems to correlate with his refusal of intellectual intuition, since what judgement grasps is a kind of necessary coherence of structure in the given, not the sheer 'presence' of things.[107] To this scheme, however, Lonergan conjoined, quite arbitrarily, a certain realism, in such a way that intellect is completed by a genuine 'insight into phantasm' mediated by the senses (and in this reduced sense he accepts a certain 'intellectual intuition'). The conjoining appears arbitrary, since the 'look' of the senses or the imagination is not confirmed for Lonergan by an intellectual gaze, but instead the judgement can only grasp the supplied insight within logical and self-consistent structures of holding-together which it grasps by unfolding its own latent powers of comprehension.[108] Absolutely nothing prevents one from taking this philosophy more consistently as an immanently confined idealism in which the human mind does not grasp anything of 'things in themselves'.

For certain later semanticist transpositions of Lonergan's transcendental Thomism, the unfolding *a priori* is located in the more objective sphere of language as constrained by logic and transcendental grammar. For this perspective, if it is possible coherently to use words to refer to God (in some remote sense), then this must be a possibility enshrined *a priori* in the logic of language and its use, a possibility within whose limits theology is confined. Here analogy is not thought initially to presuppose any account of participation in being. Rather it is seen as a 'comment on our use of certain words'. Here, once again, it appears that a specifically *theological* and revisionist construal of reality and how we refer to it, is ruled out of order and falsely associated with the approach of Aquinas.

One immediate problem with this semanticist proposal is that if analogy is sundered from metaphysics in this fashion, then, by the very same token, it is sundered from *sacra doctrina*, since if analogy is a transcendentalist theory of the possibility of human language, it cannot be, first and foremost, as it is for Aquinas, an exposition of the Dionysian revealed descent of certain mysterious 'divine names' primarily disclosed in scripture.

A second problem is contextual: Aquinas immediately precedes the question on the divine names with an account of how the vision of God in glory is dimly anticipated by some vision of God in his effects, consequent upon their participation in the divine *esse*.[109] This strongly suggests that analogy is predicated upon the metaphysics of participated being.

A third problem is terminological. Yes, to be sure, the term *analogia entis* was coined long after Aquinas, and only made generally current in the twentieth century by Erich Pryzwara. But this does not render it necessarily inappropriate, so long as it does not connote a post-Scotist 'Thomistic' analogy *within* being, taken as indifferent to infinite and finite, God and creatures. Clearly it is not entirely inappropriate, because Aquinas does speak of univocal *causes* (within the same species), equivocal causes (between different species – since despite the shared genus, specific differences are, from a generic perspective, unmediably distinct, like 'man' and 'tiger'), and analogical causes extending from *esse* to *genera*.[110] And one can note here that Aquinas specifically says that analogical likeness is more distant than equivocal (non)resemblance, yet also affirms analogy as mediating between equivocity and univocity.[111] This is because the transgeneric height of remoteness (all we know is even more unlike pure being, pure unity, etc., than one species or genus is unlike another) is nonetheless an equal closeness to everything, which reveals a hidden bond between finitely remote things and categories. In this way, for Aquinas, analogy discloses its elusive 'medium' status by abolishing any ontological equivocity whatsoever. Analogy is more equivocal than equivocation, because equivocal difference is after all only a weak degree of analogical resemblance. How could there be any equivocity, since all differences derive from transcendental unity?

This is the theological metaphysics which the theology of the divine names assumes. Aquinas is quite explicit: names stand for ideas in the mind which refer to things, and our minds can only grasp finite things by the mediation of the senses.[112] Thus, unless things themselves can be read as signs of God, names cannot be used analogically of God. The limits or unlimits of grammar reflect the limits or unlimits of the created order. But things can only be signs of God if the divine perfections are remotely visible in created perfections – or rather, if to see a created thing as possessing any perfection is to grasp its faint conveying of a plentitude of perfection beyond its scope. In other words, the metaphysics of participation in Aquinas is immediately and implicitly a phenomenology of seeing more than one sees, of recognizing the invisible in the visible.

This has to be affirmed, because Aquinas disallows any *a priori* proof 'that there must be the highest perfection', in such a way that we could just formally take it to be true that created perfections pointed to this, without experiential registering of this being the case. Inversely, it cannot be for Aquinas that analogy involves (at least initially) merely a projection from the possibilities of words that possess implicitly a range beyond what we can presently grasp – as with perfection terms such as 'beauty' which 'anticipate' artistic styles as yet unknown. For without ontological guarantee, this range might be merely equivocal save for human delusion – in such a way that relativists might say that the recognized 'beauty' of one era has nothing to do with the 'beauty' of another. In addition, the semanticist *a priori* understanding of analogy as projection from implicit linguistic resources can only issue in a purely agnostic rendering of analogy which is not Aquinas's. For the surplus of possible unknown goodness indicated by the use of the word 'good' must be, for an *a priori* consideration, simply a radically unknown Kantian sublime horizon, or a good entirely absconded. It can validly suggest from its own resources, only that God possesses his own, absolutely unknown perfection which is the efficient causal source of perfection in creatures. However, Aquinas refuses such an agnosticism: for him, we do not refer to the 'good' or 'life' of God because he is the source of good or life in creatures; rather we refer to the good or life of creatures because they manifest a good which is preeminently precontained in God in an exemplary and more 'excellent' fashion.[113] This pure light of perfection is, for Aquinas, after Dionysius, displayed in 'the many coloured veils' of

Creation. Only through such 'colours' do we see pure white light, but we do somehow see this, else we should not see colours at all, since they are, exhaustively, light's refraction.[114]

Thus analogy presupposes not just a metaphysics of participation, but also a phenomenology of participation, although this is not to say that the latter founds the former.[115] This is not the case, because there is, for Aquinas, no indefeasible original intuition of participated *esse* outside a (discursively mediated) judgement that this is the case, expressed within an entire conceptual and linguistic apparatus handed down to us from tradition. Thus for him, as for Augustine, the 'vision' of Peter approaching from the distance, will be initially also a received report of his approaching, the witness of others which conceptually frames our expectations of what we will come to see. For us, intuition is never prior to judgement supplemented by argument, which is preformed by language and tradition; there is no 'raw experience'.[116] Indeed, to ignore the non-visual dimension of oral report, historicity and judgement which fractures and yet essentially informs vision, is to reduce vision to a post-Ramist and Cartesian art of precise survey, which overlooks the truth that we only cognitively see in the light of an unseeable intellectual sun – all those obscure yet essential 'assumptions' which alone clarify everything else. For this problematic lacuna of darkness within the visible itself – which, nonetheless, for all creatures *constitutes* the visible – discursivity must seek to substitute, by rendering itself the means of showing the unshowable which illuminates.

And yet, if all being is only apparent though linguistic mediation, it is nonetheless the case that all language must be taken as only 'the showing forth' of being. If, to the contrary, one affirms that language, as relative and constricted, never discloses, this very assertion pre-constrains language within an *a priori* framework itself independent of linguistic contingencies. Thus a linguistic turn construed agnostically, and as preventing ontological disclosure (even where this is disclosure of the divine *esse*), undoes also the insight that we remain always within linguistic mediation.[117] By contrast, if we take it on trust that language does disclose, we can *remain* within radical linguisticality, since if language (or any pattern of symbolical mediation), discloses as well as articulates, we do not require in addition another disclosure. Hence only theology remains with the linguistic turn, because (after Hamann), it understands speaking to be also a seeing, or linguistic philosophy to be also phenomenology, and vice versa in either case.

In this respect, it is a mistake for theology to build on a linguistic turn construed as prior to theology, since this will always degenerate into a non-linguistic and dogmatic apriorism, which exalts an uncatholic *Deus Absconditus*. The tendency will be to construe the apophatic strategy as gesturing outside transcendentalist bounds of possible experience, and the range of constitutively meaningful linguistic expression.[118]

In this way, a bias to verbal foundations which denatures language into an *a priori* tends to engender an agnostic construal of analogy. But, curiously, a foundational phenomenology based on supposedly pure passive intuitions prior to linguistic interpretation can issue in just the same effect. For a foundational intuition must be undeniably manifest, and this can only be plausibly imputed to bounded, concrete things. The most one can say of the manifestation of the unbounded is that it is implied by bounded things as their ground. Such an implication will then be taken as a kind of minimal manifestness, so that if one's criterion for the real is appearance-to-intuition, one will take the negative showing of the unbounded as the latter's essence. Thus in Heidegger's phenomenology, Being in itself as not this or that being can only be equated with an originating nothingness 'concealed' in ontic presence, which must in turn be denied and annihilated if one is authentically to confront the absolute. Theologians working within pheno- menological assumptions tend, therefore, to assume that the horizon of being alone will issue in nihilistic conclusions, and to resist Heidegger in the name of 'the beyond being' (which must also somehow be apparent) taken as both neoplatonic Unity (in the wake of Trouillard) and transcendental Charity. But this manoeuvre can appear to hand this world over to being as construed by Heidegger, and therefore in a Manichean fashion to nihilism after all. Thus Jean-Luc Marion insists that, for Aquinas, Being in even the ontological and not ontic sense (the former identified by him with *ens commune*) is created by God, and that *esse* is a more-or-less empty name, selected (he now concedes) as the primary transcendental by Aquinas on account of its maximum indeterminate openness.[119]

Now Marion is perfectly right to say, against Etienne Gilson, that appeal to the ontological difference alone will not secure transcendence, since it can well be construed nihilistically, as by Heidegger. Moreover, he is also right to see the ontological difference as in a sense internal to Creation, since in Aquinas's case it sunders existence from essence in finite creatures, whereas (as we have seen) the divine *esse* is also infinite *forma* and *essentia* – rendering God, in a sense, the site of the collapse of the ontological differ- ence. Aquinas's divine *esse*, unlike Heidegger's crossed-out Being, does not obliterate, but eternally confirms the ontic (as not 'other' to the ontological). Nevertheless, one can be uneasy about any straightforward identification of *ens commune* with the ontological, or any consequent sense that the ontological is, also, simply 'created'. We have seen that *ens commune* may denote being in a weakly 'generic' fashion, and in consequence one could argue that, for Aquinas, divine *esse* as participated ceases to be fully transgeneric, and so ceases to be fully ontological, since it now divides into a being in general and a specified being in this and that. And even in the case of Heidegger, since his Being is distinguished from the ontic only as empty and therefore general, one may wonder whether one truly has the trans- generic: Heidegger also, is all too philosophical, all too metaphysical. So while, in a sense, Marion is right, and *esse* exceeds even the ontological difference, in another sense, being (*ens commune*) that is divided from essence or from the ontic is itself, as somewhat generic, still somewhat ontic, and fails to arrive at the difference of Being from a being or of *esse* from *ens* (in Thomist terms). By contrast, only the *esse* which exceeds the ontological difference in fact attains the ontological difference. This is surely confirmed by the fact that the real distinction in the creature is not defined as simply one between *essentia* and *ens commune*, but rather as between *essentia* and *esse*, suggesting that, for the creature, the latter is what is received of the divine self-subsisting perfection in the individual being which causes it to exist in a unique fashion. For if the ontological difference is finally the creator/created difference, then each creature is internally constituted out of nothing as that difference.

It follows that *sacra doctrina* offers a reading of the ontological difference other than that of Heidegger's, and does not take his for granted, thereby handing being and the world over to futility, boredom and nullity. Certainly Marion is right against Gilson: the ontological difference is not necessarily an ally of Christian transcendence. But he is wrong to see it as a barrier against it, since it is not a difference intuitively manifest in only one way, but manifest in different ways according to judgement. Nevertheless, of course, the judgement that we make of it (Christian, Heideggerean, or otherwise), is adopted as, for us, the most compelling, the most manifest, the most intense. The highest intensity, the highest perfection of pure infinitude[120] must needs be simultaneously expressed in judgement and shown to mental vision.

However, where intuition is conceived as prior to judgement, it will tend to halt at the circumscribably perceptible, and for this reason there is no paradox in the fact that it is specifically phenomenology (Levinas, Marion, etc.) which sometimes comes to regard the invisible as truly and authentically manifest only as invisible and so tends to demonize all visibility as idolatry.[121] Thus, for Marion, since *esse* is an empty name, all analogical predication must be a purely apophatic gesturing to a divine distance, whose giving, in order to preserve its purity as disinterested, is so impersonal that it becomes hard after all to distinguish it from pure arrival from the abyss. (Here one may note that divine 'distance' is both absolutely affirmed and absolutely denied by Aquinas.)[122] He is of course right to say that, in Aquinas, analogy concerning God is a matter of two-term *proportio*, not of four-term *proportionalitas* between two compared ratios. He is also right to say that in subordinating the latter kind of analogy, Aquinas refuses the idea that there is any ratio in God we can grasp as univocally the same as some ratio between creatures. However, proportionality, if formally dogmatic, is substantively agnostic (and is so deployed by Kant), since the God who is good in relation to his being, as we are good in relation to our being, is also the God whose good is an unknown cipher.[123]

By contrast, if we do *not* see God as a ratio comparable to a finite ratio, we can only see God at all through a finite perfection, assuming that in some fashion a finite perfection only exists by disclosing that ideal actual perfection which is its exemplar. This must be the case, because in two-term *proportio,* meaning resides more properly in one pole then another, and yet where this pole is God we are forced to begin at the wrong end. So how could we grasp any analogy if the higher divine perfection were not actually shown through the lesser perfection?

It is therefore clear that Aquinas does not build from transcendental grammatical foundations, but starts beyond the beginning with a theological supplementation which is both a metaphysics of the superadded as para-doxically the most proper, and a phenomenology of seeing more than one can see if one is to see truly at all. Both the metaphysical judgement (or 'speculation') and the phenomenological vision, are necessary and co-primary for *sacra doctrina*. Is there an intuition of Being involved here? Not in the old ontologist sense of absolute immediate grasp of the most fundamental ontological category, without the need for reflective abstraction from the differentiated. However, it *is* involved in the sense that all thought is a remote anticipation of the final beatified intuition of God, who as *esse* is also pure intellect in act identical with absolute intuition. Such anticipation is always apparent only for reflection, but apparent through reflection for all that. No doubt many will imagine that we have here reverted to Baroque delusions and fail to realize that Aquinas and Kant share the same non-Baroque intellectual chastity.[124] But, to the contrary, Baroque metaphysical rationalism is grounded in the sundering of metaphysics from *sacra doctrina*, and thus is inevitably fulfilled in metaphysics-as-epistemology before and with Kant, since finite being, supposedly fully apparent to reason (as univocal), must quickly turn into being that is only a projection of the structures of reason. Because, with Kant, reason no longer 'sees' into the realities of finite being (beyond appearances which are given merely to sensory perception), it *a fortiori* may not see through and beyond these realities. Loss of intellectual intuition therefore does not result from the critique of metaphysics (as Kant thought), but from the fulfilment (with Kant) of an entirely dogmatic metaphysics.[125]

VII

In the above fashion our preceding claim that Aquinas offers a theological ontology can be defended. As earlier set out, the leading characteristic of this ontology is a grasp of creation in the light of grace, as itself graced or supplemented, and so as a preparation for human deification. This is reinforced by evidence of anticipation of a Trinitarian structure in his account of the created order. Thus, as we have seen, relationality is integral to supplementation, and the two most intense modes of relationality concern the True and the Good. It is also the case that Aquinas regards 'life' and 'intellect' as superadditions to being which offer more being, because more intensity of perfection and more self-sufficiency. And this can be related to his account of Trinitarian traces at *Summa Contra Gentiles* 4.11 (described in Chapter One), where 'life' which exhibits emergence or emanation from the inner to the outer (whether as plant growth or animal movement) thereby shows some approach to pure inner emanation and substantive relation, while 'intellect' which exhibits an emanative movement which differentiates yet remains within, exhibits one yet stronger.[126]

However, if in this way we can see that 'faith' already informs Aquinas's ontology of Creation, it must be said in reverse that 'reason' equally informs his theology of the Trinity. Despite his explicit disavowal of the possibility of natural reason discerning the Trinity, he in fact argues for the Trinity in much the same way that he argues for the divine attributes. We have already seen that the reason he gives for disallowing merely rational approaches to the Trinity is a rather weak one: human reason can offer only remote analogies, although this is just as true for divine unity, and so forth. One can only conclude that perhaps, since the Trinity is a harder matter to grasp, its manifestness is relatively a matter of descent rather than ascent; but as Aquinas makes clear in the *Summa Contra Gentiles*, the way down is always also the way up,[127] or in the terms of the *Summa Theologiae*, the *revelabile* only fully disclose themselves with 'the helping hand' of argumentation.[128]

In arguing for the Trinity, Aquinas claims, first of all, that personhood, or a certain radical 'incommunicability', is a higher perfection of pure subsistence found in the Creation, and therefore an excellence which cannot be absent from God.[129] He further claims, in the second place, as was explained in Chapter One, that the human intellect, in forming an intention, utters a conceptual word, which is neither the thing understood (since a thing is not the idea of a thing), nor yet simply (as for Aristotle) the act of understanding by which it is inseparably carried, since a thought is more than the unfolding of the structures of mind, but rather the construction of a contingent intention either towards a contingent existing thing (even if that thing is oneself), or a contingent thing-to-be-done or produced.[130] In forming this intention, the mind does (again, see Chapter One), in a remote analogical sense, 'move',[131] and something really does inwardly 'emanate' from the mind, in such a way that it stands in a real relation to its own concept.[132] Mark Jordan has comprehensively demolished (citing multiple texts) Lonergan's work in *Verbum*,[133] which attempted, in the face of Aquinas's explicit terminology, to deny his neoplatonic and Augustinian supplements to Aristotle's theory of knowledge; hence Lonergan argued that the 'issuing' of the *verbum* from the mind does not apply to the pre-reflexive grasp of simple essences (though Lonergan's apriorism turns this into a kind of rough initial adumbration of a concept), and involves in judgement only the development of implications from a previous thought, and not a real ontological production of something 'other' than oneself within oneself. For Aquinas, however, as Jordan shows, it clearly applies to intellective grasp of essence as well as to discursive judgement, and therefore to ontological production as well as epistemological implication. If it did not involve the former, it clearly could not serve as an analogue for anything other than a modalist theology.

Aquinas claims, in the third place, that, since God is simple, and his act of intellect equals his being, or equally his being equals his act of intellect (since the latter is more intense being and is compared to the power of mind as *esse* to *essentia*), and every act of intellect involves emanation of the *verbum*, then the *verbum* must be substantive in God. It must as much embody Godhead as the Father, and is therefore also the 'Son' of the Father, since sons are equal to fathers in nature and self-subsistence, whereas cognitive intentions are not so equal to minds.[134]

In this way, Aquinas has speculatively established the Son. He holds, in general, that the thought of the True as a perfection is accompanied by desire for it as an end to be obtained.[135] However, desire in creaturely persons also extends to their relation to others and to goals outside themselves, without which they would have no ontological 'relation of order'. Such a perfection of desire must also be present in God, although because it is here removed from exteriority, and because good ends desired are 'true' as existing – just as the true is an end to be desired – it is present in God in substantive relation with the expression of truth, and, of course, as divine and simple, is equally personal and substantive.[136] In this way, Aquinas speculatively establishes the Spirit.

What is more, Aquinas does not leave the register of 'one divine essence' with all the transcendental attributes, on the one hand, as simply distinct from 'three divine persons' with their relations and 'notions' (the five aspects of origin and relationality within the Trinity), on the other. To the contrary, he goes some way towards integrating these two registers. Thus, in the first place, one can note that the essence and the persons are only distinct according to our *modus significandi*, in just the same fashion as being is only so distinct from goodness.[137] This should indeed give pause to over-enthusiastic hypertrinitarians (Moltmann, Gunton, etc.) in our own day. For it suggests that when Aquinas speaks first of all of the divine unity and simplicity (following Dionysius, not Augustine), he is not simply speaking of the one essence, but rather (already as Eckhart), of a divine depth of unity beyond our perceived distinction of essence and relation – but of course just as much relational as essential. The same point of indifference between relations and essence is, in fact, for Aquinas, as for Augustine, marked by the persons themselves – they are not identified *tout court* with the relations, even though they *are* the relations; instead, they slide uneasily between the relations and the essence, being identical with both.[138]

Secondly, we have already seen that *verbum* which is also *ars*, as an intrinsic aspect of intellection, has become 'convertible' with all the transcendentals. This means that they, inversely, are convertible with the emanation of the *verbum*, which now can be taken to convey the divine simplicity as much as anything else. Thus, thirdly, Aquinas says that if the persons of the Trinity, and in particular the Son, are identical with *essentia*, then they are so as *esse* manifesting the *essentia*.[139] Fourthly, Aquinas at times seems prepared to equate the Father with *subsistentia*, or 'the one understanding'; the Son with *essentia* (as absolute expressed *forma* or 'the intention understood'); and the Spirit with *esse* (as the completed end of the 'act of understanding').[140] This seems to correlate with that trace of Trinity which he locates even in non-intellectual creatures, as discovered in their subsistence, form and the 'relation of order' to other finite beings.[141]

From these fragmentary suggestions, one can develop a point concerning Trinitarian ontology that is only latent in Aquinas. The Augustinian ascending triad, being/life/intellect (where the two later degrees represent more intense being) is qualified in its hierarchy at the point where, within intelligent creatures, the orientation of the will towards the Good picks up again the motion of life towards a goal outside itself, whereas the intellect fulfils itself as relation to the other within itself (as has been discussed in Chapter One and earlier in the present chapter). In this way 'life' sustains a certain ecstasy as it were 'beyond' reason, as is suggested by Aquinas's other triad of first, second, and third acts (or perfections), where a superessential reach to the other as goal is superadded even to the superessential superaddition of operation to substance. The Trinitarian trace of substance, form (which can extend to operation) and 'relation of order', appears to tally with the latter scheme, while the tension of both (and of the Trinitarian psychic vestige of memory, understanding and will together with the triad substance/essence/ act of being), with the ascending triad being/life/intellect (where knowledge, not ecstatic movement is the culmination), suggests a Trinitarian hesitation between the 'priority' of *Logos* to which desire must submit, and the 'finality' of desire, which conveys also, and always already, truth. Since desire, which is the highest intensity of life as will to the Good, is found also within the divine simplicity, even the emanation of the *Logos* which remains within God must pass, as life, to an end beyond itself, yet still within God, as the Holy Spirit.

Thus if a faith-perceived Creation points to the Trinity through an ontology of descending and relational supplements, and indeed of 'double supplementation' where end-is-added-to-operation-is-added-to-substance, then a rationally-perceived Trinity confirms this pattern. In particular, it does so by implying that the supplementations received from on high by creatures are not simply abandonments of their manifold diversity, in order to receive an alien simplicity. This is not the case, because it turns out that this descending supplementation is grounded in a kind of 'reverse supplementation' in God, which instead of receiving, like a creature, unity in its manifoldness, receives manifoldness in its unity, as the Father is 'reversely constituted' by the Son and Spirit who express and desire (with simplicity) all manifold divine actuality, including the Creation, which God has decided shall exist apart from him. It is this reverse supplementation in God which finally assures us that we do not need to escape from the fact that the supernatural additions of participated unity can only arrive to us through the relationalities of space and time. For if we do receive descents leading us from diversity to unity, nevertheless, after all, also for us this is through a reverse supplementation as we pass from achieved unity into renewed dispersal, renewed ecstatic being for others – in which alone, however, transcendental as opposed to numerical unity can be intensified.

In this fashion, the 'Meno problematic' structure of our being able to search to know only what is already known, is no mere deficiency, but itself reflects God's uttering of the *Logos* only through the Spirit's desiring 'anticipation' of truth, which in God (as just discussed) is somehow both 'before' and 'after' it. This structure indeed appears to inform Aquinas's proceeding in the *prima pars* from God's being and goodness to his intelligence and truth, but then from truth to the divine will. And thus one can see just why commentators have offered apparently conflicting interpretations of Aquinas as 'existentialist', 'intellectualist', or even as primarily pivoted on 'the Good' (Marion). These are all legitimate readings, since he offers us what is ultimately a Trinitarian metaphysic. Here one can read Aquinas in either direction: the Trinity as the most intense being, or finite beings as weak participations in the relations of understanding and desiring.

In this light one can suggest (beyond, but with Aquinas), that if the *Verbum* and the *Donum* are also transgeneric as much as *esse*, then *analogia entis* is also *analogia trinitatis*. In other words, that to see the invisible in the visible is simultaneously to develop horizontally in space and time productive cognition and ecstatic reaching which both show and further realize the lateral harmonic and analogical *proportiones* by which alone we can penetrate the vertical *proportio* to God. Here again *theoria* is *poesis*, although *poesis* is *theoria*.

But what can this speculative reach to the Trinity betoken? Does it not suggest that one should re-express a non-dualism of reason and faith in 'Hegelian' terms as a naturalizing of the supernatural, in which theology succumbs to philosophy? Surely, no, because Aquinas's discursive arguments about the Trinity are ultimately confirmed by, and subordinated to, both intuition and performance. As arguments from created perfection, they are like other such arguments, grounded neither *a priori* nor *a posteriori*, but rather to be taken as expressions of a vision of the infinite in the finite. Hence there may be absolute personhood, pure relation, perfectly interior emanation, transcendental *Verbum* and *Donum* , but only if there *is* absolute perfection, and the possibility of such will not guarantee its reality nor even identify it. Only its actuality can do so, and this must be dimly perceived in order to be known. If such analogical receptions are flickering and uncertain, then this suggests that some uncertainty also hovers over our assumption that our minds do indeed relate to intentions of real being, do indeed construct and manifest the truth, do indeed desire a true good that is really to be had. Any lack of the highest perfection, which logically includes Trinity, must corrode backwards also perceived finite perfection into the remnants of illusion.

The reasoning to the Trinity may, therefore, be logically inviolable, but only if there *is* perfection, objective teleology and ontological truth. And sin renders our finite vision of infinite perfection vague and uncertain. Indeed, so blinded are we, that our vision can only be restored by the descent of perfection in time, in such a way that here we see the infinitely perfect entirely in the finite with our sensory eyes as performed thought which is also the personal substantive Son, who both realizes and lets proceed a true desire manifest in the substantive Eucharistic community. It may appear shocking that, for Aquinas, as for Augustine, the Trinity is seen as speculatively apparent in the Creation, but this is to miss the point that for both (in different ways), this speculation points us back to the fulfilment of speculation in lived history. To be sure, the Incarnation and the giving of the Spirit in time are first of all the implicit presuppositions of speculation – since these events alone have fully cleansed our minds to be able to see the Trinity in the created order (while these events themselves can only show the Trinity in terms of that order). And yet, much more radically, these events are *themselves* the achievement of speculation as vision and performance which is only for us attainable through a return to the sensorially imagistic and concretely immediate: a collective *conversio ad phantasmata*. For this reason Aquinas argues *to* Christology and the sacraments and not (or not so fundamentally) from them.

There is an additional and equally important reason for resisting the idea that Aquinas transforms Trinitarian theology into Trinitarian philosophy. This concerns the exact character of the highest perfection that is conceived and imagined. Is it simply an idealist completion of thought as a logical process, thought thinking itself and returning to itself? Werner Beierwaltes and Wayne Hankey both suggest that the basis of Trinitarian reflection lies in a neoplatonic structure of the One reflecting on its own simplicity and thereby entering division, which is, nonetheless, cancelled, with simplicity restored, through a perfection of reflexivity.[142] Aquinas, however, identifies *reditio ad seipsum* as a metaphor (albeit a necessary and accurate one) for self-subsistence. Since Trinitarian relations are for him themselves subsistent and auto-sustaining, he cannot possibly think of these relations only in terms of outgoing and return, or of reflexivity. On the contrary, the idea of reflexive *nous* as compatible with absolute unity (perhaps present in Porphyry), is an extremely shaky one, and is rejected by Plotinus, Proclus and Iamblichus.[143] These three rigorously insist that thought in its 'doubling' character – of being showing itself to itself – is non-simple and non-unified, and therefore to be characterized as only the first emanation from that which is most absolute and radically non-cognitive. Exactly the same demotion of mind (yes!) is affirmed by Fichte, the early Schelling and even Hegel, and in all three it forms the basis for a philosophy of absolute being which as nothing, must become finite in order to be, but again as absolute must return to nothing, leaving the finite in its pure naked contingency to show forth the untrammelled freedom of reality. In *Faith and Knowledge*, Hegel names this absolute idealism 'nihilism' (positively embracing Jacobi's insult), and protests that Fichte is not nihilistic enough, because he refuses to say that the absolute is fully thinkable, i.e. as graspable in its emptiness.[144] (Yes – they were all postmodern already.)

Perfection as rational reflexivity, therefore, offers only a formalism which engenders nihilism, since mind constituted as actually reflecting on its own self-consistency cannot be simple and original; both actuality in its definiteness, and thought in its mirroring reflectiveness, must fade before the abyss. It follows that neither Aristotle, nor mere monotheism, manage to render mind consistent with the absolute. To the contrary, only the concept of the Trinity does this, because here thought is not a doubling of being in mirroring, but rather it *is* being, which only consists in an 'original supplement' of self-disclosure through self-constitution. Thus whereas reflection involves a 'doubling', substantive relation, by contrast, can be just as simple and transcendentally unified as substance. In this way, it is only the highest truth of faith – the Trinity – which establishes the absoluteness of reason.

But since this mental constitution of being in the relation of self-manifestation is not a mirroring nor a mimesis, but rather that expression through which alone being is at all, this expression, though absolute, and therefore more necessary than any conceivable necessity, is still not logically necessitated, as is an imitation or an echo, constrained to observe identity. To the contrary, the *Logos* is generated in the freedom of the Spirit, which expresses its *Donum* as the exchange between Father and Son, and yet as an exchange which overflows to a third, precisely because its return is not a return in pure identity, forming a closed circle which would be such that the Spirit might as well express only the will of the Father, rather than also the 'ever-new' utterance of the Son. Thus while charity for Aquinas denotes reciprocity,[145] he also declares that 'gift', following Aristotle, denotes non-return;[146] a 'moment' of unilaterality, since the circle spirals always through the same-as-different. (In this way a gift-as-exchange view is protected from Hegelian 'return'.)

Since the *Logos* is reasonable, and does not merely convey a capricious divine will, and yet cannot, as we have seen, be logically necessitated, its rational expression is essentially an aesthetic expression (as David Burrell and Gilbert Narcisse have both argued), responding to the inner necessity of the lure of beauty which it at once constructs and envisages. Thus Aquinas never suggests, like Leibniz, that God grasps perfection through pure ratiocination, but he still affirms God's response to perfection (which is himself) as something objective. Likewise, he does not think, again like Leibniz, that God could work out what is 'the best of all possible worlds' to create, since God as infinitely perfect could always create the more perfect. So in deciding, with perfect reason, upon *this* perfection, he must respond to something like an aesthetic prompting to do 'this, now, here' (to use entirely inappropriate analogues).

Hence, in thinking the perfection of the Trinity, argument finally yields to the intuition of the necessity of the inner divine *ars* (its, as it were, 'elective necessity'), which we dimly see and dimly echo in our own creativity, which is incapable, of course, of real 'creating' of being *ex nihilo*, but is nonetheless, for Aquinas, able continuously to bring about new being 'in this' or 'in that'.[147]

VIII

It has been shown how, in three ways, Aquinas's *sacra doctrina* bends metaphysics into history: transgeneric *esse* fulfilled in theology converts the formal into the material; the redefined science of *sacra doctrina* grasps divine intuition only through descent to sensory intuition; finally, the 'reversed supplementation' of the Trinity validates history as the horizontal route of our vertical ontological supplementation: here truth is slowly engendered through our desiring anticipation of our final goal. And indeed, beneath even this initial turn towards our mode of animal 'life', divine grace which is the gift of the Spirit first meets us as a kind of quasi-physical 'motion', revealing here also the artisanal reach of divine knowledge beyond the architectonic sway of metaphysics. On the basis of the second consideration (and we can add the first and third), Michel Corbin argues that Aquinas deliberately fulfils speculation in its surpassing, as a reflection upon, and liturgical re-offering of, sacred history.[148] One might support this argument by suggesting that Aquinas here follows through the Dionysian legacy of theurgic neoplatonism. For this tradition (Proclus and Iamblichus), since the forms are only 'recollected' through ever-renewed reminders in time, the soul cannot be elevated above time and the body (as for Plotinus, less faithful to Plato's texts and the esoteric traditions of the academy). Therefore, in order to encounter the divine, we must rely less on theoretic ascent than on a divine descent, which nonetheless is partially enticed through certain regular ritual performances. Here the contingently encountered triggers of recollection are as it were 'assured' through the non-identical repetition of the liturgical cycle. (Moreover, it is arguable that the idea of a Trinitarian grounding even for the temporal and diverse anticipatory motion involved in recollection, is itself foreshadowed in Plato's own oral teaching – as indicated in several places in the dialogues and letters about the ultimate 'one' and equally ultimate manifold 'two', and the interplay between them.) In worship, supremely, we at once make and see, envisage in performing, thereby realizing Aquinas's vision of actuality as light.[149] Since God is not an object in the world, he cannot be available to us before our response to him, but in this response – our work, our gift, our art, our hymn – he is already present. Moreover, such poetic, theurgic, sacramental presence, is for Christianity, as not for neoplatonism, also a fully theoretical, intellectual presence, since, with the Trinity, Christianity has succeeded in thinking thought as absolute and simple, precisely because it no longer thinks of it as reflexion, but as relation, *poesis* and vision. (It is orthodox Trinitarianism and not neoplatonism, nor German idealism, as we have seen, which is intellectualist.)

Hence, in part three of the *Summa Theologiae*, Aquinas turns speculation into a kind of re-offering of Christ, and concludes with detailed recommendations for liturgical practice (to be discussed in the fourth chapter), before re-presenting (though this was never completed) the beatific vision as resurrection of the body and final judgement. In a sense, this suggests a very anthropological approach to Christology – not of course a Rahnerian one built on anthropological foundations, but a concluding to Christ as the realization of the human *telos* which is only here shown, beyond humanity. And Michel Corbin has further argued that the *Summa* does not follow Chenu's purported *exitus/reditus* scheme, since Part One concerns God, with much about descent as we have seen, while Part Two concerns humanity, with much about ascent through grace.[150] This suggests that Part Three is not about the foundation for return in Christ and actual return via sacramental grace, but rather concerns a kind of 'synthesis' (Hegelian but without Hegel's nihilism) of Parts One and Two, a treatment of God and Man at once, in such a way that God in executing the perfect descent of his goodness in Christ, also allows humanity in Christ to fulfil its theological speculation as perfect theurgic practice which is both miraculous and sacramental.

3   Truth and touch

For Thomas Aquinas, in a post-lapsarian economy, the Incarnation is the sole ground for the restoration of our participation in the divine under-standing. Consequently, for us, not only are things true only as participating in God; also they are only true as conjoined to the body of the incarnate *Logos*. Aquinas therefore insists that, besides being sole bearer of grace to us, Christ is alone our reliable teacher, who restores for us also truth and knowledge.

To understand in what way he believes this to be the case, it is important to grasp how in general he conceives of the reasons for God becoming incarnate. For Aquinas, seemingly unlike Anselm, it is possible that God, according to his *potentia absoluta,* might have redeemed us, and re-instructed us in truth, without the incarnation of the Son.[1] A simple cancelling of our sins by decree, allied to an act of positive recreation, would in theory have been sufficient. By this assertion, he assures us that God had no need to be appeased in order to become reconciled to us, and that, in himself, he always and eternally was so reconciled. For Thomas, therefore, the Incarnation does not bring about this reconciliation of God, but rather mediates it to us, making it effective for us and in us, thereby ensuring that we, too, are reconciled.

However, this perspective might appear to entail that the economy of the incarnation of the Son was for Aquinas little more than an arbitrarily appointed means for our salvation. And, the consequence for a con-sideration of 'truth' would be that our restored intelligence possesses no essential, intrinsic relation to our indwelling the body of Christ, since God might have repaired the reality of our participation in his understanding (and our reflexive grasp of this) by some other means. Therefore, it would seem that while truth necessarily is participation in God, only accidentally and by appointment is it participation in Christ.

Such, however, is for Aquinas not at all the case. To comprehend why, one must briefly explore Aquinas's view that while the actual means of incarnation and atonement adopted for our salvation were not absolutely necessitated, they were nonetheless 'convenient', fitting, supremely suitable for this purpose. They possessed the necessity, in Aquinas's own illustration, not of 'going in a certain direction to reach a certain goal, but that of travelling, most conveniently, or appropriately, for example, on horseback'.[2] This sense of *convenientia* hovers, therefore, between the necessitated and the arbitrary and as such (as Gilbert Narcisse has argued at length), it is clearly an *aesthetic* notion, closely allied, for Aquinas, to terms like *proportio, harmonia, ordinatio.*[3] This is confirmed by the fact that, for Thomas, *convenientia*, like *pulchrum*, is held to be convertible with being: *omnia in esse conveniunt.*[4] Furthermore, Aquinas inherits from certain Arab scholastics a strong association between the Aristotelian grammatical paronym equated with ontological *analogia,* on the one hand, and the term *convenientia* on the other. The latter term, therefore, allows us to link *analogia* with *esse,* in such a fashion that the hierarchical approximations of analogy are shown to be relative coherences grounded in an absolute harmonious fittingness or 'belonging together' in *esse* itself, which is yet something other than pure logical exigency.[5]

Thus the thematic of 'convenience' as applied to the divine economy of creation and redemption signals, in Aquinas, an aesthetic construal of participation: God creates, and is partially disclosed within, appropriate proportions which radiate according to their inherent *integritas.* And if *convenientia* is supremely and inexhaustibly shown in the Incarnation, then this is because here the created structures of analogical resemblance to God, while remaining in their condition of mere approximation even in the case of the humanity of Christ, nonetheless in their specificity of narrative and symbolic arrangement become transparent to the mode or 'way of being' of the divine *persona* of the *Logos.* This way of being of the divine logical ordering is *convenienter*, so that here that paronymic and approximate convenience which is analogy mysteriously coincides with the paronymic and absolute convenience which is *esse ipsum. Analogia entis* becomes *analogia Christi,* and the former, for Aquinas, is only available for fallen humanity through the latter. After expulsion from paradise, only the arrival of the goal in the midst of the way reveals again the way (to use Augustinian terminology).

For Aquinas, therefore, in the Incarnation there is exhibited to a maximum degree a certain pleasing *logos*, which exceeds both merely capricious arrangement, and purely forced necessity (since God is not bound to this order, as he *is* bound to conclude that a is not not a). It is true that it belongs to the *potentia ordinata,* and Aquinas's counterfactual invocation here of the *potentia absoluta* is an essential logical moment, designed to indicate that God is not impersonally and ineluctably constrained. However, this absolute power is not, as for later scholastics, following more a model derived from canon law, a kind of reserve power which may, at a whim, intervene to interrupt the conventional norms of *potentia ordinata*. Rather, for Aquinas, *all* that God actually does belongs to his *potentia ordinata,* which is not an order of caprice, but rather itself reflects the eternal divine sense of justice and appropriateness.[6] Therefore Aquinas's God is compelled, not only by the absolute exigencies of logical possibility, but also by something one may dub 'actual necessity', or the agreeable that appears in the harmonious proportions of an infinite actual order. This absolute *convenientia* of *esse ipsum* is then reflected in the relative *convenientia* of the divine economy – although relative is mysteriously conjoined to absolute at the apex and pivot of this economy, in the Incarnation.

Aquinas lists several different ways in which the order of incarnation was 'convenient', and declares that he only cites a few, since their number is infinite.[7] But especially relevant to present considerations is (first of all) the notion that it is fitting that, since we fell through Adam's pride and the rebellion of our sensual aspect, we should be restored through divine humility and re-education of the understanding by the senses.[8] Christ follows and shows us the path through suffering and despair to a despising of our mortality and the regaining of eternal life. This shows that while, for Aquinas, God *could* have restored us just through his continued *gift,* he nonetheless so respects human freedom and the legacy of human history, that he seeks also positively to *forgive* us, by tracing, himself, as only an innocent man can, the perfect ways of penitence which we are to imitate.[9]

A second instance of *convenientia* is also instructive. It is appropriate that God should draw near to humanity in this most radical and unexpected fashion, because God as infinite and replete cannot possibly be rivalled, and therefore can give himself entirely – even his own divine nature to human nature.[10] Here Aquinas is exploiting to the full the Dionysian paradox of God 'existing outside of himself' which was discussed in the previous chapter. Just because there *is* no outside to God, God can entirely externalize himself; he can most freely and ecstatically exceed himself. Just because he cannot share *anything*, he can share *everything*. It is partially because of his intense sense of this paradox, that Aquinas espouses ontologically strong notions of human deification. Adam was created to enjoy the beatific vision, and to share, without reserve, but to the measure of human personhood, in the divine nature.[11] Likewise, for Thomas (unlike some mediaeval theologians, for example Duns Scotus), Adam enjoyed already a state of semi-beatitude in Eden, receiving sanctifying grace, and possessing an impassible body.[12] Significantly, Aquinas cites the predestination of Adam to deification as a further ground for the *convenientia* of the Incarnation: humanity has a *natural* kinship with the supernatural; it bears the image of God – somewhat, albeit remotely, as the Son bears the image of the Father, since human beings as intelligent already possess close kinship with the divine substance (as we saw when expounding the 'chiasmus' of the *Prima Pars* in Chapter Two). Aquinas indeed says that, as the Word of creation, the Son has special 'kinship' with *all* creatures; however, this is far stronger in the creature able to articulate a word on its own account. Moreover, since man is capable of this rational articulation and yet remains material and animal, he is able to synthesize the whole work of creation, in a way the angels do not. It is 'appropriate' that this finite microcosm be conjoined with infinite plenitude, and in this way a certain 'cycle' is completed.[13]

These various aspects of *convenientia* suggest a triple implication for Aquinas's understanding of the incarnation of the Son, as being also the incarnation of Truth, and as providing us with our only access to Truth. (John i: 17 is cited: 'Grace and Truth came by Jesus Christ'.) First of all, while according to the bare logic of his omnipotence, God could have redeemed us another way, the aesthetic fittingness of the way actually chosen reflects the way in which the eternal divine *Logos* itself, in its free compulsion and compelled freedom, is most adequately characterized as the eminent realization of beautiful *proportio*. Hence the means appointed, in the very freedom (aesthetically compelled) of this appointment, manifest the heart of divine 'necessity'. The infinite aspects of 'appropriateness' in the pattern of Christ's temporal life, and the typological understanding of this, are the most intense possible manifestation of truth comprehended as harmony between being and understanding.

Secondly, since the hominization of the Son is 'appropriate' as restoring the deification of humanity, this shows that what it restores is analogical ascent through various degrees of *esse ipsum*. In fact, the *convenientia* of absolute descent of the intra-divine *convenientia* into human time consists in its restoration of the dynamic of hierarchic, ascending *convenientia* which is analogy. Not only is truth conveniently displayed in Christ; it is displayed as convenience.

However, from this, a third and much more difficult point follows. Through the Incarnation, the divine *convenientia* is only redisplayed, and the hierarchical, ascending *convenientia* only restored, because the two are made absolutely to coincide. Therefore, in order to remedy the fault of human sin, something 'in excess' of this occasional cause of the Incarnation is brought about, namely a new ontological state for the Creation: the causing of a human creature directly to subsist in a divine hypostasis. This new circumstance survives its occasion and purpose, and realizes a mode of divine self-sharing more absolute than the most absolute giving of the infinite to the finite according to its capacity for reception. This 'more absolute than the absolute' is the utter fusion of the finite with the infinite (though not the other way around).

This new circumstance exceeds its occasion for Aquinas (as Michel Corbin rightly insists), insofar as the reality of the hypostatic union is the thing most highly to be glorified within the created order, quite apart from the redemption which it has brought about. However, this glorification is no mere inert formality; to the contrary, it manifests a further ontological revision, which is none other than a kind of ontological reversal. For the hypostatic union involves the integration of Christ's humanity through the divine personhood, in such a way that his strictly human qualities show entirely, in their very humanity, his divine nature. This includes his body, his physical actions, and especially his transmission of the substance of his body to the Eucharistic elements. Because, for Aquinas, all our knowledge is first in our senses, this means that we first encounter Christ in reported word and image concerning his physical manifestation, and yet more directly in our partaking of the sacraments, particularly the Eucharist.[14] It is in this fashion that there is realized, for Aquinas, that aspect of *convenientia,* already mentioned, which is the instruction of our intellect in divine matters by our senses, to correct the turning of the intellect to sensory ends rather than divine ends after Adam. For when we imagine Christ who is perfect, our imagination is wiser than our fallen reason; when we hear of Christ, our hearing is wiser than this reason; when we taste Christ, our tongue is wiser than this reason, and only after the tasting will it once again speak reason.

Of course, through this process our reason is once more slowly re-instructed and thereby resumes its command. But does it altogether? For the reversal is permanent; it belongs with the permanence of the hypostatic union and its sacramental representation. And therefore it makes sense that the Aquinas who invoked the *felix culpa* pronounced at the Easter Vigil, was also the Aquinas who promoted the feast of *Corpus Christi.* For since bread and wine are now transubstantiated, forever and forever in time (and beyond?), something material is in excess of our spirits, and our minds must obey our senses, here re-attuned.

In this fashion, therefore, the Incarnation, in excess of its occasion of human redemption, effects an ontological revision which discloses an unsuspected depth to the divine *kenosis:* God is able to suffuse with his presence the material depths, in order to instruct the spiritual heights. But to grasp the real implication of this new sacramentality of the cosmos, we must recall, once again, its sole ground in the hypostatic union. For if, here, finite ascending *convenientia,* or truth, absolutely coincides with infinite eternal *convenientia,* or truth, then this implies an extraordinary elevation of human sensory intuition. This follows, because, first, the infinite truth is divine intuition; and, secondly, human knowing, which is fully preserved in its integrity in Christ's humanity, is only *entirely* intuitive (as opposed to a remote participation in intellectual intuition) in sensation. Thus if divine and human truth are to coincide, the 'immediacy' of the former will only be displayed in human existence (even if it also perfectly suffuses all of Christ's discursive deliberations), through Christ's sensory intuitions, and our sensory intuitions of Christ.

Aquinas expresses (without explicitly affirming) this new coinciding of the heavenly and earthly intuitions, by insisting that Christ's human nature, just insofar as it was conjoined to the divine hypostasis, enjoyed in this life the beatific vision (again Scotus demurred, seeing this result as a mere upshot of divine decree), while, at the same time, *all* of Christ's human knowledge (including, here, uniquely, the beatific vision, it would seem to follow) was, for Aquinas, mediated by the *conversio ad phantasmata*.[15] Christ's knowledge was, uniquely, both intuitive as beatified, and intuitive as phantasmic.

In this way, for Aquinas, Christ was uniquely the true teacher – by every act, gesture and relic as well as by word, and, indeed, *more* by relic than by word. He recalls Christ's own words that he was born to 'give testimony to the truth' (John xviii. 37). And for this reason also, Christ embodied the true theology: that which the *summa*, intensifying itself, must *build up to*, not abstract away from.

Nevertheless, through this intensification, the conclusion of *sacra doctrina* also recasts the entire character of *sacra doctrina*. For hitherto, Aquinas has said (from the inception of the *Prima Pars*) that this teaching is a science, indeed the most scientific science, because it derives its certainty from the very fount of all certainty. Nevertheless, this certainty of science is not matched by an equal certainty of derivation, since while God reveals to us something of his absolute certainty, this is only through the approximation of appropriate analogues, whose material imagery, in particular, renders them at best remote indicators. This non-demonstrative character of our modus of knowing disqualifies theology as a strictly theoretical science. In the fourth part of the *Summa Contra Gentiles*, however, Aquinas (already apparently anticipating the demand of the *Summa Theologiae* that theology, as concerning God, should be fully scientific) had already suggested that if we know the vision of God to be our true end, we must possess 'a certain foretaste' of this by faith – *and* that this foretaste must be 'most certain knowledge' if it is to act as 'the principle of everything ordered to the ultimate end'. In other words, to be *in the truth* we must orientate ourselves to absolute ontological certainty beyond our grasp, and so start with faith, and yet faith (as no longer infallibly guided since the Fall) is shaky and uncertain. To resolve this *aporia* and attain perfect certainty, man 'had to be instructed by God himself made man'. That is to say, for us to be able to begin to think with a kind of 'certainty', the goal of such thought had to arrive before our eyes. Aquinas cites John xi. 18: 'no man has seen God, but the only-begotten Son, he has declared him'. And for analogical reasoning to be reliable for fallen humanity, the very inappropriateness of material images had to be disclosed as, after all, in this one instance, wholly appropriate as the vehicle of truth. Aquinas therefore declares here that the materiality of the Incarnation *alone* renders theology a science. He repeats this point in the *Tertia Pars:* only the Truth incarnate founds faith. As Corbin suggests, this implies a negation even of the *via negativa* itself, and an extreme Christological fulfilment of the Dionysian view that use of the apparently most inappropriate symbols is a necessary path for mystical theology. For now, in Christological terms, this inappropriateness is as much affirmed as it is (also, still) negated.[16]

II

This new elevation of sensory intuition to coincidence with the divine intuition, also redoubles the sense in which Aquinas's theology of trans-generic *esse* points towards a kind of self-exceeding of metaphysics into event, image and history as already discussed in Chapter Two. For just as the individual or accident as equally 'is', as the genus or substance, so now it is as if this promissory note of *esse* has been paid up in full. For now the ontological equality of the materially individuated and sensory has, as it were, at last been allowed to express itself as also an equality in the transcendental *Verum*. And this circumstance has only come about because a single event – or rather chain of events, which eschatologically includes *every* event when Christ becomes 'all in all' – has been elevated to absolute coincidence with eternal being as such. The ontological implication of the hypostatic union is that the equal presence of Being in each single being, or of the ontological in every ontic reality, is now absolutized to the degree that one being, while remaining one being, so inheres in, or discloses Being as such, as to coincide with it. Its existing in such and such a way is no longer a restriction of Being, but somehow is now directly the Being of being itself. Although it has scarcely been discussed, this is precisely the way in which Aquinas is prepared to extend his theological metaphysics of *esse* to comprehend Christology. For Aquinas, just as there is only one divine hypostasis, so there is only one *esse* in Christ, which is the divine *esse ipsum*, even though there remains a human essence, present as one single human individual, *in atomo*.

As a matter of fact, though, Aquinas's one *esse* doctrine does more than simply interpret the one hypostasis. For while, indeed, the one *esse* is mediated to the humanity by the person of the *Logos, esse*, as Aquinas points out, includes existence and essence as well as subsistence, and thus embraces both the hypostatic *Logos* and *its relation* to the assumed humanity. Thus, as he explicitly declares, to speak of one divine *esse* in Christ is to assert an absolute existential fusion or concurrence of the two natures, since the implication is that human nature not only subsists entirely in God, but has only a divine existence, with which it is so unified as to 'add' nothing to it whatsoever. One can suggest that this is why Aquinas accompanies his one *esse* affirmation with bold citations of Cyril of Alexandra, and retrievals, indeed, of aspects of his thought too often dismissed as 'monophysite' (although, indeed, many monophysites may in reality have had similar 'orthodox' intentions).[17]

Exactly how is it that, for Aquinas, *esse ipsum* can so exceed itself as to have an 'event' conjoined to it, while, conversely, an ontic event can possess no integral consistency other than *esse ipsum*? Here, especially, *sacra doctrina* has passed beyond metaphysics, yet in what way is this possible?

Let us approach these issues first of all from the perspective of the addition of event to *esse*. One must refrain, of course, from attributing to

Aquinas any actual ascription of event as change to God. This would, for Thomas, have been incompatible with divine aseity. Nevertheless, the implication of Chalcedonian doctrine appears to be that God is not only infinite *esse*, outside time, but also the subject of a particular series of events in time, resumed as a resurrected human nature through all eternity.

Now, it is arguable that Aquinas's peculiar theological ontology (his 'metaphysics') negotiates this circumstance with particular *finesse*, in a way not often noted. It was seen in the previous chapter that, for Aquinas, the notion of God as *esse* exceeds metaphysics and belongs to *sacra doctrina*, since metaphysics (as Aristotle failed to realize) in thinking only general, transcendental categories *cannot*, after all, think the transgeneric character of Being (*as* recognized by Aristotle), since *esse* is as much manifest in the individual and accidental as in the general and the substantive. Hence the knowledge enjoyed by the divine *esse*, unlike the knowledge of the metaphysician, stretches down to every last particular. And so from the divine perspective of *esse,* there is indeed a comprehension of event that is in excess of the mere falling of events under general ontological categories, since the yet more 'general' perspective of *esse* fractures the sway of generality itself. From the point of view of 'to be', as such, an instance can break out of a preceding given framework, just as the perfection of the divine eminent knowledge of a fallen thrush is identical in the divine essence to God's knowledge of the category 'birds'.

It is this understanding of the divine transgeneric *esse* which then forms the ground for Aquinas's insistence that there is only the one, divine *esse* in the divine humanity of Christ. There cannot, for Aquinas, be another finite, human *esse* or *ens* (although there is, of course, a human *essentia*), because this would either be an accident added to the divine *suppositum* which cannot receive accidents, any more than it can itself be accidentally conjoined to Christ's humanity (since God cannot be the accident of a creature), or else it would be the addition of an essence, which is also impossible, since the divine essence is replete as containing the eminent reality of every essence.

For many modern commentators, and perhaps for the majority of scholastic theologians from the twelth century onwards, this refusal of either substantive or accidental additions to the *Logos* has seemed to exhaust all possibilities of union with humanity.[18] However, this bafflement fails to grasp the subtlety of Thomas's metaphysical innovations. Since *esse* is non-generically common to substance and accident, it is indifferent to either, and yet God is supremely 'to be'. Therefore, he lies beyond the substance/accident contrast in his essence, and since the persons of the Trinity are identical with this essence, their self-subsistence also exceeds the contrast of essential versus additional. Inversely, the divine *esse* is identical with, and manifest as, the three 'incommunicabilities' of personhood. This *esse* 'is' their peculiar, though subsistently interrelated *ways* of being. These ways, or idioms of being, can absolutely coincide in pure simplicity with all other ways, and with Being itself, since, as we recall from Chapter Two, for Aquinas *esse* only expresses the pure ontological side of the ontological difference between ontological and ontic because it also exceeds that difference and is eminently defined *essentia*. Hence what would normally be ontic and restricted – a specific way or incommunicable idiom – is in God also ontological.

It follows that when Aquinas speaks of the single *esse* of the divine humanity, he means, somewhat like Maximus the Confessor (though he is less explicit), that all there *is* in Christ is the one way of being (which Maximus termed *tropos*), which characterizes the eternal *Logos*, and is nonetheless coterminous with 'to be' itself.[19] Since *esse* is as much event and instance – 'way' or *tropos* – as general structure, and since as way of being it is somewhat like an eternal narrative constitution formative of character (in the *perichoresis* of the Trinity), it is able entirely to be communicated to a finite instance. A specific way or idiom of being, which yet absolutely coincides with all other ways, and with Being itself, and as ontic is also ontological, here slips out of the infinite into a perfect reflection in the finite. Aquinas explains that while personhood is 'incommunicable' (after Gilbert Porreta and Richard of St Victor), this absolute uniqueness does *not* preclude additions, new 'blendings' into what nevertheless remains the same character (the same subject of the same narrative).[20] Here Aquinas is true to the radical implication of incarnation: the finite, although intrinsically composed, can exhibit in and through its composition the pure character of simplicity, the uncomposed. And at this point we glimpse the Christological significance of Aquinas's Boethian focus upon simplicity rather than infinity as primarily characteristic of Godhead; since 'infinite' remains for him a negative term, it does not possess a positive conceptuality rendering it external to, and incompatible with, the finite, in a fashion that would, indeed, finitize the infinite. Thus while, for Aquinas, there is certainly no Hegelian identity through sublation of finite with infinite, there is none-theless a possible convergence of the two in terms of mode or 'character', whose absolute unity and consistency is, as such, perfectly simple, and yet can be shown also in the narrative and located complexity of the finite. By comparison, the later Scotist positive conception of the infinite and selection of the infinite, rather than the simple, as the primary characteristic of divine *esse,* issues in a certain ontic externality of infinite to finite, and a resultant difficulty in understanding how Christ's human nature, including his human soul, can relate to the divine hypostasis other than accidentally. In consequence, for Scotus, because finitude is intrinsic to Christ's humanity, there must also be finite and human, as well as infinite and divine *esse,* in the hypostatic union. It is true that Scotus had not yet fully travelled the onto-theological (and onto-Christological!) road he opened up: thus for him, as for Aquinas, the *Logos* does not come into being, God still has no real relation to the hypostatic union and the finite certainly adds nothing to the divine infinity which is a repleteness of being (even though the theses of the univocity of being as a transcendental formality and of the infinite as a positive conception of a primary 'mode', frequently threaten this affirmation in his thought).[21] Nevertheless, from the finite point of view, it appears in the Scotist conception that there is an accidental exteriority of the human nature to the divine hypostasis, in such a way that, in effect, the former enjoys a Nestorian independent individual subsistence, outside its conjoining to the *Logos*. The latter, for Scotus, is a bare positive circumstance, since human personhood is for him absent in Christ merely for the reason of the non-presence of absolute subsistence-in-self of the humanity, according to his negative, and merely substantial, definition of personhood.[22] By contrast, for Aquinas, the divine personhood is the entire *suppositum* and single *esse* of the human nature, and no mere finite fact or additional inhering, because it here supplies the narrative cohering of finite difference through specificity of 'character'. The absolute simplicity of the divine character is absolutely shown in the finite narrative, and its yet unabolished ineffability provides this narrative with its unity, coherence, and subsistence.

It can be noted here that, curiously enough, Aquinas's near-monophysitism is much less *fetishistic* of the particular than Scotus's near-Nestorianism. For where Christ's integral specificity *is* God, and so also the universal, then it is a very strange sort of specificity which we can scarcely identify. Normally, the specific is framed by the universal; it is an item visible under the sun. But here, uniquely, the specific itself frames our vision of all other specificities: it is itself the very sun we see by. Its concreteness and particularity is therefore hyper-concrete – so concrete that its reality overwhelms all else, and its very over-apparentness renders it scarcely manifest at all as a discrete item. This circumstance – especially when allied to the disclosure of the *Logos* in the *vulnerability* of Christ (as will shortly be elaborated) – absolutely prevents any Christological encouragement of Christian triumphalism or exclusivity. The Incarnation sacralizes no one site, with a resultant secular draining of all other sites: to the contrary, its sacral reality tends to the proliferation of sacred sites as uncontrollable by any institutional force.

By contrast, where, as with Scotus, Christ is allowed some independent merely human and therefore ontic existentiality, the very 'lowness' of this Christology ensures that Christ is reduced to a locatable human idol to be possessed and manipulated by a Church thinking of itself primarily as a legally-bound institution.

Aquinas's non-fetishizing position assumes that through the conjoining hypostasis, both finite and infinite can exhibit the same specific character of charity, and of forgiveness which effects reconciliation. (One may say that this is 'Hegelian', rather than Hegelian.) Thus while, for Aquinas, Christ's humanity has a fully human mind, will and even individuality (in the sense of the individuation of form by matter),[23] it still does not possess a human personhood or *suppositum*, because this would involve self-subsistence, incommunicability and uniqueness, whereas all of Christ's individual human nature subsists in, and is held together in consistency of character by, the eternal hypostasis of the Son.[24] This hypostasis as 'way' of being is beyond substance or accident, and just for this reason is able to receive an 'addition' to itself which is not really an addition (to the divine essence, with which it is identical) and yet is not substantive either. Aquinas is explicit about this: unity of the divine and human nature in Christ is a unity of *esse* rather than a unity of essence, or of accident inhering in a substance. As falling between substance and accident, this unity of *esse* is also said specifically to be a unity of *relation*.[25] This identification implies that, whereas *esse* is not of itself either essential nor accidental, nonetheless it is of itself relational – as, indeed, Aquinas's account of substantive relations in the Trinity must require. The classification of the hypostatic union as also a relation implies, however, that besides the personal, 'subjective' relation of Trinitarian subsistent relation, *esse* also admits (or partially admits, as we shall see) a kind of 'objective' relation of person to thing, for which Aquinas offers analogues of the soul inhering in the body, and of the person deploying his body as an instrument. If one regards these psycho-somatic analogues as parallel to the psychological analogues used for the Trinitarian personal relations, then one can see how the bringing of 'objective' relation within the one *esse* ensures a Christological qualification of any merely personalist account of ontological relationality – just as the 'body of Christ' thematic prevents any sanitized over-stress on our psychic externality to each other.

The 'objective' relation is nevertheless not symmetrical, like the subjective, Trinitarian one. While the hypostatic union resides in the divine *esse* alone, the divine *esse* has no real relation to this union which is a *created* union; the *Logos* does not 'become' incarnate – rather, a human soul and body come to subsist in the *Logos*. All real relationality is on the side of this soul and body, but it is a relationality so real that it is exhaustively constitutive *of* this soul and body. It is akin, says Aquinas, to a movable object's being moved to the left of a fixed object; the leftness does not impinge on the substance of the fixed object, even though it is thereby rendered to the right. But the new left position of the movable object is brought about through its being resituated in real relation to the fixed object.[26] In the Christological instance, it is as if something were subsistent arrived-at-leftness.

If this real relation of the human nature to the divine hypostasis is 'one way', then it is not exactly like a subsistent relation, since it involves an asymmetrical 'inhering in', which seems akin to the inherence of an accident. But we have already seen that this inhering cannot be accidental, any more than it can be essential. In consequence, Aquinas has to appeal here, implicitly, to the register of 'proper accidentality', as described in Chapter Two. There we saw that, for Aquinas, there can be additions to *essences*, which still nonetheless belong properly to a thing's *being*. In the Christo-logical context he cites finite examples of such instances as analogues for the hypostatic union. Besides the relation of body to soul, he mentions also the relation of a *hand* to the human soul (*not* just the human body; in the next section we will see the significance of this). Here he explains that one can have a human being who is fully and essentially human without a hand, and yet a hand is not an entirely accidental instrument of the soul, as, for example, is an axe. A hand is rather an 'organic' instrument of the soul (this crucial point is strangely overlooked in Richard Cross's unfavourable and supposedly 'analytic' assessment of Aquinas's Christology).[27] One can usefully elucidate Aquinas's discriminations here, by observing that while, indeed, a handless man is fully capable of all essentially human functions, this is in part thanks to the ministrations of the handed, and, more crucially, that it is scarcely possible to imagine the development of 'essential' human culture and intelligence without our upright posture and the related instrumental indeterminacy of our hands. (Both Aristotle and Aquinas stress at least the adaptedness of these features to our intellectual capacity, but expressing the adaptedness this way around only reinforces the power of Aquinas's analogue.) Certainly humans born without hands among handed humanity are fully human in their intelligence; nevertheless, human intelligence is the intelligence of a handed species. This point becomes even clearer when Aquinas deploys the relation between the *tongue* and the soul as an analogue in the same fashion; *even though*, after Aristotle, 'the intellect is not the act of any part of the body', yet 'the tongue is the intellect's *own* organ' (our italics).[28]

Aquinas, for the sake of what is at issue, has to imagine handedness (and tonguedness), counterfactually as an 'addition' to humanity; however, he alludes also to a closer, because supranormal, analogue: the instance of a man possessing a sixth finger. The Incarnation, he suggests, can be compared with such a growth, because while a sixth finger is an accidental deformity in relation to the human *essence*, it nonetheless becomes an integral part of this man's *personal being*, because it is useful to him (and may even, one can add, afford him greater skills and capacity in certain respects).[29]

In deploying these examples, Aquinas is concerned with the relation between the human essence, which is an animal rationality, on the one hand, and the bodily *organon* most habituated to *touch*, on the other (and the tasting of the tongue represented for Aquinas, as for Aristotle, a more intimate mode of touch). It is easy to imagine that the relation of reason to touching (as to holding and gripping) is here incidental, and that other bodily functions could just as readily have been invoked. However, this is unlikely to be the case: first of all, the relation between mind and the lowest, most material of the senses, is the most appropriate for a comparison with the conjoining of God not only with a human soul, but also with a human material body. Secondly, it has already been seen why, for Aquinas as for Aristotle, there is a link between the peculiar openness of the human mind to *truth* of all kinds, on the one hand, and the possession of the organ peculiarly adept at touch and manipulation, on the other. It will be recalled that it was argued earlier in this chapter that, for Aquinas, the Incarnation effects an ontological revision in such a way that the lower senses now instruct in truth the higher reason. Now, however, we have a hint of a preparedness for such a Christological and sacramental reversal in the initial created order of human existence itself. The hint concerns a certain crucial relation of human intelligence, not to the higher, more refined and spiritual senses like seeing and becoming, but to the lower, more material sense of touch (one should remember here that, from the Patristic tradition, beginning with Origen, Aquinas had inherited a doctrine of the 'spiritual senses' according to which *all five senses* had psychic equivalents: a doctrine which effectively 'materialized' the soul).

This hint, moreover, turns out to be more than a hint, but rather a deliberately expounded thematic, if we turn to Aquinas's commentary on Aristotle's *De Anima*.

III

In the course of the *De Anima*, Aristotle provided a remarkable analysis of touch. He noted that in the case of every other sense there is always a *medium* between sense and the thing sensed. Thus vision requires intervening light; sound, intervening air. However, in the case of touch, there seems to be no medium, and instead touching is experienced as a registering of the immediate.[30] In the case of sight, for example, the medium of light is first moved and then this medium moves us. But in the case of touch we seem to be directly moved by the source, despite the relation between different surfaces: Aristotle gives the analogy of the penetration of a body by a spear through a shield. It is not that the spear first moves the shield, and then the shield moves the body; rather the spear directly penetrates the body.[31] And this appears to be the case with all instances of touch: what senses, namely the *psyche*, is directly affected by the corporeal.

However, Aristotle judges that this appearance is somewhat of an illusion. Short of the self-knowledge of absolute *nous*, there is no real immediacy, and every material finite contact involves a third element, which is the shared domain which permits contact (for Aristotle, there is no vacuum). Sensation as a finite material movement therefore also involves a medium. This circumstance (one may interpolate) can also be grasped phenomenologically: that object which I physically encounter can only be experienced as *other* to me if its corporeality is other to mine, and it can only be experienced as an item within the world, rather than as the entire world which envelops me, if between me and the object there lies a shared worldly space. (If this space can itself be specified, it will in turn be an item within the world and not the enveloping world *in toto*.) Perception, as such, therefore has a triadic structure.

Aristotle therefore concludes that in the case of touch, there must be a hidden medium.[32] In part, he concludes that it is hidden in a banal sense, because between one contacting surface and another, there will always be an infinitesimal interval of air or water (and perhaps sometimes of fire and earth), even though this is too small for our awareness. However, Aristotle is clearly not content with this solution, and it seems that there is something unsatisfactory for him about the lack of *apparent* mediation, if the only mediation involved in touch is that of an imperceptible interval. Thus he clearly distinguishes a physical from a perceptible (phenomenological) medium, and is more interested in the latter.[33] For Aristotle, sensation must be an experience as well as a reality of mediation, and therefore he implicitly appeals to an unstated phenomenology of the kind outlined in the previous paragraph. And he is aware of the phenomenological structure at least to the degree that he provides a negative example of it in noting that an object brought right up against the eye is no longer visible.[34] Thus he gives an empirical example of the absolute necessity of *experienced* mediation for perceiving, even if he does not elaborate the phenomenological ground for this.

Aristotle must therefore show that, after all, in touching something, we experience mediation. And his demonstration here is remarkable. Since the contact of the body with the thing outside itself is experienced as physically immediate, in such a way that from an *experienced* physical point of view, the toucher entirely fuses with the thing touched, *our body itself* must be the medium. Otherwise, we would not experience the thing touched as other, and so would not experience it as anything specific at all, just as we only register an object held too close to our eye as a blinding darkness. But what is the body a surface between? Clearly it can only be an interface between (informed) matter and the pure spirit (*forma formarum*) of the soul.[35] In effect, what Aristotle has already discovered here, long before Husserl and Merleau-Ponty (who, following Brentano, drew upon this text), is that the body is not just another object in the world of which we are aware. Rather, as the embodied condition of possibility *of* awareness, it is, as body, quasi-subjective, and is also the mysterious sphere of mediation between subjective and objective, *psyche* and *hule*. The mysterious character of this mediation is apparent in the fact that it is the body in its most earthly material aspect as the immediacy of touch (which is obviously related to 'efficient' causality), which serves as the transition to *psyche*. For it is the physical capacity of the body to mediate touch which actually proves for Aristotle that there is a spiritual, psychic interior to the body which allows it to *be* body. Thus: we touch things bodily; bodies, however, do not themselves touch, since then there would be no mediation and no touch; therefore it is the soul which touches through bodies. Touching proves and manifests the *psyche*. Or, to put this in more contemporary terms: in the case of touching, one is conscious in, but also *through* the body, of contact from without. The very transcendental possibility of touch depends upon the experienced (and then reflexive) 'remove' of consciousness from exhaustive identification with the body, even though it only attains consciousness *through* the body in touching (and presently we shall see how, for Aquinas, *all* sensation is touching, and so this conclusion can be generalized). However much this consciousness might be reductively 'explained' (as by Daniel Dennett and others),[36] even our consciousness of such explanation as embodied in images we must logically construe, but also see, hear and touch in order to comprehend (according to the *conversio ad phantasmata*), will be 'removed' from these images and our bodily experience of them. In consequence the most such explanation can achieve is the insinuation that consciousness is an illusion, perhaps even providing a supposed account of how such illusion arises. But since such 'illusion' is unavoidable, and transcendentally necessary for thought, in such a way that we cannot really think outside it, there could be no demonstrating its illusory nature. Indeed, any story told about passages through fundamentally necessary illusion is the purest metaphysics. (Dennett and many others fail to see how radical a presupposition consciousness is, since we experience it *not* just as the 'remove of our minds', but as *disclosedness* of things to our minds. It is therefore *not* primarily an attribute of cognition, but rather an *ontological* horizon outside of which we could not even make sense of 'a being', since no being is thinkable outside its being able to appear to awareness.)

Nevertheless, this is not to say that articulation of such a materialistic metaphysics can be ruled out as transgressive through a transcendentalist redetermination of the bounds of pure reason. For even though one can speak of the *psyche*/touch relation in terms of a transcendental condition for what must always to us appear to be the case, it is still true that to 'save these appearances' (to use Aristotelian language), one must give an ontological account of how mind is a reality not arising from limited matter, of the kind given by Plato, Aristotle and Aquinas (or even, in the end, Kant). In the absence of such an account, one is bound, philosophically, to provide an alternative, reductive account of the apparent being of *psyche*. Thus Aquinas could never have been satisfied with a merely transcendentalist account of the mind: rather, for him, the reality of mind depends upon the experienced *proportio* between *psyche* and touch (and all the senses) being construed as a participation in the pure self-mediation – which in the Trinity is also self *as* pure mediation – of absolute eternal psychic being, just as for him (as we saw in Chapter One), the reality of truth in things sensed depends upon their participation in eternal truth (with which pure self-mediation coincides).

To return to Aristotle: in the case of touch, uniquely, it turns out that the body itself is a medium, but no longer a physical medium. Rather, it is the interface between the physical itself and the psychic. In this way, touch 'proves' the soul, which is also, for Aristotle, following Plato, 'proved' by the experience of 'common sense', whereby we are able to relate inherently disparate sensory experiences together, experiencing the same thing, for example, to be loud, red and hard – or, indeed, loud, red and yielding.[37] Here the senses must be themselves sensed, according to an 'inward' measure, which grasps invisible harmonies and proportions between them.

Nevertheless, if the *psyche* grasps the hidden proportion amongst the heterogeneous senses, it is only in touching that it experiences the proportion between *psyche* and sensing itself. This, for Aristotle, implies that, while all understanding is first in the senses, acute touch is the basis for that acuteness which constitutes understanding. Indeed it practically *defines* the latter, for Aristotle roundly declares that, without exception, men of soft flesh are well endowed with intelligence, while men of hard flesh are more merely animal in character.[38] Setting to one side the absurdity of this specific thesis, a serious contention remains: namely, that hypersensitivity of touch and intelligence are inseparable. In consequence, Aquinas, directly following Aristotle, insists that human beings are the *prudentissimum* of all animals,[39] because they have the strongest sense of touch: presumably this is related to our nakedness (relative lack of body hair), as well as to our handedness. But he specifically mentions the power of the human tongue, which has a far more exact sense of taste than with any other animal: here one can see that Aquinas is close to the insight that cuisine is a fundamental basis of human culture, and indeed intelligence.[40] By contrast, according to Aquinas, there are examples of animals being better endowed than humans in every sense other than that of touch.[41]

Clearly this set of affirmations is remarkable, because normally for the tradition (and for Aristotle and Aquinas themselves), sight and hearing (in that order) are the highest senses. This is usually affirmed since, as with mind, they can grasp several things at once, and in their case a sensory grasping by one person does not preclude a grasp by another. I can take in a landscape at one glance, and so can several people standing next to me. But I can only touch one thing at a time, and where I touch, another must await his turn.

Moreover, the *De Anima* itself mentions how touch is the lowest of the senses, found in the basest, blind and deaf organisms, and how this is because touch is directly related to *survival*. It concerns the immediate negotiation of its environment by the psychically-imbued organism. And for this reason touch has an especially intimate relation with the reverse of survival, which is destruction. This relation belongs to all the senses, to a degree. Thus whereas, says Aristotle, an especially intense and acute thought further strengthens, and can never overthrow, psychic intelligence, too strong a sensation destroys the sensory organ.[42] This is because every sense is a kind of delicate *proportio* or atunement to what is sensed, and also a kind of *mean* between all things. We can stress here that Aristotle and then Aquinas's account of sensing is ontological rather than epistemological (and to do with *convenientia*), just as we saw was the case for knowledge in Chapter One. Thus, too horrific a sound, or too violent a light, is not simply 'registered' by the senses – as a modern epistemological and empiricist account of sensation as a mere contingent and indifferent receiving, might lead one to suppose possible – but destroys the *proportio* between thing sensed and the sense itself, and so, in an extreme can destroy the sense also.[43] A loud noise can deafen; an extreme light can blind. In the worst cases the damage is permanent.

However, it is not life-threatening. By contrast, too hard a touch not only numbs this sensation, but in numbing the entire body, may also kill it. Thus the relationship of touch to the mere utility of survival, also, for Aristotle, provides it with an existential relationship to life and death.[44] This should cause us to reflect on the way in which touch, like the other senses, is also a *proportio*, a harmony. Aristotle explains, as we have seen, how to touch mediates proportionately between soul and touchable bodies; he also declares that it is a 'kind of mean between all tangible qualities'.[45] But if touching both preserves one's own life and destroys other life (though also gives it, one might add), then we can infer that it is a kind of mean between all living things, and even a kind of mediation between the life and death of the body. We can further suggest that this standing between the life and the death of the body, is the ground, in human beings, for its standing between soul and body, and the allowing of the remove of consciousness. Consciously to understand life has, as its concomitant, the possibility that one can deliberately destroy it – as well as the consciousness that one can be destroyed.

But now the paradox, whereby the baseness of touch proves soul, has been much intensified. For it will be recalled that, for Aristotle, a strong thought cannot overthrow mind. Yet now we see that touch is at the opposite, weak extreme of such intactness: whereas a loud sound deafens, but cannot kill the hearer, too strong a touch can slay. Therefore, whereas the life of thought (remembering that psychic intelligence is a kind of life, specifically for Aquinas, after Augustine, but also, by inference for Aristotle), *as* the life of thought, is absolutely inviolable, the life that touches and is touched, is absolutely and existentially vulnerable. Intelligence might salvage all life; touch might endanger all life.

Therefore, for Aristotle and Aquinas to say that the person of most sensitive touch is also the person of most intelligence, is tantamount to saying that the most secure life is purchased at the price of the most exposed life. Understanding, indeed, cannot be taken away from us, but it is only to be acquired through extreme empirical encounter, which always risks self-destruction. Only what might entirely die, entirely and indestructibly lives. (Even for Aristotle, intelligence is a kind of resurrection.)

Aquinas, in his commentary on the *De Anima,* shows a distinct interest in this complex thematic of the *psyche*/touch relationship. Given his own corporeal character, this is perhaps not surprising – yes, indeed, he agrees, men of soft flesh are always the more intelligent! However, he gives two of his own reasons for this, and in doing so provides important developments of the thematic.

Aquinas asks why touch should more correspond to fitness of mind than sight, which seems more spiritual, and 'reveals more of the distinguishing characteristics of things'.[46] In answering this, he says, first of all, that since touch is diffused over the whole surface of the body, all the senses partake of touch, and are, indeed, variants of touch (this is indicated less explicitly by Aristotle). It is in virtue of touch that anything is called sensory, and therefore better touch means better sensory adjustment in general. And since, for Aquinas following Aristotle, what is in the intellect was first in sense, high intelligence is inseparable from acute sensory perception (even if the reverse is also true).

Two comments may be made on this new assertion. First of all, Aquinas would seem to be right, because it is only reflexively, on the whole, that we become aware of the medium involved in seeing and hearing. Phenomenologically speaking, the object is seen directly without interval. Therefore, Aquinas's observation strengthens the implicit phenomenological dimension of consideration. Now it has already been seen that the argument making body the medium in the case of touch depends upon a phenomenological analysis, not a sensorially empirical one – for from that perspective the imperceptible interstices of air between touching surfaces would serve as medium. Therefore, if *all* sensation is (at least to a degree) phenomenologically immediate, then all sensation is 'touch', and *all* sensation requires that the body operate as a medium.

Nevertheless, this does not remove (nor did it remove for Aquinas, since intelligence *must* involve soft flesh, but not necessarily strong sight) the primacy of touch. For touch still exhibits immediacy in the most extreme form, and the discovery that all sensation is touch means that it also, in the end, involves bodies touching bodies in a series (especially given Aquinas's account of motion, which involves a *ricochet* of local motions and no *impetus* inherent in a body travelling always fundamentally in an ideal void, as for Newton). Thus to see a tree, for example, must be, for Aquinas, at one moment in the process of seeing, to see the species of tree as refracting the light which is its medium of conveyance. Whatever our modern perspectives on this account, we can still appreciate Aquinas's doctrine that all sensation is touch as a rigorous insistence that even the more apparently spiritual senses are the result of local, regular and physical encounters between material bodies.

But, paradoxically, it is this materialism of all sensing which proves the reality of soul, since sensing (phenomenologically) requires a medium, and the real medium, for all the senses, can only be the surface of sensation itself which is the body.

The second comment concerns the relation of the Thomist commonness of touch to all sensing, to the Aristotelian *sensus communis*. It will be recalled that the latter offered a second proof of *psyche*. However, if the senses can be sensorially mediated in terms of touch, is the second proof now redundant, especially as all the senses, taken one by one as variants of touch, now prove *psyche*? The answer is no, not exactly, because the diverse senses, including touch, still remain heterogeneous as physical experiences. If they are, nevertheless, analogically related in terms of touch, this is not only because they involve physical, surface contiguity, but also because such a surface is *only* a surface as the medium between physical and psychic. To discover that all sensation is touch, is to discover that all sensation is a proportion between psychic and material, and that, in every case, it is the soul, not the body, which senses, though always through the body, which is a harmonious mean, and no neutral uncharacterized 'instrument'. Therefore, the second proof has not been exactly rendered redundant; nonetheless, it now converges with the first proof. For now, if all sensation 'touches', and to touch is already to cross the threshold of the psychic, then every sensing is already by virtue of what is common to all the senses. *Sensus communis* must be eminently touch, and by the same movement within sensation by which we sense only through the 'remove' of consciousness, we sense in a specific way (seeing, hearing, smelling, tasting, touching), only through that sensing which is common. Here, all the media and all the means converge: the proportion between material things (including sensing and sensed) is the proportion between mind and matter, which is in turn the proportion between heterogeneous sensations. Or to put things another way: the mediation of *sensus communis* is the mediation of touch.

Besides the contention that all sensing is a mode of touching, Aquinas provides a second reason for the priority or touch. This, once again, concerns the analogous diversity of touch, and once again moves in a 'materialist' direction (even when compared with Aristotle). Aquinas asserts that touch, as material, must be constituted out of the four elements, and this assertion recalls the pre-Socratic views, discussed by Aristotle in the *De Anima*, according to which the soul's knowledge is a matter of the responding of like to like, in such a way that, for example, if the fundamental element is taken to be fire, as for Heraclitus, then the soul, also, must be a refined fire, which flares up in response to physical burning.[47] Aristotle preserves this 'like knows like' thematic, in that he argues that form passes from material individuation to pure formal generality in the mind; Aquinas of course concurs, though with crucial modifications, as we saw in Chapter One. Aristotle also indicates in a somewhat pre-Socratic fashion, that like recognizes like in the sense of affinity between different combinations of the four elements.[48] Aquinas foregrounds this more emphatically.

Now to say that knowledge always depends upon the 'touching' of sensation (and upon the reflex to a phantasmic touching as was explained in Chapter One), and to identify touching as composed of the four elements, is to insist that knowledge does require a 'pre-Socratic' basis of intra-material echo and correspondence. Touch, says Aquinas (and therefore all sensation), is a mean between all tangible qualities and their extremes, *because* it is composed of these qualities.[49] Moreover, to operate as a means of perception, the instrument of perception, the body, must *itself* be arranged as a mean, or as a well-constituted analogous proportion between the diverse elements. Therefore, the finely-attuned sensory body is not only the body of pliable flesh, but also the healthy, well-balanced body (not necessarily, perhaps, in view of Aquinas's unangelic physique, the athletic body!). Thus subtle sensing, which, as we have seen, includes the capacity of 'common sense' to relate heterogeneous sensations, must result always from the inwardly well-constituted body, possessed of good *temperantia* (this is Aquinas's term).[50]

A grasp of the harmony of the cosmos depends, therefore, upon a microcosmic echo of this order in the well-tempered body. To touch well externally, the body must be an intricate network of well-attuned self-touchings. (This thematic was also taken up by Merleau-Ponty.) Therefore, we can infer, since every touch is not only between sensory items, but the touch *of* sensory items by soul, the *temperantia* of the body *is* also 'the common touch' of *sensus communis*. And thus while the body is the surface between soul and matter, this surface is itself composed and interlinked as much by soul as by matter. Yet the material connection is equally fundamental. Therefore Aquinas concludes that 'because every form is proportioned to its matter', it follows as a result that 'the soul's lofty stature results from the body's good constitution'.[51] The inner *proportio* of body, therefore, is also the *proportio* of matter to form which in this case is of body to soul.

The priority of touch has implications for how Aquinas conceives of all sensory intuition. For Aquinas, while all finite intellects are fundamentally deliberative, and only by remote participation intuitive (as we have seen), sensation is, of course, not at all deliberative, but works by immediacy of presence. However, it can be pointed out here, that, were this a true absolute immediacy, material sensation in its simplicity would appear to rival the divine understanding. In reality, for Aquinas, while sensation lacks the complex mediation of deliberation, it does involve mediation of an intervening medium. But, as we have seen, in sensation this medium is the body itself, and the non-divine complexity involved in sensation is the integral relation between finite body and soul. Thus were there no soul, material sensation would lack the complexity essential to finitude. Matter as sensation proves the soul, yet thereby alone ensures its own limitation which is nonetheless essential to its materiality. Therefore, for Aquinas, without sensory matter, no psychic being with its eternal destiny could arise in the finite; yet without such a psychic 'remove', the sensory would not be confined in its finitude, but would idolatrously rival God (so soul alone strangely ensures limitation). In this way, body alone allows soul; soul alone bounds body, which yet is, as body, boundedness. (One is reminded here of Plato's world soul being externally 'wrapped round' the body of the cosmos in the *Timaeus*.)

If every touch, every sensation, repeats this co-constitution, then in touching, the soul does not receive impressions from the physical, but rather at once receives and produces the *convenientia* between spirit and matter. In this way, if touch rather than sight is paradigmatic of all sensory intuition, then the latter is not as purely passive or contemplative for Aquinas as one might have supposed. In fact, touch is less passive in three different ways: first of all, it is more *symmetrical* than sight or hearing. The eye, seeing, does not necessarily make the creature seeing seen, and does not, as eye, make itself seen by an unseeing object; while hearing *cannot* make the organ of hearing or the person hearing heard. However, what is touched also touches, and is acted on only to the degree that it also acts, even if only negatively, by offering resistance. Therefore, if all sensation is touching, there is only sensory affect where there is also sensory affecting – a look and a listening attention can, after all, hold someone or something and thereby draw attention to itself. And even passive unnoticed listening halts and directs towards itself certain sound-waves.

Secondly, through this symmetry of contact, touch can much more radically select, mould or alter what it grasps. We can look from different angles, move in for a close-up or stand back for a general perspective, but with our hands we can be yet more selective, and then in addition move the object grasped or change its physical shape. Negatively, as we have seen, we can also destroy it by this means, whereas only the rarest of gazes will slay. Thus again, if all sensation is a variant of touch, then to sense in general is somewhat to select, move and re-arrange. And since the visible and the audible are only *there* for sight and hearing, the ordering of the faculties can itself transform what is seen and heard (though only *as* visible and audible).

Thirdly, touch is much more *reflexive* than either sight or sound (and this is another reason for its closer kinship with intelligence). When we see an object we do not see our sight, but focus away from ourselves upon this object. But when we touch an object we also touch this touch, since we are also touched by the objects in a way that instinctively arouses personification and apostrophe (the 'soothing touch of silk'; 'that horrible bump' and so forth). Since we experience also the object touching us, there is an instant rebound to self-attention, in such a way that we at once touch also our own touching. And notice also that this is possible because of the relatively greater activity of the touched object. Since sight is more passive than touch, one might suppose that something seen is more active than something touched. Yet, instead, there is in sight (at least when its touch dimension is ignored) a curious kind of double passivity. If the gaze does not alter what it gazes upon, then neither is the gazer altered by gazing. Pure sight is theatre, where the 'active' drama on stage cannot coerce the real lives of the audience, while inversely the 'active' audience watching an objective display assembled for its delectation, cannot in any way intervene in the dramatic plot. (Listening to a concert is somewhat the same, but more ambiguous, as sound drifts round the auditorium, and is less bound within a fiction). In the case of sight and hearing, this 'double passivity' is guaranteed by the intervention of the palpable physical medium – they are like signalling by flashlight or radio across the English Channel: more like a prelude to fraternization or conflict, but not these realities themselves.

In touching, however, where there is no palpable medium, the thing touched tends much more to affect us directly: it can stop us, hurt us, alter us, soothe us or damage us. And this circumstance brings about the rebound of touch: without the interval of a palpable medium, what we touch in touch is the touching, not simply the other, held at a distance.

However, to touch touching in this way is to lose any perspective of safe distance upon the thing sensed by which we can assess it and place it in a context. Touching is not just close to us, but always 'too close', so close that we have no physical perspective upon it. Touching is sublime, saturated sensation, even if it is always somewhat beautiful, proportioned and specific. It overwhelms us and thereby moves us from our previous state. Since assessment of an object depends upon our own stability, touch does not allow us to assess the thing touched. All that we can assess is the touching, the resultant new relation, but this assessment is only possible because of our psychic distance from touching, which prevents a total overwhelming which would always be sensory death and oblivion. In the case of the other senses, it seems that we enjoy a discrete, inviolable intuition of a sensed object. But in the case of touching, we only intuit *the event of encounter*, and it is not the sense but the mind which intuits. Only, of course, our finite minds scarcely intuit at all, and so if the event of touching at the surface of bodies is only intuited by 'removed' mind, then in this case sensory intuition only occurs when it has already passed over into intellectual discursivity, discrimination and judgement. What is touched is only intuited as *intended* by active mind. Thus to the external active character of touch (which moulds as much as it is moulded), corresponds the internal active character of the *psyche* which, alone, is what consciously touches. So, once again, we see just why the touching hand is the supreme organ of intelligence.

In the previous chapter it was suggested that, in Aquinas, a latent phenomenology possessed no privilege over against a primacy of active judgement and interpretation, but that, instead, his thought implied an equipoise of seeing and making. Now we can see just how radically this is confirmed by his advocacy of the Aristotelian priority of touch. For if all sensing is in a measure touching, then in all sensing we primarily touch touching and not the touched object. In seeing, what we see is as much the object looking at us, locating us, defining us, judging us, as us looking at the object. Likewise with hearing. In this way, perception is so radically inter-objective at the outset, as to forestall any later phenomenological problematic about intersubjectivity. Likewise, if all sensation is a mode of touch, things can only be intuited by mind, which is really to be intuited as always already intended, discussed, discriminated and judged conjecturally in relation to an unlimited horizon. Thus if, for example, what we really see with our eyes is the transfer of 'gazes' between us and the object, then what we see is a ratio, which we only see, mentally, insofar as we assess and interpret it. On this view of intuition as 'touch', therefore, it could never be originary, and, since for Aquinas there is no pure finite intellectual intuition, there would be no possibility of phenomenology *stricto sensu,* founded on reduction to original given intuition. For where the most originary intuition is touch, intuition is also interactive event, mutual modification and discriminating judgement (which will always be constituted through language of some sort).

IV

Returning, now, to Aquinas's Christological concerns, one must ask about the significance of his occasional, but very marked, attention to touch, in the midst of a discourse suffused throughout by light and illumination. Normally, it would seem, the intuition of sight is offered as the best analogue for divine intuitive understanding. However, if touch is more integrally related to human intelligence, and touch reveals the essential character of all sensory intuition, then it would seem that divine intuition must, eminently, be 'touch'. And then, whereas in the previous chapter we spoke of the divine understanding as the coincidence of 'seeing' with 'making', now we can see that to describe this understanding as intuitive 'touching' would encompass both aspects. If Aquinas does not speak this way, then apart from the decisive weight of tradition, this is because the discrete, touching-one-thing-at-a-time-by-only-one-person character of touch, appears utterly inappropriate to God, compared with the stereoscopic and collective character of vision. However, this consideration also ensured that, for Aquinas, one must supplement the link of *human* intellect with touch, with a link to vision, since certainly with respect to its exclusiveness (though this also permits its greater engagement), touch is deficient.[52] However, if we allow that, for Aquinas, vision is also a mode of touch, then we can see how for him the divine intellectual vision *as* touching is also an encounter, a shaping, a making, a contriving. One can also mention again here that the Incarnation provides, for Aquinas, a 'foretaste' of the beatific vision, implying that this vision is also a tasting, the most intimate touch.

If, in this fashion, it would follow that, for Aquinas (although he never states it), the divine intelligence is eminently touch, as much as eminently vision, then we should approximate most to God in our touching of things. And whereas, normally, for Aquinas, our psychic 'seeing' of things by intellectual illumination involves a priority of mind over body (even though bodily mediation is essential), a psychic 'touching' of things would disturb this priority for all the reasons we have seen, including the specific statement that high intelligence is 'proportioned' to the well-tempered body capable of discriminating contact.

It has already been suggested that this thematic of touching provides some sort of natural ontological ground for *the event* of ontological reversal which follows for Aquinas from the Incarnation, whereby our senses must now educate our understanding. If 'touch' seems to hold the balance between mind and body, then sacramental touching *anno domini* seems to shift the balance towards body. But how can there be *revision* even of finite ontological order? For it reflects an order that eternally pertains between finite and infinite; and part of this order (at least we assume) is the priority of mind over body.

However, if intellect knows through touching, and the ratio of mind to body consists in the medium of touch, then we have seen that touch, more than other sensing, is an interactive *event* (and not a passive registering). Hence the priority of touch discloses the relation of mind and body to have the character of event, and events are revisable. Here ontology itself expects self-revision.

There are certain hints in Aquinas that the ontological reversal accomplished by the Incarnation pivots about touch. We have already seen that the absolutely new ontological possibility realized by the hypostatic union is compared by him to the conjoining of a hand to a person as his 'proper instrument' of touch and formation. As a 'proper accident', this hand is involved in the event and events of touching which are contingent, and yet fully belong to the person who touches. Likewise the human nature comes, in time, to inhere in the *Logos*, yet now existentially belongs to it, in the most absolute sense.

We have also already seen how, through the hypostatic union, which yet preserves the integrity of human nature, the divine intellectual intuition can only be fully manifest to human nature through a coincidence with our sensory intuition, where, alone for us, a certain immediacy is possible. Now we see that, for Aquinas, the site of this immediacy is touch rather than vision. And touch, it has been shown, is only intuitive as active and shaping. In keeping with this, our sacramental re-education is not primarily a matter of looking. Thus, as we shall see in Chapter Four, Aquinas considers liturgy very much as something we must with our hands shape and perform, concluding his final *summa* with detailed instructions as to what we are physically to do, and why.

Finally, for Aquinas, it belongs to the *convenientia* of the Incarnation that Christ should mediate to us what is most certain in itself, namely divine truth, through what is most certain for us, namely the directly touchable by the senses. The disciple Thomas, as the angelic doctor Thomas recalls, was permitted to ease his doubt by touching the wounds of the resurrected Christ,[53] and we are permitted to encounter God through the most intimate and discerning touch of all, which is that of the tongue in taste. For Aquinas, as for Augustine, the Eucharist most of all accomplishes a reversal. Normally food and drink are to nourish the body, which is to sustain the mind. But here the mind is not only to attend to what it eats and drinks, which can alone instruct it in the truth; it is even – after Augustine – *to become* this food and drink, which makes present the truth incarnate. Ordinarily, food and drink become us; here we are to become this food and drink. And in this case, at last, the exclusiveness of touch which permitted its penetration, is conjoined with that generality and commonality hitherto peculiar to sight and hearing. For when we touch the body and blood of

Christ, we touch everything, and infinite others may touch all the same points of this body at the same time.

Thus another ontological revision has been effected. In the Eucharist, touch as taste ceases to be restrictive in its exclusivity. Instead, from now on, if we wish to see the universal, to see God, we must aspire to touch and shape in truth, along with all other people, every last finite particular as included within and disclosing the body of Christ. Henceforward, the journey to God is equally the journey to the God-Man, and so equally to all creatures, and no longer away from them. Now, to see God is also to make the future.

V

All the above considerations concerning touch, and finite ontological revision on the basis of touch, remain, however, incomprehensible, unless we can understand how this revision affects the relation of finitude to the infinite. The latter cannot alter, and any relation of the finite to it, must appropriately reflect this binding character. Therefore, one must assume that the ontological revision of the finite which establishes the hypostatic union, since it establishes thereby a higher finite reality, discloses something new about God, hitherto unknown to us. Likewise, since the hypostatic union entails the further ontological revision which is the exalting of the sensory and further exhibition of the priority of touch (in such a way that one can, for Aquinas, even say of the finite human nature in Christ, by virtue of the one *esse*, that 'it creates'), we must assume that this exalting and exhibition also discloses something new about God. Since the way to divine truth is now somewhat different, some new character of truth in God must thereby be shown.

One could object here that the exalting of the sensory is merely a pedagogic means to restore the ideal order which is the rule of mind over body lost by the fall. However, this instrumentalist view of the sacraments suffers the same objection as an instrumentalist view of the Incarnation. In the latter case, for Aquinas, Christ became incarnate to redeem us, but this incarnation is a reality which eternally persists beyond our redemption, and in ontological dignity exceeds it. Likewise, if the body of the Incarnate God resides in bread and wine in order to feed us spiritually, this residing is eternally true – since bread and wine are not accidents of God, as nothing can be, and therefore they also are events which can never depart from him. Again, this residing exceeds in ontological dignity its occasion, and reserving of the Eucharistic elements, or the Corpus Christi processions which Aquinas helped to promote, appropriately express this. (One should note here also that we can be redeemed only by what is more than necessary for our redemption: that is, God and his presence.)

So just as 'Our Lady is now Heaven's Queen', so also the humanly sensory is forever exalted in its inexhaustible depth above the human intelligence (although *for* the human intelligence). In consequence, since all that comes to pass participates in God whose truth it displays, and never expresses any arbitrary whim, this exaltation, like the hypostatic union, must disclose some hitherto unexpected dimension of the divine truth. But exactly what, in either case?

In the case of the hypostatic union, as we have seen, since God for Aquinas is both *esse* and tri-personal, he is open to the arrival of an event which causes something else to belong to him, not accidentally and not essentially, but rather as exhibiting precisely the same *idiom* of being; the same dance, in the same measure. But for Aquinas's theological metaphysics, this existential character of the *Logos is* the real, is the true concrete reality which upholds everything. Hence to be conjoined this way, is not to be weakly or metaphorically conjoined, nor merely conjoined by similar *habitus* (a position he specifically rejects), but also to be joined in substantive actuality. Here, as we saw, there is assumed into God an 'objective relationship' of the kind which a subject has to an instrument which becomes an organic part of himself.

Nevertheless, for Aquinas, this event, this arrival, can involve nothing new for God, since he is replete. Although the human nature of the *Logos* belongs integrally to the *Logos* and its being is only that of the *Logos*, the *Logos* is not really related to its new human attribute. Or to express this more dramatically: the human nature is so perfectly conjoined to the one *esse* of Godhead that it possesses only this Godhead, yet nothing is added to the one *esse* thereby. It might seem that the ontological space of hypostatic union is thereby a black hole, or an entirely impossible space. However, the 'impossibility' of this space is really no more than the 'impossibility' of the space of Creation as such; although it is exterior to God, there cannot really be an exterior to God since he is all in all. Thus the participation of beings in *esse* involves something quite other than the external relation between beings, and is, for us, ultimately unthinkable. We have seen how Aquinas is driven to cite Dionysius to the effect that God somehow 'exists outside of himself' in the ecstasis of a lover. And we have further seen how in the Christological context this is deepened: it is because God is so utterly replete and self-sufficient that he can share without shadow of jealousy. Thus if what creation discloses of *esse* is that it somehow can exist outside of itself, what the ontological revision that is the hypostatic union discloses is that *esse* is in itself this ecstatic going outside itself. For divine *esse* is now shown to be such that a new thing can inhere in it, to be such that it can become entirely the *suppositum* of a creature outside itself, yet without real addition to itself. This last negative safeguarding of divine aseity might seem to deny that divine *esse* is also divine event, but in fact it achieves the opposite. It denies that divine *esse* can *become* event, but affirms that it *is* event, since an event can entirely come to belong to it without adding anything new. The point must be that God already was, eminently, the new event.

Of course, this eminent ground of eventuality in God is none other than the issuing forth of the Son and the procession of the Holy Spirit, which the Incarnation and the instituting of the Church fully disclose once again to fallen humanity. Through this disclosure we come to understand that there can be a created exterior to God, because God's interior is self-exteriorization. We see this because we now have seen that a created exterior can be entirely assumed into the divine *esse* without abolition, and yet without addition to the Godhead. But this regards only the ground in the Father's generating of the Son for his giving of the Creation. It reveals to us 'subjective relation' in God; it does not fully explain in what sense God can be eternally such as to be *the subject of a new event* which *comes* to belong to him, in the way that an organic instrument like a hand can come to belong to a person as something that is neither essential nor accidental. It does not fully explain how God becomes subject of this one-sided 'objective relation'. To understand this possibility, we have to grasp not only how *esse* is relational self-exteriorization, expressed as substantive relationality, but also how it somehow exceeds the contrast of given essence and accidental new additions. That is to say how the proper accident of the new organic instrument can come entirely to belong to God's being, and yet not add anything to this, nor be related to it.

To approach this issue, one should recall that while, in Aquinas, God is not really related to the Creation, he nonetheless knows perfectly the myriad ways in which he may be participated in by creatures. Therefore, it would seem that one might also say (though Aquinas does not say this), that God has eternally an eminent knowledge of the hypostatic union through knowledge of how a finite event may be absolutely conjoined to his *esse*. It would then follow that, although this only comes to be the case, God must, in his eternal nature, eminently know and therefore be, this coming to be the case. In this sense, neither Swedenborg nor Blake were wrong to think that Christianity must imply an eternal divine-humanity: a God who was always also the God-Man. The mystery here must be that in order to foreordain the Incarnation as the remedy for sin, God always was the God-to-be-incarnate, already forgiving as giving. This need not imply any Hegelian becoming of God into his own through the alienation of evil, if it is understood that the to-be-incarnate in its contingency nonetheless entirely expresses what divine goodness in any case is. Only in this way can one make sense of the fact that, while the Incarnation is a contingent eventuality in time, since it is the unique event of the absolute inhering of time in eternity, from the eternal perspective God is *eternally* the God in whom a man inheres, just as he is eternally the God who has shared his being with the Creation.

Through the Incarnation, it is revealed that divine goodness is not simply subjective self-giving as displayed in creation (which, as we have seen, in principle, for Aquinas, discloses the Trinity – though only obscurely for fallen humanity), not just the substantive relational generating of the *Logos* which is the ground of creation, but also the constitution of the *Logos* through 'assumed additions' which are neither logically essential according to a given nature, nor merely willed accidents. *Logos* is also *Ars* for Aquinas, since, as we have seen, it is a *Logos* of the aesthetically convenient, and therefore eminently contains the economy of Christ's human nature which is the highest *convenientia* of all. This *Ars*, as it were, is an aesthetic art precisely by its personal existential assumption of contingently new instruments or modes of working (along with their products). As the eminent ground of the *convenientia* of the assumption of the human nature as a new *organon*, the *Logos* as *Ars* cannot be merely the liberal art of speaking, but must also be, in an eminent sense, the craftwork of handedness. God is disclosed in the Incarnation as acting not merely by glance or speech, but also by direct touch issuing from spirit into matter (as in Michelangelo's Vatican ceiling). As somehow, in his very intelligence, this eternal touch, he is also eminently that moulding or shaping through which alone subjects communicate with each other, and together modify their shared objective medium to produce history. God, as *esse,* exceeds the contrast of being with becoming, and is eminently becoming.

And especially in becoming the subject of a human death, is God disclosed as touch. Since, as we have seen, for Aristotle and Aquinas, human intelligence is only inviolate as linked to absolutely vulnerable touch, it was appropriate that the *Logos* was only disclosed in time in and as a vulnerable body. And it was appropriate also that in dying (inevitably, because of sin), the exposure of the incarnate *Logos* to the touch of all should be revealed as the abiding intelligence able to resurrect the wounded surface of touch also to inviolable life.

It is these touching wounds, which, like the disciple Thomas, *we* touch, in order to touch for the first time God whose truth is to touch (meaning both to mould and to encounter). And since God is now revealed as touch, the new ontological exaltation of the sensory over the intellectual is no mere pedagogic means, but an appropriate new disclosure of the ultimately real. This exaltation, as we have seen, is undergirded by the priority of touch, whose direct mediation of the psychic ensures that this exaltation by no means betrays the understanding. It could always have been seen that touch as finely attuned sensation brought about understanding, but this is much more emphatically manifest after the Incarnation. Now, in order to understanding anything of divine truth (and so truth *per se*), we must touch divine physical manifestations, and we must elicit these through our crafting of liturgical enactments.

4   Truth and language

I

In his speculation on the noun-phrase 'landscape' in Paragraph 65 of the *Pensées*, Pascal explains how language fixes or designates reality and at the same time surrenders to the indeterminacy and flux of signifieds: 'A town or a landscape from afar off is a town and a landscape', he writes, 'but as one approaches, it becomes houses, trees, tiles, leaves, grass, ants, ants' legs, and so on *ad infinitum*. All *that* is comprehended in the word "landscape".'[1] A single noun-phrase is shown at once to conceal and yield an infinite asymptotic analysis of reality, and here Pascal intimates how our words remain always undefined until we actually use them, even though there is always *something* we know of a word's meaning which enables us to use it in the first place. However, it is clear from Pascal's analysis that even when we have used a particular word, we can never be entirely certain of its exhaustive definition.

Now, in the Port-Royal treatise on the categorical theory of propositions, *Logic or the Art of Thinking*, Antoine Arnauld and Pierre Nicole invoke precisely this discussion of the infinite divisibility of the world and the difficulty this presents for our use and understanding of words. They explain how every word we use summons at best a confused idea of the signified, which will always be accompanied by what they call 'incidental ideas' which the mind perforce adds to basic verbal meanings. Such confusion is at an absolute maximum in the case of the demonstrative pronoun *hoc*, 'this', used instead of a proper noun. When the supremely indeterminate pronoun 'this' is used to display, say, a diamond, the mind does not settle on conceiving it as a present apparent thing, but adds to it the ideas of a hard and sparkling body having a certain shape, besides connotations of wealth, beauty, romance and rarity.[2]

This qualification of our certainty regarding the meaning of words forms the basis of Arnauld's and Nicole's attack on the Calvinists' metaphorical interpretation of the Eucharist. For the Calvinists, they argue, assume in full nominalist fashion (probably influenced by the French Calvinist humanist Petrus Ramus), that the word 'this' establishes a firm attachment to a determinate referent, namely, in the case of Jesus's assertion, 'this is my body', a firm attachment to the bread. If one detaches the demonstrative pronoun from its obvious referent, as is the case, the Calvinists claim, when Jesus says 'this is my body', then it must be intended metaphorically. Arnauld and Nicole argue against this by drawing attention to the Calvinists' error of assuming that the demonstrative pronoun 'this' is anchored to a determinate specificity. To the contrary, they argue, specific application is only made possible in this case, because of the term's maximum of indeterminacy, its unlimited transferability. For the word 'this' always remains susceptible of further determinations and of being linked to other ideas.[3] In addition, even when something apparently determinate is invoked by the pronoun 'this', that specificity is itself infinitely divisible and in consequence retains an open-ended and mysterious character. One might think, in the case of the bread to which the pronoun 'this' refers in Jesus's assertion, that there is at least some limit to the open-endedness of our mental compassing of the bread. But later in the *Logic*, again invoking Pascal, Arnauld and Nicole protest that even 'the smallest grain of wheat contains in itself a tiny world with all its parts – a sun, heavens, stars, planets, and an earth – with admirably precise proportions; that there are no parts of this grain that do not contain yet another proportional world'.[4] Thus, even the most literal-seeming reference in fact preserves an infinity of mystery, even as it seems to command or delimit that extension.[5]

It should of course be added that behind the assertions of the infinite divisibility of matter lie the seventeenth-century disciplining and enhancement of the senses provided by such devices as the microscope, telescope and air-pump, which revealed things that were previously invisible, and cautioned against relying upon the observations of unassisted sense.[6] Thus Pascal and his allies deployed aspects of the New Science *against* nominalism and the cruder variants of empiricism. And they brought into apologetic alignment the scene of experimentation with the scene of sacrificial offering, to the extent that both are read as exposing and releasing unexpected depths within seemingly brute matter.

For the Port-Royal grammarians, therefore, there is a triple bond between the theory of physical matter, the question of how language operates and the theology of the Eucharist, and in particular the doctrine of transubstantiation. Echoing this threefold concern we will now demonstrate how discernment of the Body and Blood of Christ in the material species of bread and wine in the Eucharist, as interpreted by Aquinas, allows for – even demands – the greatest inexhaustibility of meaning, but at the same time, overcomes the problem of a sheer indeterminacy of sense, thereby allowing a basis for the possibility of 'truth'.

But before going on to consider this oxymoronic status of meaning and language in the Eucharist, one should perhaps ask why, having referred to the Port-Royal critique of how the Calvinist 'fixing' of language ignores language's indeterminacy, one should regard 'sheer indeterminacy' without qualification as a problem – for surely the attempt to secure meanings and thereby rescue 'truth', is inherently futile. Is not this view, after all, a key feature of post-modern – especially Derridean – philosophy which hails *différance* and the eruption of flows and postponement of meaning as the ineliminable outwitting of metaphysical attempts to secure present truth from the ravages of time and indeterminacy? Such a position exalts the release of language into a play of traces which, far from being 'commanded' or fixed by the person wielding signs, rather ensures that that person is commanded *by* those signs.[7] Moreover, this command is a strange anarchic sort of command, which never finally declares *what* is commanded, since meaning is held forever in abeyance by the postponing protocol of *différance*. So, given this rigorous release of language, why should one reinvoke a nostalgia for even the relatively determinate? Put briefly, the problems, as we see them, with the Derridean sign as they relate to our theme, are as follows.

In the first place, by cleaving to absence, Derrida leaves the metaphysical correlation of meaning and presence in place, even as he claims that presence is that which is perpetually postponed. For the vehicle of Derridean *différance*, namely the sign, must perforce remain the same in its repeatedly pointing to something which never arrives. This renders both signification and repetition transcendentally *univocal*, precisely because they point to the nothing of postponed essence – and it should perhaps be noted that nothing is more identical than nothing is to nothing. In this way, the very unmediability of an absolute radical difference, immune to any likeness, must collapse into its opposite, into identity, sameness and indifference. It resolves, as a transcendental category, into absolute equivalence which comprehends or measures each difference after all.

The second problem with the Derridean theory is that when difference is held at such optimum pitch, each assertion of discontinuity is identically superlative and attains a kind of homogeneous heterogeneity. Indeed, in the third place, for all his high talk, this in some ways reduces the Derridean sign to the ideality of a perennially available and wordless thought which overcomes its own mediations and cleaves to presence. The logic of deconstruction allows no mediating relationship between *différance* and the various appearances of meaning which it organizes or disorganizes. In consequence, the universality of the 'grammatological flux' is perhaps to be seen as a saturation of language which empties language of itself. For, in the words of one of Derrida's faithful followers, John D. Caputo, meanings are allowed 'to slip loose, to twist free from their horizons, to leak and run off'.[8] Thus, the Derridean sign relinquishes commitment to any specific epiphanies of meaning, or preferences for the lure of certain metaphors, and substitutes an universalized, autonomous and impersonal *mathesis* for language as such (as Gillian Rose rightly argued). For true difference and openness to the Other demand a sensitivity to the fact that some things are more alike than others, or are driven by the provocation of preference or desire which celebrates that difference all the better.

In the fourth place, one might even say that, grammatically-speaking, the Derridean sign, in privileging absence, which becomes after all the superlative present object, is cast in the indicative mood of the present tense, which is the very prototype of all language, only for a specifically *Cartesian* linguistics. One should nonetheless note here that Derrida invokes the category of the middle voice to suggest that *différance* does exceed the dichotomy of active and passive. However (as has been argued elsewhere),[9] because for Derrida the sign commands the subject bespeaking or inscribing language, however much a speaker or writer intends a meaning, the infinite play of autonomous 'corridors of meaning' by definition always arrives over-against the subject to cancel the specificity of his or her desire.[10] In this way, the impersonally objective rules, but such a notion of the objective, from Descartes onwards, is only available for the dispassionately representing *subject*. Hence any suggestion of postmodernism that the Cartesian subject has been erased is a ruse: in fact what it removes is the situated, embodied, specifically desiring historical subject, whereas it must secretly retain a transcendental subject who merely knows, since otherwise the indifferent rule of the sign would never 'appear' as a transcendental truth. (Such pure appearing at the transcendental level, supposedly without interpretation, also shows that Derrida remains confined within the canons of phenomenology.)

Finally, one should perhaps say a little more about the *subject*, as Derrida sees him or her. Insofar as Derrida hastens to undo any substantiality on the part of the subject's intention or desire when he or she elects a meaning in language – by insisting upon meaning as being withheld in an abstruse realm of postponement, and by subjugating the speaking self to the sway of the grammatological flux – he after all assumes that the subject's intentionality is something that *requires* cancellation. In other words, he simply repeats the assumption that human will can only be construed as something that issues from a self-identical subject which commands all that it wills. He here enthrones a voluntarist subjectivity which wields dominion over all that it surveys, even as he insists upon the inevitable abdication of that subjectivity. His fear of the engulfing power of human desire – that same fear which forces Derrida to deny the giving or receiving of a gift, or any reciprocal relationship with the Other – too much equates desire with exhaustive *acquisition*, and suggests that there are no modalities other than that of the indicative and the imperative, even if those modalities are consummated through deconstruction, in Derrida's sceptical discourse. And if one can have no intimation at all of the postponed meanings of a sign through anticipation or desire – just as one cannot for Derrida ever present oneself, as oneself, to the Other, either with one's gifts, praise or prayer – then, like the air which surrounds us, that postponed meaning has in fact no distance from us at all. Thus, in refraining from every risk of reducing meaning to presence, one finds that meaning is accorded a kind of hyper-presence which surrounds us with its untouchability. The preciosity of Derrida's demur accords absent meaning a stifling inaccessibility and unmediable enclosure within a revered guarded fortress. Yet such a construal renders absence dialectically identical with a metaphysical fetishization of presence.[11]

The foregoing critique of Derrida's account of the sign is by no means exhaustive, but what we have been trying to show is that it is neither presence as such, nor absence as such, which is culpably metaphysical, but rather the dichotomy itself, and that for all Derrida's exaltation of the indeterminacy and flux of meaning, by simply inverting the metaphysical structure of the sign, he stays within its paradigm, and ends up fetishizing presence after all.

II

At this point, we must return to the theme of the signs of the Eucharist and ask whether by contrast they in any way outwit this difficult dichotomy of presence and absence. If *all* they do is render explicit the indeterminacy of a sign, then there would be no contribution that eucharistic theology could make to semiotics surplus to that of a sceptical philosophy. However, one might also entertain an opposite anxiety: a cursory glance at the history of post-mediaeval Catholic theology, and its focus upon transubstantiation and 'real presence', might seem to suggest that the Eucharistic signs clearly privilege presence over absence. But if one looks further back to mediaeval theology, particularly that of Thomas Aquinas, and some of its later refractions, such as the work of the Port-Royal grammarians already mentioned (despite their possible Cartesian aspects), one can construct a different account of the theological signs of the Eucharist which – beyond the postmodern – more genuinely outwits the metaphysical dichotomies of presence and absence, life and death, continuity and discontinuity, and so forth. In order for such an account to be possible, however, one must understand the Eucharist, following the work of Henri de Lubac, as an essential action within the Church which constantly reproduces the Church, and not simply as either an isolated authoritative presence or merely illustrative symbol, which came, following the early modern period, to be the dominant readings.[12]

Briefly, the key to the transcending of the dichotomy of absence and presence in the Eucharist lies in the 'logic' – if one can here use such a term – of *mystery* which, according to patristic negotiations of the word *musterion,* implies a positive but not fetishizable *arrival,* in which signs essentially participate, but which they cannot exhaust; for that mystery arrives by virtue of a transcendent plenitude which perfectly integrates absence and presence. Thus a more positive account of the sign is suggested, for the sign here is neither emptily 'left behind' through postponement, nor is it the instrumental Ramist sign which secures the real in an artificial exactitude.

What this amounts to is an ontological coincidence of the mystical and the real, a coincidence which, as de Lubac shows, lies at the heart of mediaeval Eucharistic theology. If this coincidence becomes fissured, the

Eucharistic signs perforce become either a matter of non-essential, *illustrative* signification which relies upon a non-participatory and conventional (if mimetic) similitude between the bread and the Body, and the wine and the Blood, or else the site of an extrinsicist miracle which stresses the alienness of bread from Body, and wine from Blood. These alternatives, in disconnecting the symbolic from the real, in an attempt to prioritize either one or the other, are *both* equally reducible to a synchronic mode of presence which fails to allow the sacramental mystery its full, temporally ecstatic potential within the action of *ecclesia,* namely, the continuing coming-to-be of the Church as Christ's body through an ingesting of this same body, which is at once a real and a symbolic consuming. Without such a context, the merely static localized presences of instrumental sign or intrusive miracle are ultimately situated within the order of the sign mentioned already in association with philosophical privileging of either presence or absence – for, in being disconnected from ecstatic ecclesial action, the Eucharistic signs must implicitly separate the signifier from the signified.[13] Even in the case of an arbitrary miraculous presence, the exclusive prioritization of the 'real' over the merely 'symbolic', gives rise to a tendency to think of the Eucharist as an arbitrary present sign concealing an equally present meaning (the giving of a merely extrinsic 'grace') subsisting within a synchronic or rationalized realm of logical demonstration on the basis of certain authorized assumptions.

So, by stressing the *ecclesial* and *relational* context of the Eucharist, and its character as linguistic and significatory *action* – shaped by human hands – rather than extra-linguistic presence, one can start to overcome the logic of the secular Derridean sign. But in doing so, one finds also that one has – almost by default – defended an account of transubstantiation. For it is when the Eucharist is hypostasized as either a thing or a sign in separation from ecclesial and ecstatic action, that it becomes truly decadent. Thus, Jean-Luc Marion, implicitly building upon de Lubac, convincingly argues that transubstantiation *depends* upon the idea that Christ's Body and Blood are 'present' only in the sense of the ecstatic passing of time as gift, and *not* in the mode of a punctual moment abstracted from action, under the command of our gaze. And he shows furthermore that modern theories of transignification presuppose a mundane temporality, in which Body reduced to meaning is fully 'present' to us, rendering such theories crudely metaphysical in a way that transubstantiation avoids.[14]

To explain further how one can construe the theory of transubstantiation in terms of a theory of the sign as mediating between presence and absence, two points can be emphasized. First, following Louis Marin, there is the question of the relation between this theory and a general philosophic scepticism. On the face of it, transubstantiation seems to collude with the sceptical notion that the way things *appear* to be is no guarantee as to how they really are. For here, it seems, we have an absolute denial of the apparent presence of bread and wine, and an affirmation, by faith, of the presence of the Body and Blood of Christ, despite the fact that none of the normal sensory indicators of such phenomena is present at all. How is the ontological reversal which prioritizes touch manifest here? Does one not rather have a fideistic denigration of vision and taste, and of the reliability of sensory evidence as indicators of truth? It might seem so, since there is discontinuity and rupture between the bread and the Body, or between wine and Blood. However, the sceptical disruption of normal certainty in the case of transubstantiation is balanced by the certainty of the affirmation of faith: here *is* the Body and Blood. Moreover, the appearance of bread and wine are not disowned as mere illusions. To the contrary, it is allowed that they remain as accidents, and indeed as accidents which convey with symbolic appropriateness their new underlying substance of Body and Blood. One might say that only the symbols of an outpoured body nourishing us, give us an expanded sense of the character of this divine body: disclosing it as an imparted and yet not exhausted body, quite beyond the norms and capacities of an ordinary body.

Hence, although one passes here through a moment of the most apparently extreme philosophical scepticism – a thing is not at all what it appears to be; its reality is radically absent – this is only to arrive at a much more absolute guarantee of the reliability of appearances. For now, it is held that certain sensory phenomena mediate, and are upheld by, a divine physical presence in the world (though this is invisible). The extreme of scepticism has been entertained in one instant, only comprehensively to overcome all possible scepticism and to arrive at a more absolute trust in our material surroundings. Through the faithful reception of the Eucharist we can now experience these surroundings as the possible vehicle of the divine. And the only mode of scepticism thereby finally endorsed is a benign, doxological one. If bread and wine can be the vehicle for the divine Body and Blood, then we must now assume that nothing exhaustively is as it seems. But instead of this unknown surplus being construed as the threat of deception, it is now the promise of a further depth of significance and truth: of a trustworthiness of appearances even beyond their known, everyday predictable trustworthiness. And since the fact of unknown depth behind things is unavoidable, it really is *only* this benign scepticism upheld by a faith in a hidden presence of God which could ever fully defeat the more threatening scepticism of philosophy.

For in a fallen world, we do not infallibly experience the unknown depth as a participated unknown which partially discloses its truth in the manifest; to the contrary, we experience it also as a rupture from God and ultimate truth or meaningfulness. Such hesitation is only overcome when we encounter, with the eyes of faith, the divine bridging of this rupture so that (here in the Eucharist) we see and taste a material surface as immediately conjoined to the infinite depth. Participation is, in this case, so entire that God as the participated truth is fully present, without lack, in the material bread and wine which participate. The situation here is exactly parallel to that which was disclosed in Chapter Three in relation to the Incarnation.

Because human reason no longer discerned God through its material sensing of the material world, God had to descend bodily into this world to reinstruct our reason. However, were it the case (as for some Protestant views), that the Incarnation is in no sense perpetuated through time, then, after Christ's ascension, one would revert to a priority of our rational remembering and understanding of Christ both for our salvation and our access to truth. Yet this appears unsatisfactory: first of all, because our fallenness persists and is still to be fully healed; secondly, because – as was explained in Chapter Three – the new priority of the sensory (especially of touch) amounts to an ontological revision whose 'fittingness' for our redemption nonetheless (beyond its mere means) discloses something new about God. Since God is not, for Aquinas, an arbitrary God, the 'convenient' means he newly elects, also further disclose how he eternally *is*.

Thus, for both these reasons, if the truth is to continue to be disclosed to us for our redemption, the Incarnation must continue to be 'made present' to us – albeit in the ecstatic fashion described by Marion. Aquinas accordingly argues that the divine humanity must be 'applied to us', and that for this reason the material and signifying participation of the sacraments in his humanity is also 'convenient'. As 'signs', the sacraments are said to be 'like' the humanity assumed by the eternal sign, the *Logos*.[15] Christ as the divine presence can only be made known to us signifyingly and sensorily, in the sacraments, just as his 'truth' is in part disclosed in the later historical *improvement* of humanity he has effected. Baptism, first of all, transmits to us the renewed divine image in humanity of purified visibility, but the Eucharist, far more intimately, through taste, conjoins us to the divine *substance*, since by becoming part of the body of Christ we are conjoined to the hypostatic union itself.[16] Here, once again, the ontological revision accomplished by the hypostatic union is inseparable from the further ontological revision which is the reinforced priority of touch, and one should note that we are only conjoined to the *Logos* as we are conjoined to the broken-as-vulnerable touch of the divine body, which is resurrected in the abiding intelligence of this vulnerability. Just as Christ's broken and resurrected body was the 'organic instrument' of the *Logos*, so also the broken and eaten bread is an 'instrument of the God made flesh'.[17] Thus we now, for Aquinas, encounter the truth that is Christ through a sacramental development strictly parallel to a natural one: baptism is like birth, confirmation like growth, the Eucharist like nutrition, penance like healing.[18] And yet this transmission is also described by Aquinas as a 'personal' one: it is the only possible mediation of the divine person of the *Logos* in time.[19]

The second point concerning the mediation between presence and absence in the Eucharist is as follows. One can note that there is still a rupture here of the normal functions of sense and reference. Under ordinary circumstances, one can present a sense or a meaning in the absence of any anchoring reference (at least of a specific sort): for example, one can speak of an imaginary town, and still make sense. Inversely, if one is to *refer*, there has to be something palpable one can point to: if one says 'London', then one knows that this is a place one can visit, somewhere one can indicate on a map of a real place, 'England'. However, in the case of the words of institution, it seems that sense and reference peculiarly change places, or collapse into each other. Thus, pointing to a piece of bread and saying 'This is my Body' does not even make fictional or imaginative sense, as we do not tend to imagine an unknown body as bread. The phrase only makes sense if it does, however absurdly, actually *refer*: that is, there is only a meaning here if the words *do* point to the Body via the bread; only a sense if the bread has been – as in Aquinas's understanding – transubstantiated. Inversely, however, the phrase 'This is my Body' does not refer in the normal sense, because it does not indicate anything palpable which fulfils the expectation of the words – as would be the case if one used them while pointing back at oneself. In the latter case, 'reference' would be satisfied because one could then look at the Body and say 'ah, it's like that': one would have *identified* it. But in the case of the reference of the words of institution, no ordinary identification can take place, since there is no immediately manifest Body: reference is here affirmed without identification, since sense – the imaginative supposition of 'Christ's Body' – must continue to do all the identifying work. Thus while sense is drained of its usual absence, since there is only sense via specific reference, equally, reference is drained of its usual presence, as we are presented with no palpable content.

This second point about the collapsing together of sense and reference (in such a way that both appear to be missing), can now be brought together with the first point about a faithful trust in the bread and wine as disclosing an invisible depth of Body and Blood. Combining both points, it can now be seen that 'this is my Body' – as said while pointing to bread – means that a missing sense for Body (how can it be bread?) and a missing identifying reference for Body (we do not see it) are both simultaneously supplied when we take the bread as symbolically disclosing an inexhaustible Body (or wine as disclosing the Blood); in other words, when we reunderstand Christ's divine-human body as what nourishes our very being.

However, this does not mean that sense and reference are exhaustively supplied. To the contrary, if we say that the real sense and reference of this bread and wine is the Body and Blood of Christ, then since the latter are ultimately mysterious, sense and reference here are only supplied in being simultaneously withheld. Yet once again, this faithful trust is the most guarantee of sense and reference one could ever obtain. This is the case because, ontologically-speaking, for anything to be 'here' it must be in excess of here; for something to arrive, it must withdraw. And the strange effect of such withdrawal into the inaccessibly real is to return reference to the 'surface' of signification, to the realm of interpretation of senses or of meanings. For this reason, the Eucharistic collapse of sense and reference into one another only dramatizes a situation which always obtains: sense and reference are *never* discrete, since even the fictional city is only imaginable because we identify it by reference to some *real* cities, while, inversely, London will be diversely identified according to the different senses we make of its appearances (including where we draw its boundaries). Thus reference is not denied, but secured in the only way possible, when, in the case of transubstantiation, it ceases to be that 'other' of language which anchors all signs, but instead becomes that which folds back into sense, into language. For here, instead of the referent being confirmed by our glance towards the bread, it is confirmed by Jesus's phrase itself, uttered with a simple authority which kindles our trust.

From all the above, we can conclude that whereas, according to Derrida, Christian theology privileges something pure outside language, it is on the contrary the case that the Eucharist situates us more inside language than ever. So much so, in fact, that it is the Body as word which will be given to eat, since the word alone renders the given in the mode of sign, as bread and wine. Not only is language that which administers the sacrament to us, but conversely, the Eucharist underlies all language, since in carrying the absence which characterizes every sign to an extreme (no body *appears* in the bread), it also delivers a final disclosure, or presence (the bread *is* the Body), which alone makes it possible now to trust every sign. In consequence, we are no longer uncertainly distanced from 'the original event' by language, but rather, we are *celebrants of that event* in every word we speak (the event as transcendental category, whose transcendentality is now revealed to be the giving of the Body and Blood of Christ).

In this way, we can see how the 'convenient' sacramental transmission to us of the personal *Logos* by *taste* (intensified touch, which as touch both 'sees' and 'makes'), is always accompanied by a linguistic transmission which issues in speaking. The *tasting* by the tongue is only possible with the *speaking* of the tongue – and conversely. And it is for this reason that sacramental transmission (*unlike* that of original sin), is 'personal' and as Aquinas says, 'through the zeal of good will' and desiring faith, as well as material.[20] But here we can further come to understand how the *Logos* descends into tasting, and how such tasting itself becomes instructive of the intellect. For the corporeal mediation between matter and soul, which (as we saw in Chapter Three) is involved in all touching, and so in taste, itself involves a moment of absence, in such a way that the touched thing is always already something indirectly and psychically judged. Nothing is present unless already interpreted and therefore as signified by a sign. And so already, for a person's tongue to taste food and drink, is for that person also to taste – judge – them in his mind (thus a person's 'taste' is equivalent to his judgement). In this way, his testing tongue is also an assessing and speaking tongue. All it can ever eat is signs.

As a result, it seems that language accompanying taste throws the reliability of tasting into doubt; signs are indeterminate. However, in the Eucharist, where the words of language 'this is my body' affirm that the absent depth tasted is here entirely present on the surface, then the physical taste of the believer itself confirms this. Whereas, normally, language makes taste to be taste, and yet throws it into doubt, here language speaks beyond its own doubting, and taste confirms its trust, thereby helping to remove the doubt from language. So now, taste makes language to be language, but this is only because taste is now entirely fused with the *Logos*: for this reason, Aquinas can speak of Christ's passion as efficacious for us through 'spiritual contact' which works both by 'faith' (in the absent) and the 'sacrament of faith' (which make the absent present).[21] So now we have seen how language accompanies touch, we can also see that what the new finite primacy of touch really discloses is an eternal *co-primacy* of *Logos* with 'contact' (of intellect with 'sense').

With regard to the doubt inherent in language, we have discussed how the use of the word *hoc* or 'this' hovers between specific designation and an open expectancy of infinite arrival. Such a hesitation brings together a specificity of presence – *this* tomato, etc. – with a generality of absence, where 'this' may denote anything whatsoever. The point can be further elaborated by realizing that this indicated hovering is in fact a linguistic presentation of the general epistemological problem of the aporia of learning (as discussed with reference to Aquinas in Chapter Two), namely, the question first articulated in the *Meno* as to how, if one is ignorant of something and *knows* one is ignorant of that thing, one can nonetheless already know something of it in order to know that one is ignorant of it. At what imperceptible moment is the barrier of ignorance pierced? And once one has reached the stage of knowing one is ignorant of something, how does one know that there is more to be known, beyond this initial relation? One of the ways in which Augustine resolves the aporia of learning is by recourse to the mediations of desire, which not only provoke the knower ever forward without quite knowing what he or she is looking for, but also issue from the thing to be known, drawing the knower towards it, as if electing to be known by a particular person. But it should be noted that desire – which is divine grace in us – offers a resolution to the conundrum of knowledge only insofar as it lets it stand *as* a conundrum. The provocations of desire reveal that the truth to be known is never exhausted, but is characterized by a promise of always more to come. One can suggest that there is a linguistic variant of this Augustinian thematic, for when one uses words, one perforce uses them without quite knowing the true proportions of their referent, for those true proportions lie ever beyond our grasp. To a certain extent, words remain undefined until one elects a particular path for them, until one *uses* them, and yet this indeterminate or half-arbitrary specification is not wholly defined by us, for there always remains in the words we use some *lure* by which we can infer the paths of their meaning.

In a similar way, the simultaneous indeterminacy and specificity always involved in the deployment of the word 'this' is mediated by the desire provoked by an initial indeterminacy in pronouncing the word 'this', which yet requires a specific instantiation. Moreover, this work of mediation is doubled in an instance where one uses the word 'this' in a seemingly redundant way by saying 'this is', of something which is manifestly bread. And yet again, this element of desire is here trebled, because if one continues by saying 'this is bread from the bakery', the dimension of desire would drop away with the satisfaction of one's curiosity about what was going to be said. However, where one pronounces a seemingly bizarre identification, desire *remains,* partly because one wishes forever to penetrate this mystery, and partly because the specification is itself of something infinite, and therefore not exactly specific at all. So whereas in every specific use of the word 'this', the indeterminate horizon remains, in this instance this is all the more the case.[22]

One can further illuminate this peculiar situation by mentioning an alternative use of the phrase 'this is'. Not only might it precede a statement of *identification,* which can often include an element of derivation as in 'this is my grandmother's ring', it might alternatively precede a statement of re-identification or unmasking, as in 'this painting is a forgery'. However, in the case of 'this is my Body', neither of these seemingly exhaustive alternatives pertain. As we have already seen, one is not here giving accidental information, as in the first example, where the fact that the ring used to belong to my grandmother does not displace its essential and visible ringness (which does not require to be identified, except in the initial learning of language). This contrasts with the Eucharistic scenario, because when the priest says 'this is my body', although he is not saying 'this bread is not really bread', he is not attributing an accidental property: instead it would seem that he is providing an absurd identification, where actually no identification at all needs to be rendered. On the other hand, there is no suggestion of exposure of false appearances, as if Jesus had said 'this bread is really Body'. Therefore, when Aquinas claims that transubstantiation has been effected in such a way that the accidents of bread and wine nonetheless remain, one could say that he is strictly adhering to the peculiar linguistic pragmatics of this New Testament usage.

Nevertheless, there does seem to be one major problem about Aquinas's interpretation, namely, that it runs counter to common sense. The natural reaction to the claim that the bread is more essentially Body is one of tremendous shock, because no Body can be seen.[23] Why does this shock not lead to rejection? The answer here is manifold, because it has to do with the complex circumstance in which this phrase is uttered. For one thing, the sheer plainness of the phrase tends to produce trust, and for another, the circumstances in which it is uttered – the ceremonial context, the priestly authority, the echoing of the original institution at an evening banquet, the choice of simple elements – which as Aquinas says possess a natural sweetness – all tend to ensure our consent. Although the shock could not be greater, it nonetheless concerns the conjoining of the supernatural with the ordinary, in such a way that we are persuaded of a certain analogical continuity which makes us *desire* the claimed presence of the Body and Blood of Christ. In short, the shock is acceptable because desire, instead of being cancelled, as in the case where one's expectations are fulfilled – as when one says, 'this was my grandmother's ring' – is here sustained and intensified. Aquinas repeatedly observes that it is actually desire *for* the Body which ensures discernment of the presence of the Body.[24] Because our tasting of the body is accompanied by signs, and so remains always a judging interpretation, the dimension of absence is not abolished even in this saturated degree of participation, whereby we are physically conjoined to a direct substistency in God as one *esse*. Since it remains, to taste truly and sweetly can only mean to taste as still desiring. Such discernment by a taste which desires, restores to us a foretaste of the beatific vision lost at the Fall, and thus (according to the conclusions we reached in Chapter Two), the very possibility of access to truth as such. Therefore, the following account of Aquinas's instructions for the liturgical promotion of a state of mind able to discern the body, is also an account of how, for Aquinas, one is to become capable of, and also fulfil, *theoria* as such.

III

In Aquinas's description of the liturgy surrounding the Consecration, it seems that there is a determined effort to *incite* passions. These allusions to emotion can be divided into two categories: (1) relating to preparing the right *sort* of feelings during the liturgy leading up to the consecration, in keeping with the solemnity of the mysteries about to be celebrated; and (2) an additional, more intense, even physical, stirring of emotions, which, as we will see later, is closely linked to Aquinas's theology of the Eucharist.

The first set of allusions can be surveyed quite briefly. Aquinas introduces the theme of emotional preparation with an invocation of the Old Testament injunction to 'Keep thy foot when thou goest into the house of God' (Eccles. iv.17). The celebration of this mystery, he writes, 'is preceded by a certain preparation in order that we may perform worthily that which follows after',[25] which would seem to suggest that liturgy is not an end in itself, but an act of preparation, very closely allied to human desires. The first stage of this preparation is divine praise, and, for Aquinas, this meant the singing of an Introit, usually taken from the Psalms; this is followed by a recalling of our present misery, and an invocation of divine mercy, through the recitation of the *Kyrie*. Next, heavenly glory is commemorated in the *Gloria*, so that, as Aquinas puts it, such glory becomes that towards which we might incline ourselves or tend. And finally, before the next main stage of this long act of preparation, the priest prays on behalf of the people that they may be made worthy of such mysteries. What this final prayer amounts to is in fact a prayer for emotional preparation, a preparation for preparation, a desire for there to be desire. What one might call this incipient stage, then, is a liturgical liturgy.

The second advance towards preparation is, as Aquinas puts it, the instruction of the faithful, which is given dispositively, when the lectors and subdeacons read aloud in the church the teachings of the prophets and apostles. At this point, we notice a slight change in the provocation of right desire – for whereas in the first stage, as we have already seen, the desires provoked were immediate responses or solicitations of joy, misery, glory and so on, now the passions of the people are lured via the mimetic enactment by choir or priest of certain spiritual or elevated emotions: for example, a sense of progress towards God, which is a sense of spiritual delighting or, sometimes, of spiritual sorrowing, according to Aquinas. Thus, after the Lesson, the choir sings the Gradual, which Aquinas says is to signify 'progress in life'; then the Alleluia is intoned, and this denotes 'spiritual joy'; or, if it is a mournful Office, the Tract is intoned, which, he writes, is 'expressive of spiritual sighing'. So, it seems that having first elicited the raw and uninstructed passions of joy and sorrow, the liturgy then provides a spiritual model whereby these motions might be guided to make the people worthy of the mysteries to come. It is as if desire is at first fulfilled only by a reinforcing and increasing of desire, which we must learn from the desired goal itself.

At first sight, it might seem strange that liturgical progress here runs from initially spontaneous and authentic emotions towards feigned and borrowed ones. For this inverts the normal assumed sequence whereby one first learns by copying and then grows into authentic possession. However, the placing of *mimesis* in this case ahead of the autonomous, suggests that, from the liturgical point of view, a borrowing is the highest authenticity that can be attained. For where all desire for God and praise of God must come from God, imitation is no mere pedagogic instrument which subserves a more fundamental self-originating substantiality. Here, to the contrary, one must copy in order first to begin to be, and one continues to be only as a copy, never in one's own right. However, as has been seen, what we first imitate and copy in the divine is desire or love. And here again, normal expectations are subverted. For just as being does not here precede copying, so also the apprehension of the thing copied does not precede our copying. We do not first apprehend and then desire and imitate; rather, we first apprehend in acts of desiring which begin to disclose, through mimesis, that which is imitated. This liturgical logic of imitation in fact performs a theology of Creation for which it is the case that outside participation in the divine, the creature is, of itself, nothing. Towards the end of this chapter we will show how the narrative logic of imitation in the liturgy is underpinned by a metaphysical logic of participation (as described in Chapters One and Two), and how the culmination of the Mass in the transformation and reception of the elements displays the fusion of these two levels. For now, one can note that Aquinas's logic of imitation both anticipates and surpasses in advance a postmodern treatment of mimesis. For the latter also, imitation is constitutive of the imitator and precedes the original. And yet postmodernism, as if still echoing negatively a suspicion of all mimesis which it (falsely) attributes to Plato, regards these circumstances as entirely disruptive of all identity. More radically, Aquinas thinks of identity *as* reception, and of perception as receiving.

The third stage in the preparation of emotions is to proceed to the celebration of the Mystery, which, as Aquinas explains, is an oblation and a sacrament. Both of these dimensions of the mystery, the sacrificial and the sacramental, entail their own respective passions as well. Regarding the Mystery insofar as it is an oblation, the peoples' praise in singing the Offertory is now realized as they imitate in turn the mimetic performances of the choir or priest, for, as Aquinas says, this expresses the joy of the offerers. Insofar as the Mystery is to be seen as a sacrament, he declares that 'the people are first of all excited to devotion in the Preface . . . and admonished to lift up their hearts to the Lord, and therefore when the Preface is ended the people devoutly praise Christ's Godhead, saying with the angels: Holy, Holy, Holy; and with His humanity, saying with the children, Blessed is He that cometh'.

One might think that after all this elevating and instructing of the passions, the people would finally be ready to receive the Mysteries. And we have seen how this involves a turning away from the rawness of spontaneity and a sublimation to a higher kind of passion. This would surely seem an appropriately elevated moment for proceeding to the Mysteries. But not so. At this most mysterious of moments, just prior to receiving God into one's body, the people are reminded of more earthly emotions; far from this being a moment to look into a spiritual and abstruse realm of higher desire, the people are now brought back to their desire and love for one another. This is done by the communal recitation of the Lord's Prayer, in which the people ask for their daily bread, and by the exchange of the *Pax* which is then given again with the concluding words of the *Agnus Dei*. As the precondition of touching God, we are to touch one another. In this final intrusion of community, we can see a further elaboration of the logic of *mimesis*. The doubling of the choir's imitation of God and the angels by the peoples' imitation of the choir, reveals that the inversions of copy and original involved in relation to God are repeated at an interpersonal level. For our existing only as first created, as first an imitating of God, is echoed in the passage of time, as we exist (naturally and culturally) only through first receiving our specific mode of human existence, by the mediation of our forebears and contemporaries. They indeed give birth to us, and speak us into articulate being. Hence *metaphysical* participation extends to the political domain, ensuring that here a participation in the *social* sense precedes the individual self. Thus, once the people have been restored to themselves in earthly proximity to one another, after the earlier elevation of desire, they are now ready to receive the sacrament.

When Aquinas has thus narrated the modulations of desire during the liturgy, he then turns to more local observations in his replies to the various objections. And one or two of these replies are relevant to our theme. In his Reply to the Sixth Objection, Aquinas notes the way in which the liturgy seems to involve a great many different genres and perspectives, and that each of these seems to have a corresponding purpose linked to the provocation of desire. He declares that the Eucharist is a sacrament which pertains to the entire Church, in such a way that every different quarter of the Church must be included. Consequently, 'some things which refer to the people are sung by the Choir, so as to inspire the entire people with them', and there are other words which the priest begins and then the people take up, the priest then acting as in the person of God, and so on. And even when the words which belong to the priest alone, and are said in secret, are to be uttered, he calls the people to attention by saying 'The Lord be with you', and waiting for their assent by saying 'Amen'. At all times, it seems, the desire of the people is provoked, channelled and maintained. This is no automatic ritual, but one which, like the order of ancient sacrifices, must be accompanied by the right devotion in order to be acceptable to God.[26] So much is this the case, in fact, that at the Consecration, the priest does not seem to pray for the consecration to be fulfilled, but, as he says, 'that it may be fruitful in our regard'. Here Aquinas cites the words of the priest, 'That it may become to us the body and blood'. One can see here how the necessity for the Holy Spirit's reach of life as desire beyond understanding for attainment of truth (as described in Chapter Two) is fully elaborated in Aquinas's account of the primacy of desire in making truth present through the sacraments.

But just why is the Body of Christ so desirable? We have already mentioned that this is partly to do with its infinite absence and inexhaustibility, but it would be a mistake to suppose that this is the only reason. To do so would be to associate the instigation of desire with lack and frustration. On that account, desire is primarily a *possibility*. However, such an account of desire, although a common one, is false, because if desire is primarily instigated by frustration, it reduces to the mere epistemic imagining of a *possible* satisfaction. But in order for desire to be felt at all, it must be granted at least some scope of expression, which amounts to some measure of fulfilment, since desire expresses itself only in response to some reception of the desired object. Were such reception to be *altogether* withheld, then no desire could be expressed, nor any desire felt. Moreover, while it is true that we may appear especially to want the impossible, the knowledge that something *is* impossible, always in some fashion blocks the spontaneity of desire, in such a manner that one is not really relaxed in desiring, and remains self-conscious in a way which inhibits ecstasis, or else forces one to contrive an artificial or rational mathesis of desire. In the opposite situation of a desire that can be fulfilled, it is true that familiarity can breed a slackening of interest. But all that this implies is that for desire fully to operate, there must be both the possibility of fulfilment, and a sustained strangeness and distance. In this optimum and therefore defining situation, desire is something primarily *actual* rather than *possible*, because it is maximally in existence when flowing freely, as well as being continuously provoked.

Such a construal of desire as primarily actual accords with a Thomistic understanding of desire in relation to the Eucharist. For us to desire Christ's Body in the Eucharist, according to Aquinas, it must not only be withheld, but also, in a measure, be given. Thus Aquinas places great stress on the analogical *appropriateness* of the elements of bread and wine right down to the details of the multiplicity of grape and grain being compressed into a unity and so forth.[27] He also stresses how the elements of the Eucharist taste and smell good, and regards this as part of a complex rhetoric whereby the Eucharistic presentation of Christ is made attractive to us.[28] Indeed, as we have already seen, one could argue that Aquinas implies an Eucharistic re-working of what it is to *know*. On the one hand, it would appear, as we have seen, that transubstantiation accords with an optative scepticism about sensory evidence or 'touch'. Normally this would preface a spiritualizing or idealist philosophy which takes refuge in the certainty of ideas or logic. However, Aquinas denies sensory evidence only to announce that the real concealed substance is nonetheless manifest in sensory appearances, if these are now reconstructed as both metaphors and sources of delectation – that is, as both signs and morsels, as both what the tongue utters, and as what it savours. The elements are reduced to accidents, and yet their accidentality is then seen as all-important. One can go so far as to say that, having denied knowledge by sensory evidence, Aquinas then affirms a knowledge by sensual enjoyment. Beyond the disciplining of desires by reason lies a higher desire for God only made possible when God conjoins Himself with the seemingly most base forms of sensory delighting in the form of bread and wine, thus bringing to an extreme pitch the descent of the artisanal (and not merely architectonic) God, spoken of in Chapter Two. In the Incarnation, perpetuated in the Eucharist, the participation of *sacra doctrina* in the divine self-knowledge is perfected. In a fallen world, no longer capable of ascent to truth, this perfecting is the necessary condition of possibility for the resumption of *sacra doctrina*, of theology as such. But, as we have seen, we must go even further. Since the *convenientia* of this new ontological revision is yet disclosive of God, we now understand the beatific vision itself to be akin to sensory enjoyment in a way not realized before.

As was seen in Chapter Two, there is no induction of God *a posteriori,* and there is no deduction of God *a priori*, and yet, in the Eucharist, there is a tasting of God through direct physical apprehension, conjoined with a longing for the forever absent. Thereby, one can see that the ultimate reason for the acceptance of the shock of the phrase of institution is that it is one's body which here guides one's reason in the name of an infinite reason. Such a pedagogic order is, for the patristic inheritance which Aquinas received, strictly in keeping with the kenotic logic of salvation history: since it was the higher, Adam's reason, which first betrayed the lower, his body, redemption is received in reverse order through the descent of the highest, God, into our bodies which then start to re-order our minds.

IV

In the foregoing, we have seen how one can read the Eucharist as a particularly acute resolution of the aporia of learning in terms of the category of desire. This reading also has the advantage of showing just how fundamentally in line with Augustine, Aquinas's thinking about transubstantiation really is. Something similar can be glimpsed in a fourth example of mediation between presence and absence, namely, the persistence of the accidents after the event of transubstantiation. This phenomenon, it turns out, is only comprehensible for Aquinas in terms of his neoplatonic ontology of participation in Being, which surpasses Aristotelianism in seeking to do justice to the doctrine of Creation.

Not often noted in Aquinas's account of the Eucharist is the way in which, besides transubstantiation, at least two subsidiary miracles are invoked, although they are all part of the same miracle.[29] First, the conversion of water – representing the people – into wine, re-enacting naturally the miracle at the wedding feast at Cana, occurs before the transubstantiation of the wine into Christ's Blood. (And one can note here that Aquinas at one point appears to hint that the sacramental order of marriage stands in one sense above the sacramental order of priesthood, since it combines both natural and spiritual nurturing.)[30] This is important, because it shows that the Body of Christ is a nuptial body, which is always already the unity of Christ with the Church, His people. In a similar fashion, Aquinas emphasizes that bread and wine include a vast synthesis of disparate human labours, including the labour of transport and trade.[31] All these features tend to confirm the idea that, in the Eucharist, God is only made apparent in a sensual fashion which involves the mediation of all human physical interactions. Now, this exaltation of the sensual runs parallel with the glorification of the accidents which is the second – and this time miraculously re-enacted – subsidiary miracle involved.[32] It might seem that if bread and wine are reduced from substance to accident, that their natural materiality is thereby degraded. However, one can only think this, if one, remains ignorant of just how transubstantiation relates to Aquinas's most fundamental ontology. This is a matter ignored, for example, by P. J. FitzPatrick. We will elaborate this presently. The miraculous character of the remaining accidents is patent for Aquinas in the fact that, since the persistent accidental properties of bread and wine go on having a generative effect – for example, nourishing and delighting us – God causes the accidents to act *as if* they were substantive. This means that here the operation of matter in a normal fashion has been rendered miraculous. It is as if Aquinas is saying that the rendering of the normal and continuous as miraculous is the greatest miracle of all, and helps us to reunderstand the miraculous created reality of the everyday.[33]

Under normal circumstances, the accidents of bread and wine – for example, their shape and their taste – would manifest the substance of bread and wine, but now they have to be taken as directly manifesting God in whom they subsist. However, they are not accidents *of* the Body and Blood of Christ, since Christ being God, and therefore being simple, cannot be the subject of accidents. Nor, however, does this means that they are simply *signs* of the divine, as if they were mere persisting miraculous appearances. This cannot be the case, because Aquinas insists that the bread and wine remain as ontological accidents even though they are no longer accidents of any substance.[34] Here is the point objected to by FitzPatrick, on the grounds of its utter incoherence in terms of Aristotelian philosophy.[35] But what he ignores is that Aquinas's metaphysic is not ultimately Aristotelian.[36] Aquinas is quite explicit: in question 77, article 1 of the *Summa*, he raises the question of whether free-floating accidents are not utterly simple and therefore blasphemously like God in character.[37] But the answer he gives is that although they are torn away from the composition of substance and accident, they still retain a composition of existence and essence, since their essence, unlike that of God, does not cause them *to be*. This invocation of the real distinction between essence and existence constitutive of all creaturehood explains how it is possible for accidents to persist without substance, for they possess a ground in which to inhere, namely, created being, *esse commune*, which is nonetheless only ever displayed in specifically characterized formations. The real distinction of *esse* from *essentia* displays a deeper ontological level than that of substance and accident, because substance is always present in its own right as this or that kind of creature which can be accidentally qualified, whereas created being, *ens* (or *esse*) *commune* is not present in its own right at all, but only as this or that kind of being, whether substance or accident. For created being is really only a participation in Being as such (*esse*), which belongs to God alone. Hence, paradoxically (as we indicated in Chapter Two), *beyond* substance, which is self-standing, lies something, for Aquinas, *not* self-standing, namely, *ens commune*, which only exists in an improper borrowed fashion, just as earlier we saw that the human creature is imitative without remainder.[38] But since participation in Being is the most fundamental ontological dimension of creation, the real distinction of essence and existence can in theory sustain finite reality before and without the division of substance and accident. And this explains why free-floating accidents are possible, although it would probably be better to say that the remaining accidents have passed beyond the contrast of substance and accident. They are neither essential – since they are not God; nor are they non-essential – since they manifest God and are His creation.

Once one has understood that the remaining accidents exceed the contrast of substance and accident, one can also see that they are not relegated beneath the level of substance. On the contrary, they are now promoted to a character that most essentially reveals the condition of createdness, and they are accorded the honour of directly subsisting in Being, which is the most immediate divine created effect. For this reason, one can say that merely accidental bread and wine have become more themselves than ever before, and this coheres with the fact that they have also become completely attuned to a signifying and spiritually active purpose.[39] So much is this the case, that Aquinas insists that partaking of the Body and Blood of Christ under the species of bread and wine has become the means of deification. It is as if one is saying that bread and wine now remain eschatologically alongside God, in such a way that the most ordinary is here exalted, and it becomes not absurd to adore a mere piece of bread.[40] This is especially the case, because the remaining accidents are no longer like food that only becomes food when we take it up and eat it, and otherwise is only *potential* food. Rather, to exceed the contrast between substance and accident is to attain to createdness as pure transparency, as pure mediation of the divine. At this point the underlying metaphysical logic of participation, as it were, surfaces or erupts into the narrative logic of *mimesis* which it supports (in accord with the swerve of metaphysics into history which allows *sacra doctrina* to fulfil the transgeneric – as described in Chapter Two). For as purely subsisting in the divine, the accidents also achieve a pure flow of ceaseless and self-sustaining creative mimicry. Thus, the bread and wine which persist as accidents, have become always and essentially *food* – figurative food which shapes our imitative humanity – and, in this way, they are the appropriate vehicles of the *Logos*, since like the *Logos*, they now exist in a pure passage, or relationality. For this reason, Aquinas repeats Augustine's statement that the Eucharistic food is not like ordinary food which is cancelled as food by being incorporated into our nature when we eat it. It is rather the other way about: we are incorporated into the food. This implies that we are speaking here about an essential food which never starts to be food and never ceases to be food, because it is entirely the mediation of a God who is in Himself mediation.

The fifth way in which the contrast of presence and absence is outwitted by the Eucharist, concerns the operation of desire. It has already been seen how desire mediates the usage of the word 'This' in the case of the Eucharist; now we will show how for Aquinas the central role of desire helps to ensure that for the phenomenon of the Eucharist and the liturgy there is no fetishization of presence or absence.

First of all, the Eucharist might seem to risk a fetishization of presence, if all that mattered for the sake of salvation were to receive the elements, since this is authorized by the Church. And, indeed, such a fetishization was risked by many Counter-Reformation approaches. Aquinas, by contrast, insists that what is primarily salvific, even if one does receive, is desire for the Body and Blood of Christ.[41] And this tends to make sense of the fact that we can never receive once and for all, and have to go on receiving. If there is no end to receiving the Eucharist, and we have never received enough, this does indeed imply that desire is as good as receiving, just as receiving the Eucharist with the right desire is essential.[42] Thus Aquinas repeatedly suggests that the whole of the liturgy is primarily directed towards preparing in people a proper attitude of receptive expectation.[43] Everything is intended to affect us in an appealing manner directed towards every aspect of our common humanity, including the more sensory aspects; and, as we have seen, if anything, an appeal is made to our minds through our bodies, rather than the other way around.

Indeed, Aquinas construes the circumstances of the instauration of the Eucharist – the drama of the late evening supper, the unexpected directedness of the words used – as deliberate rhetorical means deployed to fix truths in his disciples' and our memories, and incite desire of the truth itself in our hearts.[44] Nevertheless, Aquinas insists that the primacy of desire does not mean that abstention is as good as reception, for it is in the very nature of desire that it should want what it desires, just as we have already seen that desire is only actualized when it is in part fulfilled and can flow freely, not when it is frustrated or contrived. So while avoiding a fetishization of presence, and insisting that it is the personal desire for God which is salvific, rather than adherence to ecclesial authorities, Aquinas nonetheless avoids an opposite fetishization of absence and postponement.[45] Thus God does provide us with a foretaste of His eschatological presence, the beatific vision, and, indeed, Aquinas insists that we only *have* desire for Christ, not because of some abstract promise, but because our imaginations have been engaged right from the outset of the first Maundy Thursday by the use of beguiling verbal and sensory devices.[46]

It will be recalled that in the background of this interest in desire lies the Augustinian deployment of desire to resolve the aporia of learning. Desire is the answer to this aporia, but not desire alone. It has to be desire for God, for only if God is real can we trust that a desire for further knowledge will be fulfilled and that signs are not empty. However, the question of desire for God should not be taken merely in an individualistic way, but rather in collective and historical fashion. Human beings have only been able to believe in God through the mediation of signs conveying His reality which they believe they can trust. Indeed, one might describe our fallenness as a situation of the absence of such trustworthy signs. The Passion of Christ drives that situation to an extreme, because here one has a maximum visibility of the divine presence in humanity that is nonetheless destroyed. The God who can be touched is the God who can be overthrown by touch, and in fact has been so overthrown. This can provoke a kind of death of God nihilism which affirms that we glimpse the truth in and through destruction. However, such nihilism is qualified in the Christian gospel because it offers, even in the extreme of the death of the divine, an image of something trustworthy, in such a way that vulnerability to the point of destruction discloses the eternity of reason. The death of Christ becomes a sign of promise since, in the resurrection, the shedding of Christ's Blood is transformed into the gift of the Eucharist. And in every Eucharist, the extreme contrasts that one sees in the Passion are repeated, and repeated in their reconciliation. Every Eucharist is a representation, a re-actualization of the sacrifice of Christ; therefore it is a continuation of His loss and destruction – this bitterness is also tasted. However, since the loss *feeds* us, such ultimate dereliction is also revealed as the pure essential food that is substantive passage. And this death as food can therefore act as the ultimate trustworthy sign – the passage of the Eucharistic food is also the unique passage of sacrifice to sign which constitutes the very nature of a sacrament.

V

One can sum up this balancing of the Eucharist as the presence of the truth with a non-elided *desire* for the Eucharist, by invoking the mediaeval allegorical linking of the Eucharist with the quest for the Holy Grail. Such an invocation is far from arbitrary, because the period of emergence of Grail literature (roughly 1170–1220) is contemporary with the increasing articulation of a doctrine of transubstantiation.[47] The allegory of the Grail helped to ensure that the seemingly most commonly available thing in every church in every town and village was made the object of a difficult quest and high adventure, a quest indeed so difficult that it was almost impossible to attain, as if it were scarcely possible even to locate and receive the Eucharist. Nonetheless, the ultimate vision accorded Galahad ensures that the postmodern fetishization of pure postponement is also here avoided.

In the above, we have seen how the Eucharist is situated between presence and absence. Because of this situation, it does not pretend that indeterminism of meaning can be cancelled by pure presence; on the one hand, since presence is not denied, the Eucharist remains something meaningful. But now the further question arises as to how this can possibly benefit meaning in general and the possibility of our access to truth. In conclusion, we will try to indicate the outlines of an answer to this question.

Outside the Eucharist, it is true, as postmodern theory holds, that there is no stable signification, no anchoring reference, no fixable meaning, and so no 'truth'. This means that there is no physical thing whose nature one can ultimately trust. We have seen how the Eucharist dramatizes this condition, pushes it to an extreme, but then goes beyond it. The circumstance of this greatest dereliction of meaning is here read as the promise of the greatest plenitude of meaning, since the *Logos* could only touch fallen humanity in being touched by destruction. However, if we do trust this sign, it cannot be taken simply as a discrete miraculous exception, if we are true to a high mediaeval and Thomistic construal of the Eucharist. First of all, we have seen how Aquinas regards bread and wine as the most common elements of human culture. Hence, if these become the signs of promise, they pull all of human culture along with them. Secondly, 'this is my Body' cannot be regarded as a phrase in isolation, any more than any other linguistic phrase. Here, the Saussurean point holds true, that every phrase of language in some sense depends for its meaningfulness upon the entire set of contrasts which forms the whole repertoire of language, in such a way that, for example, 'this' only make sense in contrast to 'that', 'my' in contrast to 'your' and 'his', 'is' in contrast to 'is not' and 'was' and to other verbs, and so forth *ad infinitum*.

For this reason, if this phrase is guaranteed an ultimate meaningfulness, it draws all other phrases along with it.

In the third place, these words and events only occur in the Church. And we only accept transubstantiation because the giving of Body and Blood in the Eucharist gives also the Body of the Church. The Eucharist both occurs within the Church and gives rise to the Church in a circular fashion. In consequence, a trust in the Eucharistic event inevitably involves trusting also the past and the future of the Church. In receiving the Eucharist, we are in fact receiving an entire historical transmission which comprises the traditions of the Church and then those of Greece and Israel. This tradition includes the Bible, in which it is declared that God is in some fashion manifest to all traditions and in the physical world as such. Thus, trust in the Eucharist draws all historical processes and then every physical thing along with it. One could even say that just as the accidents remain, so the supreme event of the Eucharist, which other things anticipate, is only present in a kind of dispersal back into those very things. One is referred back to a primitive trust in the gifts of creation. For all peoples, these things have enabled a beginning of trust in the divine. The Incarnation, the Passion and the gift of the Eucharist ensure that this trust does not run into an ultimate nihilistic crisis and lets us experience that there is indeed *actually* perfection (even though this *might* not be).

This idea, according to which the Eucharistic fulfilment of prophecy turns one back towards the original prophecies and ennobles them (just as reception does not cancel desire; just as the accidents remain; just as the body teaches the mind), is dramatized in the mediaeval allegorical text, *The Quest of the Holy Grail*, which reflects a Cistercian spirituality focused upon desire, and which reads devotion to the Eucharist in terms of a search,[48] just as Aquinas said that we are 'wayfarers' who can only discern the Body of Christ through faith.[49]

On their way to the Grail castle, the knights in the story are led to a mysterious ship which has been voyaging since the time of King Solomon. This ship has a mast made of the Tree of Life from the Garden of Eden, and other insignia which foreshadow Christ. It had been built by Solomon's wife who was concerned that future times should know that Solomon had prophesied Christ's coming. Her female left-handed *ingenium*, which is a crafty capacity to make things, is contrasted to Solomon's male con-templative *sapientia*.[50] The ostensible concern in the story is that we should recognize the prophetic power of our ancestors, but surely the deeper point is that if there were no record of the anticipation of Jesus and the Eucharist, we would not recognize them as significant or true at all, nor discern them, for they are only meaningful as fulfilment; without the record of Israel, there could be no manifest Incarnation. It follows that Jesus and the Eucharist are in some way a ship, just as the Tree of Life was read allegorically in terms of the God-Man. The ship is already the Church and the Eucharist, as a tentative human construction, whereas the fulfilled Eucharist is perfect human and yet divine art. Inversely, one can say that the Eucharist remains the ship, because it persists as quest despite fulfilment. This allows us to link the notion of non-cancelled desire with the idea that trust in the Eucharist points us back towards a trust in everything, and especially the ordinary and the everyday. Such everyday trust therefore becomes the precondition for finding truth. For if we are to go on questing, then all the things pointing towards the Eucharist retain their pregnant mystery without cancellation. We are still knights looking for the Grail, just as we are still Israel on pilgrimage. Since knowledge consists in desire, we must affirm that the aporia of learning is resolved all the time in the promise of everyday human practices. We are usually unaware of this recollection, and yet in a way we do have a certain inchoate awareness of it. Thus we can see that the Eucharist as disclosure of truth through touch and sign is itself desire. Although we only know via desire, or wanting to know, and this circumstance also resolves the aporia of learning, beyond this we discover that what there is to know is desire itself: desire which has already actuated all that for which we long.

Notes

1 Truth and correspondence

1 Bruce D. Marshall, '"We Shall Bear the Image of the Man of Heaven": Theology and the Concept of Truth', in L. G. Jones and S. E. Fowl (eds), *Rethinking Metaphysics* (Oxford: Blackwell, 1995), pp. 93–117. See also, *Trinity and Truth* (Cambridge: Cambridge University Press, 2000) pp. 108–41, 242–75.
2 Ibid., pp. 98–114; *Trinity and Truth*, 90–108.
3 Ibid.
4 Ibid.
5 We are grateful to Dr Arthur Gibson of the Roehampton Institute, University of Surrey, for discussions regarding these issues.
6 Graham Priest, *Beyond the Limits of Thought* (Cambridge: Cambridge University Press, 1995); John McDowell, *Mind and World* (Cambridge, Mass: Harvard University Press, 1994. 1996); for a critique of disquotationalism from a different perspective, see also Hilary Putnam, *Words and Life*, ed. James Conant (Cambridge, Mass: Harvard University Press, 1994), especially pp. 264–310, and *The Threefold Cord: Mind, Body and World* (New York: Columbia University Press, 1999). We are grateful to the Revd John F. Montag for drawing our attention to Putnam's treatment of this topic.
7 Op. cit. 'We Shall Bear the Image of the Man of Heaven', pp. 105–14.
8 See especially Eric Alliez, '1300: The Capture of Being' in *Capital Times: Tales from the Conquest of Time*, tr. Georges Van Den Abbeele (Minneapolis: University of Minnesota Press, 1996), pp. 197–239.
9 Op.cit., 'We Shall Bear the Image of the Man of Heaven', pp. 94–8, especially pp. 95–6.
10 See Chapter Two, Section VI below.
11 See n. 7 above. Marshall's occasional tendency to generalization when referring to these matters is epitomized by his adverbial clause, 'Like the scholastics generally . . .' (p. 95).
12 E.g. A. J. Ayer.
13 E. de Bruyne, *Etudes d'aesthetique médiévale* (Louvain: Editions de l'Institut Supérieur de Philosophie, 1946) volume III, p. 284; Umberto Eco, *The Aesthetics of Thomas Aquinas*, tr. Hugh Bredin (London: Radius, 1988); Leo Elders, S. V. D., *The Metaphysics of Being of St Thomas Aquinas in a Historical Perspective* (Leiden: E. J. Brill, 1993), pp. 136–44; Władysław Tatawkiewiez, *History of Aesthetics* (The Hague: Mouton, 1970), volume II, p. 285. On *convenentia* see Gilbert Narcisse O.P., *Les Raisons de Dieu: Arguments de convenance et Esthétique Théologie selon St. Thomas d'Aquin et Hans Urs von Balthasar* (Fribourg: Editions Universitaires Fribourg Swisse, 1997), esp. pp. 184–92.

14 Fran O'Rourke, *Pseudo-Dionysius and the Metaphysics of Aquinas* (Leiden: E. J. Brill, 1992), p. 100.

15 Op. cit. *Beyond the Limits of Thought*, pp. 130–2.

16 *De Veritate*, Q. 1 a. 1 resp; Q. 1 a. 4 resp. All citations from Aquinas's *De Veritate* are taken from V. J. Bourke's translation, *Disputed Questions on Truth* (Chicago University Press, 1952–4).

17 *De Veritate*, Q. 1 a. 1 resp; Q. 22 a. 1 ad. 12; *S. T.* I-II. Q. 27 a. 1 ad. 3; Comm. in I Sent. 31, 2, I ad. 4; Rudi A. te Velde, *Participation and Substantiality in Thomas Aquinas* (London: E. J. Brill, 1995), pp. 46–53; Elders, *The Metaphysics of Being*, p. 59; O'Rourke, *Pseudo-Dionysius*, pp. 109–13; Eco, *Aesthetics*, pp. 22, 31–2, 37, 46.

18 See further op. cit., *Pseudo-Dionysius*, pp. 109–13; *S. T.* I Q. 5 a. 1, a. 2, a. 3.

19 *De Veritate* Q. 1 a. 1 resp; *S. T.* I-II. Q. 27 a. 1 ad. 3; *In Div. Nom.* IV, 5; Elders, *The Metaphysics of Being*, p. 57; O'Rourke, *Pseudo-Dionysius*, see especially the final chapter; Monroe C. Beardsley, *Aesthetics from Classical Greece to the Present* (New York and London: Macmillan, 1966), p. 102; Eco, pp. 36–46

20 Op. cit. te Velde, *Participation*, p. 273.

21 *De Veritate*, Q. 1 a. 1 resp; ibid., te Velde, p. 273.

22 *De Veritate*, Q. 1 a. 1 resp. Truth is the *convenantiam unius entis ad aliud*. That *convenientia* is the ontological ground of analogy is shown by Q. 2 a.11 resp: '*Si non esset aliqua convenientia creaturae ad Deum secundum rem, suum essentia non esset creaturam similitudo.*' And see Narcisse, op. cit. p. 179. Narcisse shows at length that Aquinas's ontology and gnoseology assume an understated yet central aesthetic dimension expressed in terms of an inscrutable *convenientia* or *proportio* between one being and another, and between Being, Truth and Goodness. One should note that this reading of correspondence in Aquinas as an aesthetic fittingness was already proposed by Franz Brentano in 1889, in 'On the Concept of Truth'. This essay is the ultimate source for Heidegger's account of *aletheia*, or of truth as ontological manifestation. However, such a notion requires transcendence; within Heidegger's immanentism, in the end, *nothing* is manifested, and there is no truth. See Franz Brentano, *The True and the Evident,* trans. R. M. Chisholm *et al.* (London: Routledge and Kegan Paul, 1966) pp. 3–25, and Dermot Moran, *Introduction to Phenomenology* (London: Routledge, 2000) pp. 30–31.

23 *S. T.* I.Q. 5 a. 4 ad. 1; I-a II-ae Q. 27 a. 1 ad. 3.

24 Tatawkiewiez, *History of Aesthetics*, pp. 257–8; Elders, *Metaphysics*, pp. 136–44; de Bruyne, *Etudes*, p. 14; see also Dom Henri Poullion, 'La Beauté, Propriété Transcendentale Chez Les Scolastiques, 1220–1270', *Archives D'Histoire Doctrinale et Littéraire du Moyen Age* XV (1946), pp. 263–328.

25 *S. T.* I.Q. 5 a.5 ad. I: 'Beauty and goodness in a thing are identical fundamentally; for they are based upon the same thing, namely, the form; and consequently goodness is praised as beauty. But they differ logically, for goodness properly relates to the appetite (goodness being what all things desire); and therefore it has the aspect of an end (the appetite being a kind of movement towards a thing). On the other hand, beauty relates to the cognitive faculty; for beautiful things are those which please when seen [*quod visio placet*]. Hence beauty consists in due proportion; for the senses delight in things duly proportioned, as in what is after their own kind – because even sense is a sort of reason, just as is every cognitive faculty. Now, since knowledge is by assimilation, and similarity relates to form, beauty properly belongs to the nature of a formal cause.'

26 *De Veritate*, Q. 1 a. 1 resp.

27 *De Veritate*, Q. 4 a. 2 resp; Q. 10 a. 1 resp.

28 *De Ente et Essentia*, IV, 2.

29 Oliva Blanchette, *The Perfection of the Universe According to Aquinas: A Teleological Cosmology* (Pennsylvania: The Pennsylvania State University Press,

1992), pp. 270–9, 291–6; O'Rourke, *Pseudo-Dionysius*, pp. 269–70; *S.T.* IV. a. 5; a. 6.

30 Aristotle, *De Anima*, III, 8, 431b, 21; Aquinas, *De Veritate*, Q. 1 a. 1; Q. 2 a. 2; see also Anton Charles Pegis, *St Thomas and the Problem of the 'Soul' in the Thirteenth Century* (PhD dissertation, Toronto: St Michael's College, 1934), especially pp. 180ff.

31 *De Veritate*, Q. 2 a. 2.

32 Tatawkiewiez, *History of Aesthetics*, pp. 276ff.

33 *De Veritate*, Q. 1 a. 1; a. 3; a. 5.

34 *De Veritate*, Q. 1 a. 2 resp; *S.T.* I. Q. 17 a. 1 resp: 'A craftsman is said to produce a false work if it falls short of the proper operation of his art. . . . Something that begets a false opinion is false', thus 'gall is false honey, and tin, false gold'; *S.T.* I. Q. 16 a. 1 resp. 'Natural things are said to be true in so far as they express the likeness of the species that are in the divine mind. For a stone is called true, which possesses the nature proper to a stone, according to the preconception in the divine intellect.'

35 *De Veritate*, Q. 1 a. 8: 'But negations or privations existing outside the soul do not have any form by which they can imitate the model of divine art or introduce a knowledge of themselves into the human intellect.'

36 *De Veritate*, Q. 1 a. 4: 'For this reason, a thing is said to be true principally because of its order to the truth of the divine intellect rather than because of its relation to the truth of a human intellect'; *De Veritate* Q. 1 a. 8: 'All this is entirely from God, because both the very form of a thing, through which it is conformed, is from God, and the truth itself in so far as it is the good of the intellect, as is said in the *Ethics*; for the good of any thing whatsoever consists in its perfect operation. But since the perfect operation of the intellect consists in its knowing the true, that is its good in the sense just mentioned. Hence, since every good and every form is from God, one must say, without any qualification, that every truth is from God.'

37 *De Veritate*, Q. 1 a. 2; *S.T.* I. Q. 1 a. 4 resp; Q. 16 a. 1.

38 *De Veritate*, Q. 1 a. 8: 'As is clear from what has been said, among created things truth is found both in things and in intellect. In the intellect it is found according to the conformity which the intellect has with the things whose notions it has. In things it is found according as they imitate the divine intellect, which is their measure – as art is the measure of all products of art . . . By its form a thing existing outside the soul imitates the art of the divine intellect; and, by the same form, it is such that it can bring about a true apprehension in the human intellect. Through this form, moreover, each and every thing has its act of existing. Consequently, the truth of existing things includes their entity in its intelligible character, adding to this a relation of conformity to the human or divine intellect'; Q. 2 a. 1: 'But since God infinitely exceeds the power of our intellect, any form we conceive cannot completely represent the divine essence, but merely has, in some small measure, an imitation of it. Similarly, extramental realities imitate it somewhat, but imperfectly. Hence, all different things imitate God in different ways; and, according to different forms, they represent the one simple form of God, since in His form are found perfectly united all the perfections that are found, distinct and multiple, among creatures.'

39 *De Veritate*, Q. 1 a. 2; *S.T.* Q. 1 a. 2, a. 3, a. 5; Q. 14 a. 16; Q. 15 a. 2 ad. 2; Q. 16 a.6.

40 *S.T.* I. Q. 8 a 3 resp: 'God is said to be in a thing in two ways; in one way after the manner of an efficient cause; and thus He is in all things created by Him; in another way He is in things as the object of operation is in the operator; and this is proper to the operations of the soul, according as the thing known is in the one who knows; and the thing desired in the one desiring. In this second way

God is especially in the rational creature, which knows and loves Him actually or habitually. And because the rational creature possesses this prerogative by grace, as will be shown later (Q. 12) He is thus said to be in the saints by grace.'

41 This does not mean judgement as it were of a fact, but more a matter of recognizing a thing insofar as it is an imitation of God. See *De Veritate*, Q. 1 a. 3 resp; a. 4 resp. Even divine inner illumination requires judgement: see *S.T.* I. Q. 12 a 11 ad. 3; Q. 79 a. 9.

42 *S.T.* I. Q. 5 a. 5 ad. 1.

43 See te Velde, p. 279.

44 *S.T.* I. Q. 14 a. 4; O'Rourke, pp. 226, 234–5.

45 *De Veritate* Q. 2 a. 1; Q.12 a. 1 resp. Also *S.T.* I. Q. 79 a. 1 resp: 'The intellect is a power of the soul, and not the essence of the soul. . . . In God alone is His intellect His essence; while in other intellectual creatures, the intellect is a power.'

46 *De Veritate*, Q. 2 a. 2; *S.T.* I. Q. 12 a. 2 resp; Q. 12 a. 13 resp.

47 *De Veritate*, Q. 4 a. 4: 'Moreover, in both types of procession the difference between procession from God and procession from us is similar. For a human son, proceeding in the manner of nature from a human father, receives only a part of his father's substance, not all of it; but the Son of God, proceeding in the manner of nature from the Father, receives all of His Father's nature in such a way that both the Father and the Son have absolutely one and the same numerical nature.'

48 O'Rourke, pp. 226, 262.

49 *De Veritate*, Q. 2 a. 1 resp: 'If there were anything that could perfectly represent God, that thing would be unique, for it would represent Him in one way and according to one form. For this reason, there is in God only one Son, who is the perfect image of the Father.'

50 Q. 2 a. 5 resp: 'As proof of this, note that the divine knowledge which God has of things can be compared to the knowledge of an artist, since He is the cause of all things as art is the cause of all works of art.' And *De Veritate*, Q. 2 a. 5 resp: 'Now, in order that a thing be known, its likeness must be in the knower, though it need not be in him in the same manner as it is in reality. Hence, our intellect does not know singulars, because the knowledge of these depends upon matter, and the likeness of matter is not in our intellect. It is not because a likeness of the singular is in our intellect in an immaterial way. The divine intellect, however, can know singulars, since it possesses a likeness of matter, although in an immaterial way.'

51 *S.T.* I.Q. 16 a. 1 resp: 'Everything is said to be true absolutely in so far as it is related to the intellect from which it depends; and thus it is that anticipated things are said to be true as being related to our intellect. For a house is said to be true that expresses the likeness of the form in the architect's mind.'

52 *De Veritate*, Q. 2 a. 5: 'The likeness of a thing which is impressed upon our sense and purified by several stages until it reaches the intellect is a likeness only of the form.' One can note here that the *ontological* dependence of our knowledge on sensing and *conversio ad phantasmata* was denied by Duns Scotus, who thought that this was an *historical* deficiency resulting from the Fall. See Duns Scotus, *Ordinatio*, I d. 3 Prima Pars Q. 3 §187. For the wider implications of this, see note 76 in Chapter Two below.

53 *De Veritate*, Q. 2 a. 5 resp: 'Therefore, others, such as Avicenna and his followers, have said that God knows every singular, but universally, as it were, in knowing all the universal causes from which a singular is produced. An astronomer, for example, knowing all the motions of the heavens and the distances between the celestial bodies, would know every eclipse that will occur even for the next hundred years, yet he would not know any one eclipse as a distinct singular so as to have evidential knowledge that it actually exists or not – which a country

bumpkin has when he sees an eclipse. It is in this manner, they say, that God knows singulars; He does not, as it were, see them in their singular nature but through knowledge of universal causes. But neither can this opinion stand; for from universal causes there follow only universal forms, unless something intervenes through which these forms are individuated. But from a number of universal forms gathered together – no matter how great this number may be – no singular can be constituted, because the collection of these forms can still be understood to be in many. Therefore, if one were to know an eclipse by means of universal causes in the manner described above, he would know, not a singular, but only a universal. For a universal cause has as proportionate to it a universal effect, and a particular cause, a particular effect. Hence there would still remain the inadmissable consequence mentioned earlier, that God should be ignorant of singulars.'

54 *De Veritate*, Q. 4 a. 1 resp.
55 *De Veritate*, Q. 4 a. 1 resp; Q. 4 a. 2; *Summa Contra Gentiles*, 4. 11. (6), (16), 12; (5); *S.T.* I-II. Q. 93 a. 1 ad. 2; I. Q. 85 a. 2 ad. 2; I. Q. 34 a. 2 resp.
56 *De Veritate*, Q. 4 a. 2 resp: 'Now, for us every object of understanding really proceeds from something else. For example, conceptions of conclusions proceed from principles, conceptions of the quiddities of later things proceed from quiddities of things prior, or at least an actual conception proceeds from habitual knowledge. Now, this is universally true of whatever we understand, whether it be understood by its essence or by its likeness; for conception itself is an effect of the act of understanding. Consequently, when the mind understands itself, its conception is not mind but something expressed by the mind's act of knowledge. Hence, two things pertain to the nature of our intellectual word: it is understood, and it is expressed by an agent distinct from itself.'
57 On self-expression as a contained emanation and as craft-like, see *De Veritate*, Q. 4 a. 1 resp: 'Consequently, just as we consider three things in the case of a craftsman, namely, the purpose of his work, its model, and the work now produced, so also do we find a threefold word in one who is speaking. There is the word conceived by the intellect, which, in turn, is signified by an exterior vocal word. The former is called *the word of the heart*, uttered but not vocalized. Then there is that upon which the exterior word is modelled; and this is called *the interior word* which has an image of the vocal word. Finally, there is the word expressed exteriorly, and this is called the vocal word. Now, just as a craftsman first intends his end, then thinks out the form of his product, and finally brings it into existence, so also, in one who is speaking, the word of the heart comes first, then the word which has an image of the oral word, and, finally, he utters the vocal word.' See also *S.T.* II-II. Q. 79 a. 9 resp: 'For the act of reason is, as it were, a movement from one thing to another.'
58 *In Phys* II. 4: 'Art imitates nature; and the reason for this is that the principle of artistic activity is cognition. Therefore, natural things can be imitated by art, because, by virtue of a certain intellectual principle, all nature is directed to its aim, so that a work of nature appears to be a work of intelligence, since it moves towards sure goals by definite means – and it is this that art imitates in its activity.'
59 *S.C.G.* 4. 1 (11)
60 *De Veritate*, Q. 1 a. 5 resp.
61 *De Veritate*, Q. 4 a. 4 resp: 'This difference is also found with respect to the intellectual processions. The word considered in us by actual consideration and arising, as it were, from a consideration of a thing known previously, or at least from habitual knowledge, does not receive into itself the whole of that from which it had its origin. For in the conception of one word, the intellect expresses not all but only part of what it possesses in its habitual knowledge. Similarly,

what is contained in one conclusion does not express all that was contained virtually in its principle. However, for the divine Word to be perfect, it must express whatever is contained in that from which it had its origin, especially since God sees all things, not in many intuitions but in one. Consequently, whatever is contained in the Father's knowledge is necessarily and entirely expressed by His only Word and in the very same manner in which all things are contained in His knowledge. In this way it is a true word, whose intellectual content corresponds to that of its principle. Through His knowledge, moreover, the Father knows Himself, and, by knowing Himself, He knows all other things. Hence, His Word chiefly expresses the Father and, as a result, all other things which the Father knows by knowing Himself. Therefore, because the Son is a word that perfectly expresses the Father, the Son expresses all creatures.'

2 Truth and vision

1 See John Milbank, 'Théologie Politique', in *Dictionnaire Critique de Théologie*, ed. J.-Y. Lacoste (Paris: Editions du Cerf, 1998).
2 See John Inglis, 'Philosophical Autonomy and the Historiography of Mediaeval Philosophy', in *British Journal of the History of Philosophy* 1997, vol. 5, no. I, 21–53 and *Spheres of Philosophical Inquiry and the Historiography of Medieval Philosophy* (Leiden: Brill, 1998).
3 For example, *S.T.* I.Q. 1 a. 2 ad. 2, and II. I. Q. 109 a. 1.
4 For example, *S.T.* I.Q. 2 a. 2; Q. 12 Q. 12 resp: *In Boeth De Trin* Q. 5. a. 4; *S. C. G.* 1, 3(2).
5 Rudi te Velde, *Participation and Substantiality in Thomas Aquinas* (Leiden: Brill, 1995), pp. ix–xiv.
6 For example, *S.T.* I.Q. I a. 5 ad. 1; *In Boeth de Trin* Q. 5. a. 4 and *Super Libr. De Causis Expos*, lect. 1, after Aristotle, *Metaphysics* 11.4.1070a 31.
7 *S.T.* I.Q. 12 a. resp: 'Hence also the intellectual power of the creature is called an intelligible light, as it were, derived from the divine light, whether this be understood of the natural power, or of some perfection superadded of grace or glory.'
8 *S.T.* I.Q. 79 a. 4: 'Now the human soul is called intellectual by reason of a participation in intellectual power; a sign of which is that it is not wholly intellectual but only in part.' Were the human soul entirely intellectual it would always be in the act of completed thought, enjoying pure intuition, whereas to the degree that the soul's thinking is intermittent this thinking is merely discursive. Aquinas further describes participation in pure intellect at *S.T.* I.Q. 84 a. 5: resp: 'For the intellectual light which is in us, is nothing else than a participated likeness of the uncreated light, in which are contained the eternal types.' (Hence there must be for Aquinas in some sense an intuition of *esse* along with all the other transcendentals and divine attributes.) Aquinas continues, 'By the seal of the Divine light in us, all things are made known to us.' Further clear evidence that for Aquinas the human intellect enjoys a share of the divine intuition (divine intuition being identical with the immediacy of divine light) is provided *In Boeth de Trin* Q. 6 a. 1 resp (c): 'intellect first contemplates a truth one and undivided and in that truth contemplates a whole multitude, as God, by knowing his essence, knows all things.' Also *S.T.* I.Q. 12 a. 11 ad. 3, where commenting on Augustine (*DeTrin*, xii) 'even in this life we see God himself', Aquinas says 'All things are said to be seen in God and all things are judged in Him, because by the participation of this light, we know and judge all things'. The intellectus/ratio contrast in taken by Aquinas from Augustine and corresponds to an eternity/time contrast as at *S.T.* I.Q. 79 a. 9: 'by way of

judgement, from eternal things already known, we judge of temporal things, and according to laws of things eternal, we dispose of temporal things.' He also mentions that for Boethius, likewise, reason is to intellect as time to eternity, as well as a circle to its centre: see *In Boeth de Trin,* Q. 6 a. 1; also (c). Although Aquinas does not explicitly speak of 'participation in divine intuition', participation in the divine light must amount to this; and it is clear that judgement by *intellectus* is relatively immediate.

9 John I. Jenkins, *Knowledge and Faith in Thomas Aquinas* (Cambridge: C.U.P. 1997), pp. 107–11. Jenkins resists Lonergan's epistemologization of Aquinas's theory of truth which is still fundamentally an Augustinian illuminationist one. And see *S.T.* I.Q. 85 a. 6 resp: 'the proper object of the intellect is the quiddity of a material thing; and hence, properly speaking the intellect is not at fault concerning this quiddity . . . Also in regard to those propositions which are understood as soon as the terms therein are understood the intellect cannot err, as in the case of first principles . . .'.

10 In relation to 'rivalling God' see Aquinas, *In Boethius de Hebdomadibus* 3 for the parallel point that creatures cannot be good by substance without possessing divinity. On division and indivision see *S.T.* I.Q. 85 a. 8 resp and *S.T.* I.Q. 16 a. 2.

11 *S.T.* I.Q. 79 a. 7, a. 8, a. 9.

12 *S.T.* I.Q. 16 a. 1. And *De Veritate* I.Q. 1 a. 4 resp.

13 See *S.T.* I.Q. 16 a. 1 resp: as regards 'ontological manifestness' Aquinas cites Augustine (*De Vera Relig.* xxxvi), 'Truth is that whereby is made manifest that which is' and Hilary (*De Trin,* V): 'Truth makes being clear and evident.' As regards the 'truth of things of themselves', he here says that 'natural things are said to be true insofar as they express the likeness of the species that are in the divine mind. For a stone is called true which possesses the nature proper to a stone, according to the preconception in the divine intellect . . . truth resides . . . secondarily in things according as they are related to the intellect as their principle.' See also *De Veritate* I. Q. 1 a. 1 and a. 4 resp.

14 See *S.T.* I.Q. 5 a. 5 ad. 1: 'beauty relates to the cognitive faculty; for beautiful things are those which please when seen. Hence beauty consists in due proportion . . . Now since knowledge is by assimilation, and similarity relates to form, beauty properly belongs to the nature of a formal cause.'

15 *S.T.* I.Q. 12 a. 13 resp: 'human knowledge is assisted by the revelation of grace. For the intellect's natural light is strengthened by the infusion of gratuitous light; and sometimes also the images in the human imagination are divinely formed, so as to express divine things better . . . while sometimes, sensible things, or even voices, are divinely formed . . .' And see John Montag, 'Revelation: The False Legacy of Suarez', in *Radical Orthodoxy: A New Theology,* ed. J. Milbank, C. Pickstock and G. Ward (London: Routledge, 1999), pp. 38–63.

16 Montag ibid.

17 *S.T.* II.Q. 171 a. 1 ad. 1; a. 2 resp; a 3 resp; I.Q. 12. a. 13 ad. I.

18 Aquinas, *In Metaph. Proemium.* And see J.-F. Courtine, *Suarez et le Système de la Métaphysique* (Paris: P.U.F., 1990), pp. 31–99.

19 Op. cit. and *In Boeth de Trin,* Q. 5 a. 4.

20 *S.T.* I.Q. 14 a. 4.

21 *S.T.* I.Q. 1 a. 2 resp.

22 *S.T.* I.Q. 12 a. 12. resp; ad. 1; ad 3; *In Boeth de Trin,* Q. 6 a. 1 (c) ad. 2; *S.C.G.* 1. 3 (3).

23 See, for example, Nicholas Lash, 'Ideology, Metaphor and Analogy', in *Theology on the Way to Emmaus* (London: SCM, 1986) pp. 95–120, esp. pp. 107–8.

24 See John Inglis, 'Philosophical Autonomy'. Inglis shows how not only Aquinas, but even Scotus and Ockham simply ignore certain more purely philosophical

aspects of Aristotle's treatment of the soul which do not relate to theology. See also his *Spheres of Philosophical Inquiry*, p. 267 where he stresses that Aquinas did not think a Christian could live the life of a philosopher, since he regarded philosophy as an essentially pagan practice as well as theory, belonging to a long-distant past. In addition, see also Olivier Boulnois's 'Quand Commence L'ontothéologie? Aristotle, Thomas d'Aquin et Duns Scot' in *Revue Thomiste* Jan.–Mar. 1995, TXCV, no. 1, 84–108: 'metaphysics is for him (Aquinas) only a programme given by certain definitions of science . . . he never develops a metaphysics properly speaking' (our translation).

25 On ascent and descent see *S.C.G.* 4. 1 (11).
26 *S.C.G.* I. 9 (2) and (3).
27 See Jenkins, op. cit. And see Michel Corbin, *Le Chemin de la Théologie Chez Thomas d'Aquin* (Paris: Beauchesne, 1972), p. 685.
28 *S.T.* I.Q. 1 a. 5 resp: '. . . other sciences derive their certitude from the natural light of human reason, which can err; whereas this one (*sacra doctrina*) derives its certitude from the light of the divine knowledge, which cannot be misled . . .'. See also *S.C.G.* 1 9 (2).
29 Corbin, op. cit. (note 27 above) pp. 677–80, 713–27.
30 *S.C.G.* I. 8 (1).
31 *S.T.* I.Q. 1. a. 2 resp.
32 *S.T.* I.Q. 1 a. 1 resp.
33 *S.T.* I.Q. 1 a. 8 and Q. 5 ad. 2.
34 *S.T.* I.Q. 5 ad. 2: '[*sacra doctrina*] does not depend upon other sciences as upon the higher, but makes use of them as of the lesser, and of handmaidens . . . That it thus uses them is not due to its own defect or insufficiency, but to the defect of our intelligence, which is more easily led by that which is known through natural reason . . . to that which is above reason . . .' On *sacra doctrina* in relation to the liberal arts, see *In Sentenia* I, Prologue: a. 2 *solutio* ad. I: 'The divine light, from the certitude of which this science proceeds, is efficacious in making manifest the many things which are treated in the different sciences of philosophy, which proceed from conception of these things to knowledge.' In this respect (see later in the main text) its scope surpasses the merely architectonic scope of metaphysics. See a. 2 *solutio*: 'this science . . . considers diverse things, and not just universally, like metaphysics, which considers all things universally insofar as they are beings, without descending to proper knowledge of moral matters or of natural things.'
35 *S.T.* I.Q. 2. a. 2. ad. 2, ad. 3: 'From effects not proportionate to the cause no perfect knowledge of the cause can be obtained', Aristotle, *Posterior Analytics* 75a 40–620; Aquinas, *In Post Anal*, lecture 15: 'In demonstration the middles and the extremes must belong to the same genus'; It is required . . . that the principles and conclusion be taken with respect to the same genus.' And see Olivier Boulnois, 'Quand commence L'ontothéologie?' p. 101.
36 Aristotle, *Metaphysics E* I.1026a. 28–32.
37 *S.T.* I.Q. 3 a. 3: '[God] must be his own Godhead' (that is to say, as individual and nature in one, he is really neither in our sense); see also, *S.T.* I.Q. 3 a. 5: God is here said not to be in a genus and at ad. 1 it is declared 'that God is not in the genus of substance' because (one has to interpret here a difficult passage) he is neither 'a' general sense, nor 'an' individual over–against others. Nor, of course, is he an 'underlying' substance to which accident could be added. However, elsewhere he is allowed to be 'subsistent' in the sense of being absolutely without prior cause or dependency.
38 *S.T.* I.Q. 2–6.
39 *S.T.* I.Q. 5 a. 1, a. 2. a. 3. In the *responsio* to article 1 Aquinas says: 'viewed in its primal (i.e. substantial) being a thing is said to be good relatively (i.e. insofar as

it has being), but viewed in its complete actuality a thing is said to be relatively and to be good simply.' On this basis it is at least arguable that Aquinas grants a co-primacy of good alongside being.

40 *S.T.* I.Q. 2 a. 1 ad. 2: 'Nor can it be argued that it [that 'than which nothing greater can be thought'] actually exists unless it be admitted that there actually exists something than which nothing greater can be thought; and this precisely is not admitted by those who hold that God does not exist.'

41 *S.T.* I.Q. 6. a. 4: 'from the first being, essentially such, and good, everything can be called good and a being, inasmuch as it participates in it by way of a certain assimilation which is far removed and defective; as appears from the above . . . everything is called good by reason of the similitude of the divine goodness belonging to it . . .'. And Q. 6 a. 1 ad. 2: 'All things, by desiring their own perfection, desire God himself, inasmuch as the perfections of all things are so many similitudes of the divine being.'

42 For Aquinas and Dionysius, see Fran O'Rourke, *Pseudo Dionysius and the Metaphysics of Aquinas* (Leiden: E.J. Brill, 1992).

43 *S.T.* I.Q. 1 a. 1: 'Even as regards those truths about God which human reason could have discovered, it was necessary that man should be taught by divine revelation; because the truth about God such as reason could discover, would only be known by a few, and that after a long time, and with the admixture of many errors.' And a. 6 ad. 2: 'Whatsoever is found in other sciences contrary to any truth of this science [*sacra doctrina*] must be condemned as false: Destroying counsels, and every height that exalted itself against the knowledge of God (2 Cor. x. 4–5).'

44 For example, *S.T.* I.Q. 1 a. 7 ad. 1: 'Although we cannot know in what consists the essence of God, nevertheless in this science [*sacra doctrina*] we make use of His effects, either of nature or of grace, in place of a definition. See also Q. 2. a. 2 resp. and especially Q. 12. a. 13 ad. I: 'Although, by the revelation of grace in this life we cannot know of God what He is, and thus are united to Him as to one unknown, still we know Him more fully according as many and more excellent of His effects are demonstrated to us . . .'.

45 For an account of the French Catholic attempt to refound Catholic thought on a neoplatonic henological rather than Aristotelian/Thomist ontological basis, and the various influence of this on Stanislas Breton and Jean-Luc Marion (and the convergence with Levinas), see Wayne Hankey, 'Denys and Aquinas: antimodern cold and postmodern hot', in *Christian Origins*, ed. Lewis Ayres and Garth Jones (London: Routledge, 1998), pp. 139–85.

46 For a critique of Marion along these lines, see D. Bijou-Duval, 'Dieu avec ou sans L'Être' in *Revue Thomiste*, Jan.–Mar. 1995, TXCV, no. 1, 547–66.

47 *In Boeth de Trin*, Q 6. a. 3: 'it should be noted, however, that we cannot know that a thing is, without knowing in some way what it is, either perfectly or at least confusedly, as the philosopher says we know things defined before we know the parts of their definition.'

48 See Graham Priest, *Beyond the Limits of Thought* (Cambridge: CUP, 1995), esp. pp. 94–123.

49 Jacques Maritain, *Distinguer Pour Unir* (Paris: Desclée de Brouwer, 1941), pp. 827–943; Etienne Gilson, *Le Thomisme* (Paris, Urm, 1972), p. 126.

50 Rudi te Velde, *Participation and Substantiality*, pp. 201–33; Aquinas, *De Potentia Dei*, Q. 5 ad. 1: *nam quantum uniciuque inest de forma, tantum inest ei de virtute essendi*, translated by te Velde as 'the more of form each thing has, the more intensely it possesses being'. On p. 233 te Velde says 'the form can be said to be distinct form God, not as an independent principle besides God but insofar as in each particular form God (= Being itself) distinguishes himself in a particular way from the simple identity of his essence. Form is something "of God" in

things created by God.' See also *S.T.* I.Q. 7 a 3 for the equation of *esse* with *forma*: 'Since God is himself form, or rather himself being. He cannot be in any way composite.' Also Q. 17 a. 3: 'Just as the thing has being by its proper form, so the knowing faculty has knowledge by the likeness of the thing known.' Finally a passage at *S.T.* I.Q. 8 a. 1 rules out any notion that Thomist *esse* is a Kantian non-predicamental existential qualifier: 'Being is innermost (*magis intimum*) in each thing and most fundamentally inherent in all things (*quod profundus omnibus inest*) since it is formal in respect of everything found in a thing.'

51 Jean-Luc Marion, 'Saint Thomas d'Aquin et L'Onto-theo-logic', in *Revue Thomiste,* Jan.–Mar. 5 1995, TXCV, no. 1, pp. 31–66. Marion claims (46) that Albert the Great's usual and Aquinas's frequent preference for *causatum* over *effectus* for 'effect' indicates the Dionysian rather than Aristotelian character of his account of causality.

52 *S.T.* I.Q. 34 a. 3 resp: 'the word of God . . . is both expressive and operative of creatures.'

53 *S.C.G.* 4.1 (3).

54 See the discussions of Boulnois and Marion in the issue of the *Revue Thomiste* frequently cited above (e.g. n. 51). We tend to agree with Marion rather than Boulnois in stressing the 'circularity' in Aristotle claimed by Heidegger. But Boulnois's article is very important.

55 *In Metaph. Proemium.* Regarding the latency of conclusions within principles, see Aristotle, *Posterior Analytics* 71a 24.

56 *S.T.* I.Q. 2 a. 3. And II. I. Q.109 a. 1 resp.

57 *In Metaph.* L. IV. I IV. 574: '*Philosophia igitur ex principiis ipsius procedit ad probandum ea quae sunt consideranda circa huiusmodi communia accidentia entis.*' These are the *communia praedicta* or transcendental terms that need not, but can be, applied to matter, including substance.

58 See note 50, above, and *De Potentia Dei* Q. 5 a. 4 ad. 3. Here Aquinas has come to stress that *esse* is only an accident 'by a kind of similitude', since it is more 'interior' even than substance and does not 'arrive' to an *essentia* independent of *esse*. On *esse* as accident in Aquinas, see Marion's penetrating discussion in *Étant donné: Essai d'une phénoménologie de la donation* (Paris: P.U.F., 1997) '*Adveniens extra*', pp. 217–21.

59 Again, see note 50.

60 *S.T.* I.Q. 6 a. 3 resp: 'the first perfection of fire consists in its existing, which it has through its own substantial form; its secondary perfection consists in heat, lightness and dryness and the like; its third perfection is to rest in its own place. This triple perfection belongs to no creature by its own essence; it belongs to God alone, in Whom alone essence is existence, in Whom there are no accidents . . . .' By contrast the second perfection of a creature such as fire lies 'in respect of any accidents being added as necessary for its perfect operation', and the third in 'the attaining to something else as the end.' For the first act as *essentia*, second act as *esse*, see *In Boeth de Trin,* Q.5 a. 3. It is very important to realize here that Aquinas is enriching the Aristotelian accounts of motion with neoplatonic notions of communicative emanation. Thus in Aristotle motion is not the communication of an accident but the realization of the intrinsic activity of a substance. This appeared to render the 'event' of causation utterly and inexplicably accidental, thus helping to give rise to Arabic occasionalism. Aquinas moves beyond both Aristotle and the Arabs in terms of 'proper accidentality'. (On proper accident see *De Potentia Dei,* Q 4. a. 4 ad. 3.) Thus for him there is a passive principle of motion which is the receiving of a proper accident and a creative principle of motion, which is the 'actively potential' power to communicative activity, not the formal activity by which being subsists. But as we have seen, this second communicative act can as much or more define a thing's

essence as the original form. We are indebted for discussions on theology and motion to Simon Oliver.

61 *S.T.* I.Q. 79. a. 1 resp: '. . . the intellect is a power of the soul, and not the very essence of the soul. For then alone the essence of that which operates is the immediate principle of operation when operation itself is its being: for as power is to operation as its act, so is the essence to being. But in God alone this action of understanding is His very Being. Wherefore in God alone is His intellect His essence: while in other intellectual creatures, the intellect is a power.' And see ad. I. And also Q. 77 a. 1 resp: '. . . the soul itself, as the subject of its power, is called the first act, with a further relation to the second act.' And, critically, ad. 5: '. . . the proper does not belong to the essence of a thing, but is called by the essential principles of the species. Wherefrom it is a medium between the essence and the accidental thus understood. In this sense the powers of the soul may be said to be a medium between substance and accident, as being natural properties of the soul.' Aquinas also here, and at ad. 1 affirms the agreement of this view with Augustine, since for the latter, knowledge and love do not inhere in the soul as accidents in a substance – as relational terms they are for Augustine neither substantive nor accidental, and yet for Augustine constitute the essence of the soul, since, argues Aquinas, the participated, superadded and later can be more essential than the first essence. Thus despite the usual commentaries, Aquinas does not perhaps here depart from Augustine, in incorporating Aristotle's view of intellect as a mere power of the soul. Moreover, by invoking Augustine he is implicitly linking this view to the idea of mind as an image of the Trinity.

62 Marion, 'Saint Thomas d'Aquin', cited in note 51.

63 *S.T.* I.Q. 3. a. 3, a. 4 and a 6. On the complex issues to do with Socrates not being humanity, see Aquinas, *De Ente et Essentia, passim.*

64 *In Metaph. Proemium.*

65 Here, if we understand him right, we are slightly more inclined to attribute to Aquinas a thoroughgoing Platonic theoontology than is Olivier Boulnois in the article in *Revue Thomiste* also cited: see note 24 above.

66 *S.T.* I.Q. 3. a. 6. resp: Q. 3 a. 7, '. . . just as in sensible forms there is a participation of the higher substances, so the consideration of speculative sciences is a certain participation of true and perfect happiness.'

67 *S.T.* I.Q. 1. a. 7: 'The object of the principles and of the whole science [*sacra doctrina*] must be the same, since the whole science is contained virtually in its principles.' Since (a. 4. resp) 'God, by one and the same science, knows both Himself and His works'. Subalternate *sacra doctrina* (a. 3. resp) 'bears, as it were, the stamp of the divine science, which is one and simple, yet extends to everything'. In consequence (and how drastic is this!) 'objects which are the subject-matter of different philosophical sciences, can yet be treated of by this one single sacred science under one aspect precisely so far as they can be included in revelation'.

68 *S.T.* I.Q. 2. a. 1 ad. 1 : 'To know that God exists in a general and confused way is implanted in us by nature, inasmuch as God is man's beatitude. For man naturally desires happiness, and what is naturally desired by man must be naturally known to him.' See also *S.C.G.* 1. 2 (1).

69 *In Boeth de Trin*, Q. 6. a. 3.

70 See the whole of Q. 12 of the *Summa Theologiae.* Transcendental Thomism tends here to miss this collapse of contrast between object and medium of vision, and to misread the restriction of even the beatific vision, as restriction to a grasp of the divine *Lumen* as *a priori* condition of seeing. But if, at this ultimate juncture, we attain God as subject rather than as object, then this suggests, idolatrously, an ontic residue of objectivity in God apart from his intellectuality. James

Hanvey perpetrates this error in *Radical Orthodoxy: A Catholic Enquiry*, ed. L. P. Hemming (London: Ashgate, 2000) p. 166.

71 At *S.T.* I.Q. 8. a. 1–4. This section still comes under the discussion of divine 'infinity', as the prologue to Q. 8 makes clear, and the prologue to Q. 3 declares that infinity will be dealt with under the treatment of divine essence (or substance).

72 *S.T.* I.Q. 20. a. 2 ad. 1: 'just as "a lover is placed outside of himself", so [citing Dionysius *Div. Nom.* IV. 1.] "on behalf" of the truth we must make bold to say even this, that He himself, the cause of all things, by His abounding love and goodness, is placed outside Himself by his providence for all existing things.'

73 *S.T.* I.Q. 8 a. 3 resp: 'God is said to be in a thing in two ways; in one way after the manner of an efficient cause; and thus He is in all things created by Him; in another way He is in things as the object of operation is in the operator; and this is proper to the operations of the soul, according as the thing known is in the one who knows; and the thing desired in the one desiring. In this second way God is especially in the rational creature, which knows and loves him actually or habitually. And because the rational creature possesses this prerogative by grace, as will be shown later (Q. 12), He is thus said to be in the saints by grace.' Note here that the 'especially' indicates some sort of gracious or teleological eschatological presence to all creatures, while as to humanity 'the saint' is ontologically normative.

74 See my remarks in footnote 73 above.

75 The overcoming of a grace/nature duality (with Blondel, de Lubac and, in a very flawed manner, Karl Rahner), finally arrived at a theologically 'postmodern' questioning of modern assumptions, whereas Karl Barth remained basically within those assumptions and so within modernity. See Henri de Lubac, *The Mystery of the Supernatural*, trans. Rosemary Sheed (London: Geoffrey Chapman, 1962).

76 *S.T.* I.Q. 12 a. 1: '. . . there resides in every man a natural desire to know the cause of any effect which he sees; and thence arises wonder in men. But if the intellect of the rational creature could not reach so far as to the first cause of things, the natural desire would remain void'; one can note here that there is an historical and conceptual relation between the univocalist drift towards an ontic God, on the one hand, and the rise of a 'two-tier' model of nature and grace, on the other. (Thus Gilson's recovery of 'the existential' and de Lubac's recovery of the one natural supernatural end of humanity belong together.) This is the case, because already with Scotus a grace-supplied 'elicited desire' was distinguished from a 'natural desire'. Ironically, however, this probably arose because Scotus *already* read Aquinas wrongly in terms of a grace/nature dualism and wished *to avoid* 'extrinsicism'. Thus he argued against the 'Thomist' view that the proper object of the human intellect is material, although it can extract spiritual form from matter. For Scotus this suggested some purely natural access to the spiritual world, on the one hand, but, on the other hand, *no* natural capacity for pure spiritual intellection, as involved in the beatific vision. Therefore, it must seem that for Aquinas such capacity is merely 'added on' by grace. Scotus suggests, instead, that the need for *conversio ad phantasmata* merely results from our fallenness, and that while, of course, capacity for the supernatural vision is an infused gift of divine grace, it is nonetheless proper to human *potentia* since it can be exercised as a *habitus*. In that case, however, he reasons, our minds must always have the capacity to grasp something non-material, and the materially instantiated cannot be 'the first object of the intellect'. He nevertheless denies, against Henry of Ghent, that God (taken by Henry to be absolutely equivocal from creatures) is the first object, and instead declares that Being taken as

indifferent to matter and spirit, and also to finite and infinite, is the first object. The univocity of this concept accompanying its indifference then provides the natural foundation for the power in all human beings to see God. However, as against the assumed Thomist purely 'natural' desire of human beings to rise to abstracted cognition of spiritual realities (but *not* to the beatific vision), Scotus confines natural knowledge and desire to the realm of univocal formalities as yet having *no* orientation toward God. Correspondingly, desire for the beatific vision is entirely a desire elicited by grace, although this *alone* gives human beings their *telos*. De Lubac explains that when more sophisticated sixteenth-century Thomists like Domingo de Soto reacted against Cajetan's misreading of Aquinas in terms of two human ends, one natural and the other supernatural, they tended to adopt Scotist notions which were, relatively speaking, more loyal to the Patristic integralist tradition. However, the Scotist distinction between proper innate desire and elicited desire still *begins* to undo the paradox of 'a natural drive beyond natural drive' found in Aquinas. And the primary univocal object of knowledge which is Being creates the space for a new natural/supernatural dualism in terms of a formal, virtual, immanent, epistemological nature *disjoined* even from natural ends: this space is finally exploited by Kant. In fact, of course Scotus misread Aquinas: the prime object of knowledge for Aquinas is Being which as analogical can allow an ascent beyond a needed material mediation in this life towards an anticipation of the beatific vision. Although we shall outgrow the need for this mediation, it itself encourages this outgrowing, on the basis of analogical participation. And the 'natural' capacity to abstract is, as we show in this chapter, itself inseparable for Aquinas from supernatural orientation to beatitude. See Henri de Lubac, *Augustinianism and Modern Theology*, trans. L. Sheppard (S. Chapman, London, 1964), pp. 118–64; Duns Scotus, *Ordinato* I. d. 3 first part, Q. 3; Olivier Boulnois, *Duns Scotus: Sur la connaissance de Dieu et l'univocité de L'Etant* (Paris: P.U.F.), pp. 47ff.

77 *S.T.* I.Q. 12 a. 4 resp: '. . . the created intellect cannot see the essence of God, unless God by his grace unites Himself to the created intellect, as an object made intelligible to it.'

78 Jean-Hervé Nicolas, 'Les Rapports entre la Nature et le Surnaturel dans les Débats Contemporaines', in *Revue Thomiste,* Julliet–Sept. 1995, TXCV, no. 3: 399–418.

79 S.C.G. 1 28–37. Here the assertion of creaturely participation and analogy intervenes between 'divine perfection' and 'divine goodness'. For truth under operation see the prologue to *S.T.* I.Q. 14. Here, immediately after treating of the divine names, Thomas says 'Having considered what belongs to the divine substance, we have now to treat of God's operation.'

80 Bruce Marshall, 'Faith and Reason Reconsidered: Aquinas and Luther on Deciding What is True', in *The Thomist*, Jan. 1999, vol. 63, no. I: 1–49. And see *S.T.* II.II. Q. 2 a. 7; Q. 5 a. 1; III. Q. 1 a. 3.

81 *S.T.* II.1. Q. 93 a. 6 resp: 'Both ways [of partaking of the natural law by first knowledge and second inclination] . . . are imperfect and to a certain extent destroyed in the wicked . . . But in the good both ways are found more perfect; because in them, besides the natural knowledge of good there is the added knowledge of faith and wisdom; and again, besides the natural inclination to good, there is the added interior motive of grace and virtue.' So there are only two categories of people for Aquinas: the fallen wicked and the engraced good; not three: the bad against nature, the good by nature and the extra-virtuous by grace. See also I.Q. 94. a. 3 resp: '. . . in order to direct his own life and that of others, man needs to know not only those things which can be naturally known, but also things surpassing human knowledge; because the life of man is directed to a supernatural end: just as it is necessary for us to know the truths of faith in

order to direct our own lives.' In addition, see *S.T.* II. I. Q. 65 a.2 and John Inglis, *Spheres of Philosophical Inquiry,* p. 267.

82 See Marshall, op. cit. and *S.T.* II.II. Q. 2 a. 3 ad. 3: 'unbelievers cannot be said to believe in a God as we understand it in relation to the act of faith. For they do not believe that God exists under the conditions that faith determines; hence they do not truly believe in a God, since, as the Philosopher observes, to know simple things defectively is not to know them at all.' That is to say not as essence, not as cause, not as anything. And see also another passage discussed by Marshall: Aquinas, *In Joan,* C. 17 lect 6 (no. 2265).

83 Eugene F. Rogers, Jr, 'Thomas and Barth in Convergence on Romans I', in *Modern Theology* 12: 1, Jan. 1996. See also Hermann Pesch, *Die Theologie der Rechtfertigung bei Martin Luther and Thomas von Aquin* (Mainz: Matthias Grunewald, 1985).

84 See, for example, *In Meta. Proemium c:* '. . . *ens commune* which is the genus of which the above mentioned substances are the common and universal causes.' Armand Maurer comments on this passage, 'Being is not a genus in the strict sense of the term. It is here called a genus because it is the subject of metaphysics and hence analogous to the subject genera of the other sciences' (in St Thomas Aquinas, *The Division and Methods of the Sciences,* ed. A. Maurer Toronto Pontifical Institute, 1963, Appendix III, p. 88). But our analysis below shows that this may not be the case. First of all, how should one interpret *In Boeth de Trin* Q. 5 a. 4 ad. 6? 'The metaphysician deals with individual beings too, not with regard to their special natures, in virtue of which they are special kinds of being, but insofar as they share the common character of being.' Would it not be the case, that if metaphysics dealt with *esse,* which is primarily infinite, not *ens* or *esse commune* which is an abstraction from the finite, then it would, like *sacra doctrina,* be concerned with 'specific natures', since *esse* includes all plenitude of form, and as transgeneric does not hover remotely beyond specificity? But still more conclusive is *S.T.* I.Q. 3 a. 4 ad. 1: '. . . the divine *esse* has nothing added to it in the first sense' [of repletion as e.g. 'irrational animal precludes the addition of reason'], 'whereas *ens commune* has nothing added to it in the second sense of indifference to what nonetheless might be added', as e.g. the 'genus of animal is without reason, because it is not of the essence of animal to have reason; but neither is it to lack reason'. This is unequivocal: *ens commune* is a genus. But Being is not a genus! And so *ens commune* serves to mask the improperly 'generic' character of finitely participated *esse,* 'really distinct' from the *essentia* or *forma* which it nonetheless activates, and which itself, in turn, 'gives' *esse* to be participated. Thus, when Aquinas agrees with Aristotle that *ens* and *unum* are not *genera,* he is not conceding that metaphysics can adequately treat of them. See *In Metaph.* III. 1. viii n. 433, for this agreement.

85 *S.T.* I.Q. 14 a. 6 resp: 'Some have erred on this point (whether God knows things other than himself 'properly'), saying that God knows things other than himself only in general, that is only as beings.' In that case, this must mean a supposed knowledge of *ens commune* as (or at least as if) it were a genus, since God's knowledge of creatures as beings participating in *esse* is a proper knowledge extending to their full individuality. See also Q. 14 a. 11.

86 See, for example, *In Boeth de Trin,* Q 5. a. 3 esp. ad. I.

87 *S.T.* I.Q. 14 a. 5, a. 6, a. 11; Q. 15 a. 3. I; Q. 1 a. 5.

88 *S.T.* I.Q. 14 a. 16; Q. 16 a. 6; Q. 34 a. 1, Q. 1 a. 4; a. 2, a. 3. And also Q. 15 a. 2 ad. 2. 'By wisdom and art we signify that by which God understands.'

89 See Chapter One above.

90 Marion, op. cit.

91 *S.T.* I.Q. 84 a. 1 and Q. 15 a. 3 ad. 4.

92 See *Super Librum de Causis Espositio* commentaries on propositions 1–6. And see *S.T.* I.Q. 14 a. 1 ad. 1, 2 and a. 3 ad. 3.

93 *In Boeth de Hebdom.* 3–5; Rudi te Velde, *Participation and Substantiality*, pp. 87ff. and *passim*. See also L. Bruno Puntel, *Analogie und Geschichtlichkeit I* (Freiburg: Herder, 1969).

94 See, in particular, Catherine Pickstock, *After Writing: On the Liturgical Consummation of Philosophy* (Oxford: Blackwell, 1998), chapter one, and *A Short Guide to Plato* (Oxford and New York: Oxford University Press, forthcoming).

95 *In Boeth de Trin,* 4. a. 4: 'Thus the principles of accidents are reducible to the principles of substances.'

96 *S.T.* I.Q. 1 a. 6 ad. 2: 'therefore it [*sacra doctrina*] has no concern to prove the principles of other sciences but only to judge of them', and 'whatsoever is found in other sciences contrary to any truth of this science must be condemned as false'. See also, and for what follows, note 43 above.

97 Michael Corbin, *Le Chemin de la Théologie*, p. 726; commenting on the first question of the *Prima Pars*, Corbin says that metaphysics 'semble ici englobée'.

98 At Q. 1 a. 7 ad. 2, Aquinas cites 2 Cor. x. 5: 'Bringing into captivity every understanding unto the obedience of Christ.' John Inglis points out that in the thirteenth century, members of the Dominican order were forbidden to study Arts and Logic as such at the University, and could only study philosophy under special dispensation. This indicates at least some hesitancy about the study of the Arts as an autonomous discipline outside a theological context and also shows that the Dominican order at this time did not envisage any study of philosophy as a living independent discipline as opposed to the deployment of philosophemes within theology. See John Inglis, *Spheres of Philosophical Inquiry*, p. 267.

99 Corbin, *Le Chemin*, pp. 714ff.

100 Corbin, *Le Chemin*, pp. 724, 793, 800ff.

101 *S.T.* I.Q. 13 a. 7 resp. For Aquinas, those who say 'relation is not a reality, but only an idea', are wrong, because 'things themselves have a mutual order and habitude'. This shows the links of *relatio* to *ordo, proportio* and *pulchrum.*

102 *De Veritate* I .Q. 1 a. 1 resp.

103 See Nicholas Lash, 'Ideology, Metaphor and Analogy'. Here he cites David Burrell, *Aquinas: God and Action* (London: R.K.P., 1979), p. 48: 'commenting on Aristotle's metaphysics, Aquinas reflects that a metaphysician differs from a logician only by his power. Not by a separate faculty; a metaphysician is distinguished only by the astuteness with which he employs those faculties we all share and which logic can help to refine. The mode of metaphysics is not intuitive for Aquinas, but logical.' The present authors agree with Burrell that there is no separate metaphysical 'faculty'. However, it is hoped that our analysis above in the text, and citations in the footnotes, shows that for Aquinas, all our thought, in order to be thought, is primarily intuitive, albeit in a very weak degree, and so *in toto* 'metaphysical' or rather 'theological'. What has to be said here is that while ontologist intuitionism represented one Catholic rejection of Kant, the neo-Thomist purging of Augustinian illuminationist elements from Aquinas was itself a rejection of anything that might be tinged with Kant's idealist legacy. Thus (ironically) Lonergan's 'Kantian' and transcendentalist suspicion of vision and intuition is itself also a perpetuation of neo-Thomist misreadings of Aquinas, just as it is ultimately allied to Baroque Thomist reliance on a univocalist ontology prior to theology, which itself eventually generated Kant and idealism. See Eric Alliez, *Capital Times*, trans. G. van den Abbeele (Minneapolis: Minnesota U.P. 1996), pp. 240–1. However, Burrell's truly inspiring work on Aquinas and medieval philosophy since *Aquinas: God and Action* abandons his earlier transcendentalist–semanticist premises.

104 See Courtine, *Suarez et le Système, passim.*

105 *In Metaph.* L. IV.I.IV. 574.

106 See the subtle and vital arguments of *De Ente et Essentia.* Only after Scotus did logic emphatically cease to be concerned with the actual mode of things in the mind and become instead to do with 'algebraic' possibilities. Although there were many tendencies in this direction already in the twelth century, by comparison, the thirteenth century represented a reversion to the real 'metaphysical' concerns of philosophy and theology as inherited from antiquity. This is the fundamental reason why semanticist accounts of Aquinas are anachronistic. And clearly any 'primacy of logic' conflicts with the Thomist priority of act over possibility. For all this, and a critique of Peter Geach's anachronistic approach to Aquinas, see the old but excellent work of Henry Veatch, esp. 'St Thomas's Doctrine of Subject and Predicate' in *St Thomas Aquinas (1274–1974): Commemorative Studies,* ed. A. Maurer (Toronto: Pontifical Institute, 1974).

107 Bernard Lonergan, *Insight: A Study of Human Understanding* (New York: Harper and Row, 1978), pp. 320, 323, 412–15.

108 Lonergan, *Verbum: Word and Idea in Aquinas* (Notre Dame, Ind.: Notre Dame U.P., 1967), pp. 25, 49, 50–1, 64, 197.

109 *S.T.* I.Q. 12 a. 11, a. 12, a. 13. esp. a. 12 ad. 2: 'God is known by natural knowledge through the images of His effects' and a. 13 ad. 1: '[by grace we know God] more fully according as . . . more excellent of His effects are demonstrated to us . . ..' This provides the ontological presupposition for the account of 'divine names' in Q. 13.

110 Here is the text which confirms that one may speak of *analogia entis* in Aquinas and disallows analogy as primarily a reflection on language: *S.T.* I.Q. 4 a. 3 resp: '. . . if there is an agent not contained in any genus, its effects will still more distantly reproduce the form of the agent [their generic, equivocal agency] not, that is, so as to participate in the likeness of the agent's form according to the same specific or generic formality, but only according to some sort of analogy, as existence is common to all.' In this way all created beings, so far as they are beings, are like God as the first and universal principle of all being. See also Q. 4 a. 2; Q. 6 a. 1. The same primary interest in causality and participation is perpetuated in Q 13: see Q. 13 a. 2 resp and Q. 13 a. 5. resp and ad. 1.

111 *S.T.* I.Q. 13 a. 5. resp.

112 For example, *S.T.* I.Q. 13 a. 10 sed contra; citing Aristotle, *Perihermeneias* I: 'The idea in the intellect is the likeness of what is in the thing.'

113 *S.T.* I.Q. 13 a. 2 resp: '. . . it does not follow that God is good because He causes goodness; but rather, on the contrary, He causes goodness in things because He is God; according to what Augustine says (*De Doctr. Christ* I. 32) Because He is Good We Are' and ad. 2.: '. . . these names are not imposed to signify the processions themselves, as if when we say God lives, the sense were, life proceeds from Him, but to signify the principle itself of things insofar as life pre-exists in Him in a more eminent way than can be understood or signified.'

114 Aquinas identifies actuality with light: *Super Libr. De Causis Expos.* Proposition 649 (4–5).

115 On this matter, see Emmanuelle Gabellieri, 'Saint Thomas: une Ontotheologie Sans Phenomenologie?', in *Revue Thomiste,* Jan.–Mar. 1995, TXCV, no. 1, 150–92.

116 Nicholas Lash, *Easter in Ordinary: Reflections on Human Experience and the Knowledge of God* (Charlottesville: U.P. of Virginia, 1998).

117 Here, as elsewhere in the chapter, we are indebted to conversations with Phillip Blond, David Hart and John Betz. See also Conor Cunningham's crucial essay 'Language: Wittgenstein after Theology', in *Radical Orthodoxy,* pp. 64–91.

118 This confused blending of Kant with the *via negativa* is pervasive in recent theology.

119 Marion, 'Saint Thomas d'Aquin et l'Onto-theo-logie'.

120 See Fran O'Rourke, 'Intensive Being in Pseudo-Dionysius and Aquinas', in *Dionysius*, vol. XV, Dec. 1991, 31–81. O'Rourke mentions that Cornelio Fabro, not without warrant in Thomistic terms, spoke of *esse intensivum*. Needless to say, when we speak in this chapter of 'degrees of intensity', we do not of course mean this in the Scotist sense that divine infinite Being is merely a more 'intense' instance of being-in-general. Rather we mean that being as such is unknown to us and only consists in his absolute intensity, in which nonetheless, in varying degrees, we participate.

121 On this, see Phillip Blond's decisive analysis of Levinas, 'Emmanuel Levinas: God and Phenomenology', in Phillip Blond (ed.) *Post-Secular Philosophy* (London: Routledge, 1998), pp. 195–229.

122 Marion, 'Saint Thomas d'Aquin et L'Onto-theo-logie'. 'Distance' between humanity and God is denied by Aquinas at *S.T.* I. Q. 7 a. 1 ad. 3: 'Hence nothing is distant from Him, as if it could be without God in itself', although the locution is allowed elsewhere.

123 See John Milbank, 'A Critique of the Theology of Right', chapter one of *The World Made Strange* (Oxford: Blackwell, 1997), pp. 7–35.

124 See Lash, 'Ideology, Metaphor and Analogy'.

125 For the background to this, see once again, J.-F. Courtine, *Suarez et le Système de Métaphysique*.

126 *S.C.G.* 4, the whole chapter 11. And see Gilles Emery, *La Trinité Créatice* (Paris: Vrin, 1995).

127 *S.C.G.* 4. 1, (1) (2).

128 *S.T.* I.Q. 1 a. 4 ad. 2; Q. 1 a. 8 resp. and ad. 2.

129 *S.T.* I.Q. 29 a. 3.

130 *S.T.* I.Q. 34 a. 2.

131 For example, *S.T.* II II. Q. 109 a. 1. and Q. 79 a. 9 resp: 'for the act of reason is, at it were, a movement from one thing to another.'

132 *De Veritate* 1 Q. 4 a. 2: '. . . when the mind understands itself, its conception is not the mind itself, but something expressed by the mind's act of knowledge.' Hence while Aquinas accepts the Aristotelian identity between the act of understanding and the act of the thing understood, nevertheless, beyond Aristotle, the act of understanding is for him the emanative relation to a conceptual object. This is confirmed by *S.T.* I.Q. 85 a. 2 ad. 2: 'words do not therefore signify the intelligible species themselves, but that which the intellect forms for itself for the purpose of judging things.'

133 Mark Jordan, *Ordering Wisdom: the Hierarchy of Philosophical Discourse in Aquinas* (Notre Dame, Ind.: Notre Dame U.P., 1986), pp. 31–9. At *S.T.* I.Q. 34 a. 2 resp. Aquinas says categorically that the 'word . . . signifies that which emanates from another'. Some other texts speaking variously of 'intuition', 'manifestation', 'expression', 'procession', 'emanation' are *De Veritate* Q. 4 a. 1 resp. and ad. 5; *S.C.G.* 4. 11 (6), (16); 12 (5); *S.T.* I–II. Q. 93 a. 1 ad. 2; *S.T.* I.Q. 28 a. 4 a. I; Q. 34 a. 2.

134 *S.T.* I.Q. 34, a. 1, a. 2. For the comparison of power of mind/intellect to *essentia/esse,* see notes 61 and 50 above.

135 See *De Veritate,* I Q. 1 a. 1.

136 *S.T.* I.Q. 37 a. 1, a 2.

137 *S.T.* I.Q. 39 a. 1.

138 *S.T.* I.Q. 29 a. 4. resp.

139 *S.T.* I.Q. 34 a. 2 ad. I. And *S.C.G.,* 4. 11 (11).

140 *S.C.G.* 4. 11 (13).

141 *S.T.* I.Q. 45. a. 7.

142 See Wayne Hankey, 'Denys and Aquinas' and 'Stephen's Menn's Cartesian Augustine', a review of Stephen Menn, *Descartes and Augustine* (Cambridge:

Cambridge University Press, 1998) in *Animus* 3 (on the internet at http://www.mun.ca/animus) and Werner Beierwaltes, 'Unity and Trinity in East and West', in B. McGinn and W. Olten (eds) *Eriugena: East and West* (Notre Dame, Ind.: Notre Dame U.P., 1994), 209–31 and 'Cusanus and Eriugena' in *Dionysius*, vol. XIII Dec. 1989, 115–52. Hankey's contrast of a Porphyrian Augustine and theurgic Dionysius is unconvincing. Augustine also places the soul within the cosmos and in the *Confessions* finally realizes his own selfhood through losing it in cosmic liturgy. Nor is the Augustinian *cogito* Cartesian, for in Augustine our certainty of our own being, life and understanding is a certainty of intentional opening to these things, which are taken as innately transcendental realities exceeding their instantiation in us. Thus no *res cogitans*, enclosed upon itself, is here reflexively established, as by Descartes. See the excellent article by Susan Mennel, 'Augustine's "I": The knowing subject and the self', in the *Journal of Early Christian Studies*, Fall 1994, vol. 2, no. 3, 261–75.

143 See Hankey, 'Stephen Menn's Cartesian Augustine' (see note 142 above), and Gregory Shaw, *Theurgy and the Soul: The Neoplatonism of Iamblichus* (Pennsylvania: Pennsylvania State U.P., 1995).

144 Hegel, *Faith and Knowledge*, trans. Walter Cerf (Albany: S.U.N.Y. U.P., 1997), p. 168.

145 *S.T.* II.II. Q. 25 a. 7, a. 8.

146 *S.T.* I. Q. 38. a. 2.

147 *S.T.* I.Q. 44 a. 5, a. 8. Although Aquinas reserves the capacity for 'creation' to God alone, since no instrumental help can possibly be given in the bringing about of being as such, Aquinas does in effect say that we are 'co-creators' (participating in the creative act), since we do communicate *esse* in limited ways. Therefore Milbank's account of Aquinas on this matter, in his *The Religious Dimension in the Thought of Giambattista Vico 1668–1744, Part I: The Early Metaphysics* (Lewiston: Edwin Mellen, 1991), pp. 23–6 should now be discounted.

148 Corbin, *Le Chemin*, pp. 800ff.; see also, for the same conclusion elaborated in a different fashion, Catherine Pickstock, *After Writing, passim*. And, in addition, Roland Spjuth, 'Redemption without Actuality: a Critical Interrelation between Eberhard Jüngel and John Milbank's ontological endeavours', in *Modern Theology*, vol. 14, no. 4, Oct. 1998.

149 *Super Libr. De Causis. Expos.* Proposition G 49 (45).

150 Corbin, *Le Chemin*, pp. 788ff.

3 Truth and touch

1 *S.T.* III. Q. 1 a.2 resp. 'God of his omnipotent power could have restored human nature in many other ways'; *S.C.G.* IV. 55 (4).

2 *S.T.* III. Q. 1 a.2 resp.

3 Gilbert Narcisse O.P., *Les raisons de Dieu: Arguments de convenance et esthétique théologique selon St. Thomas d'Aquin et Hans Urs von Balthasar* (Fribourg: Editions Universitaires Fribourg Suisse, 1997). See also Michel Corbin, *L'inouï de Dieu: Six Études Christologiques* (Paris: Desclée de Brouwer, 1979), pp. 109–59 for *convenientia* and the incarnation.

4 *S.C.G.* I. 42. See also *S.T.* I. II. Q 29 a.1 ad. 1: 'Being as such has not the aspect of repugnance, but only of fittingness [*convenientia*]: because all things concur fittingly in being [*omnia conveniunt in ente*]'. Also *S.T.* III Q. 1 a.2 resp.

5 *De Ver.* Q. 2 a. 11: '*Si non esset aliqua convenientia creaturae ad Deum secundum rem, sua essentia non esset creaturarum similitudo.*' On the links between convenience, analogy and paronym, see Olivier Boulnois' article 'Analogie', in *Dictionnaire Critique de Théologie*, ed. J.-Y. Lacoste (Paris: P.U.F., 1998).

6 On this, see the fine discussion by Frederick Bauerschmidt in his book *Julian of Norwich and the Mystical Body of Christ* (Notre Dame, Ind.: Notre Dame U.P., 1999), Introduction.

7 *S.T.* III. Q. 1 a.2 resp: 'And there are many other advantages which accrued, above man's apprehension'; *S.C.G.* IV. 54 (1).

8 *S.T.* III. Q. 48 a. 6 ad. 1, 2; I, Q. 1 a. 9 ad. 3; III Q. I a. 1 resp; Q. 16 a. 4 ad. 2; *S.C.G.* IV. 53 (4); 55 (14), (15), (28), 56 (1) – (5) and see Corbin, p. 157.

9 See John Milbank, 'Forgiveness and Incarnation', to be published in the Proceedings of the second Villanova Conference on Religion and Postmodernity, ed. Jack Caputo.

10 *S.C.G.* IV. 55 (3): 'He loses no dignity however closely a creature draws near to him.'

11 *S.C.G.* IV. 55 (2): 'although the divine nature exceeds the human nature to infinity, man in the order of his nature has God himself for end and has been born to be united to God by his intellect.' And see *S.T.* I. Q. 97 a. 1 and III. Q. 1 a. 2.

12 *S.T.* I Q. 99 a. 1 ad. 3; a. 2 resp. And see Richard Cross, *Duns Scotus* (Oxford: Oxford University Press, 1999) pp. 113–26 for a clear exposition of the difference from Scotus at this point.

13 *S.C.G.* IV. 41 (13): the *Logos* is 'united to the entire human nature with the intellect as medium'. God can be 'more eminently and ineffably united' with intellectual creatures 'from a kind of kinship of likeness', since they 'can properly enjoy the word and share with him'; 42 (3): 'the word has a kind of essential kinship ... with the whole of creation' as 'all creatures are nothing but a kind of real expression and representation of those things which are comprehended in the conception of the divine word'. See 55 (2) for the argument that the human destiny to deification renders the Incarnation appropriate: this stress discloses a certain anthropological starting point for Aquinas's Christology as mentioned at the end of Chapter Two. At 55 (7), Aquinas declares that 'man, since he is the term of creatures in the natural order of generation, is suitably united to the first principle of things to finish a kind of cycle in the perfection of things.' This latter statement should of course caution us against too abrupt a contrast of Aquinas with Scotus on the issue of the ground for incarnation: i.e. salvific or ontological. On this, see Corbin, *passim*. In the *Summa Theologiae,* see especially III. Q. 1 a. 2 resp. where the Incarnation is said to be 'more fitting' ... with regard to the full participation of the divinity, which is the true bliss of man and end of human life; and this is bestowed on us by Christ's humanity, for Augustine says in a sermon: God was made man, that man might be made God.' And see III. Q. 3 a 8 resp. for 'kinship' between the *Logos* and humanity.

14 *S.C.G.* 55 (29): 'the remedies of Christ's salvation . . . must be applied especially to each one, that he may receive the effect of the universal cause.' This is done through the sacraments, and concerning these, Aquinas says at 56 (1) that 'it was necessary to show men some remedies in which the benefit of Christ's death could somehow be conjoined to them'. These signs are *like* (4) the incarnate word in character and are appropriate to our condition and mode of understanding (3). Also they ensure that we will not think 'visible things' are evil because they were the cause of our first downfall. If the sacraments can mediate a strong sense of divinity, then this is because Aquinas takes a very high Alexandrian view of the hypostatic union, especially in the final phase in his work. At *S.T.* III. Q. 2 a. 7 ad. 3, he declares that 'a man is called creator and is God because of the union', although this is 'inasmuch as it [the union] is terminated in the divine hypostasis'. See also Q. 3 1 a. 2 ad. 2 where Aquinas indicates that the human nature could display divine qualities through 'a concourse of natures' possible only 'for a divine person on account of its infinity'. Here the implication seems to be that there can be no restriction preventing the

infinite from adding to itself substantively, even though and even because it is replete. See also Corbin, pp. 116–209.

15 *S.T.* III. Q. 9 a. 2 resp; a. 4 ad. 2: 'The human mind has two relations – one to higher things, and in this respect the soul of Christ was full of the infused knowledge. The other relation is to lower things – i.e. to phantasms, which naturally move the human mind by virtue of the active intellect. Now it was necessary that even in this respect the soul of Christ should be filled with knowledge, not that the first fullness was insufficient for human mind in itself, but that it behoved it to be also perfected with regard to phantasms.'

16 *S.C.G.* IV. 54 (4); *S.T.* I. Q. 1 a. 2: 'faith ... is made more certain by believing God himself who speaks'; hence Augustine says (CD X 19), 'In order that man might journey more trustfully towards the truth, the Truth itself, the Son of God, having assumed human nature established and founded faith', a. 9 ad. 3; Corbin, pp. 161–209.

17 For *esse* as conjoining person and nature, see *S.T.* III. Q. 17 a. 2 resp. For concurrence, see Q. 2 a. 3 ad. 2. At *S.T.* III. Q. 2 a. 1 ad. I, Aquinas is prepared to uphold Cyril's statement that 'from the Divine and human natures (a union in subsistence having taken place) one Christ results'. He also agrees with Cyril (a. 2 resp.) that the hypostatic union is not merely one 'of dignity or authority or power', but is also 'a concourse of natural union'. See also Q. 16 a. 4 resp. For the human nature being in Christ *in atomo*, See Q. 2 a. 5. ad. 2.

18 See Richard Cross, op. cit. and also his article (unfavourable to Aquinas), 'Aquinas on Nature, Hypostasis and the Metaphysics of the Incarnation', in *The Thomist*, April 1996, vol. 60, no. 1, 171–202. And see, in addition, Rowan Williams's article on mediaeval Christology, Jesus Christus III, Mittelalter 2 and 3, in *Theologische Realenzyclopaedie*, vol. 16 (1987), pp. 748–53.

19 For Maximus, see Andrew Louth, *Maximus the Confessor* (London: Routledge, 1996), pp. 54–59, where Louth gives a lucid exposition of Maximus's account of *tropoi* and of his development of Dionysius's 'new theandric activity' as the active existential emergent unity of the God-Man. For some equivalent concepts in Aquinas, see *S.T.* III. Q. 2 a. 1 ad. 2 where he defends, though reinterprets in a non-monophysite sense, Cyril's 'one incarnate nature of the Word of God'; and again Q. 2 a. 3 resp, where he speaks of 'a concourse of natural union' as opposed to a mere union of *habitus*. At ad. 2 he speaks of the human nature 'concurring' with the divine hypostasis.

20 *S.T.* III. Q. 2 a. 12 ad. 2: 'A Divine Person is said to be incommunicable inasmuch as it cannot be predicated of several *supposita*, but nothing prevents several things being predicated of the Divine Person ... Hence it is not contrary to the nature of person to be communicable so as to subsist in several natures.'

21 For these theses, see Duns Scotus, *Ordinatio,* I. d. 43 Q. unica 14–16; Q. 4. d. 3 Pars I.Q's 1–2, 4; I. d. 8 Pars I. Q. 3; II. d. 3 Pars 2 Q. 3; *Opus Oxoniense,* I. d. 3. Q. 1 and 3; d. 8 Q. 3.

22 For Scotus's Christology, see Cross, *Duns Scotus,* op. cit., and Rowan Williams, op. cit.

23 *S.T.* III Q. 4 a. 4.

24 *S.T.* III Q. 4 a. 2.

25 *S.T.* III Q. 16 a.6. ad. 2; 'to be man belongs to God by reason of the union, which is a relation'; Q. 17 a. 2 resp: 'in Christ there is "no new" personal being, but only a new relation of the pre-existing personal being to the human nature', Q. 2 a. 7 ad. 3.

26 *S.T.* III. Q. 16 a.6. ad. 2: 'a man may be made to be on the right side without being changed and merely by the change of him on whose left side he was .... Hence in such cases, not all that is said to be made is changed, since it may happen by the change of something else.'

27 *S.C.G.* IV. 41 (7) (11): '.... for by an axe many can operate, but the hand is deputy to the soul in its very own operation ... the hand is an instrument of the soul and its very own, but the axe is an instrument both external and common ... human nature is compared to God as a proper and conjoined instrument is compared, as the hand is compared to the soul.' For the same analogue in the *Summa Theologiae*, see III. a. 3 ad. 2, where 'foot' is also added.

28 *S.C.G.* IV. 41 (12).

29 *S.C.G.* IV. 41 (12).

30 Aristotle, *On the Soul*, trans. W.S. Helt (Cambridge, Mass.: Harvard U.P., Loeb Editions, 1995), II. xi-xii 422b1–424b19, pp. 127–39 and III. xii 434a23–435b26, pp. 195–203.

31 *On the Soul*, II. xi. 423b5–25, p. 133.

32 Op. cit. 423b5–27, pp. 133–4.

33 Op. cit.

34 II. x. 422a8–19, p. 125; xi 423b17–26, p. 133; III. ii. 426b1–8, p. 151.

35 *On the Soul*, II. xi pp. 423b1–424b19, pp. 133–9.

36 See Daniel C. Dennett, *Consciousness Explained* (London: Penguin, 1993), esp. pp. 280–2. Notoriously, Dennett's book is mistitled and gives us only a populist account of brain science, apart from two pages where Dennett claims that to have shown (debatably) that there is an analogue to 'software' in the brain is to have isolated the cause and site of consciousness. We do not imagine, he says, that cats described in terms of modern biology are not real cats, lacking some 'vitalist' principle, so why should some directing centre of an organic entity overlaid with 'software' be thought to be lacking in consciousness? But the comparison is invalid: vitalism is only a hypothesis, consciousness is an experienced 'pre-reality', within whose horizon all reality arises. Hence it is, after all, entirely to the point to say that one can imagine all informational 'software' functions (allowing that they can only be described in these terms by a judging, desiring animal) and even many calculative and instructive functions of human beings occurring unconsciously. (The instances of ethical and aesthetic judgement must, however, be excepted.) The problem is that consciousness is transcendental disclosure *without* function, which only 'intervenes' in causal processes when it renders subjective judgements on the basis of an ineffable disclosure which it manifests. Hence, *a priori* it cannot be 'explained'. Hence also, John Searle's contention that mind, as subjective conscious awareness irreducible to brain software, can even so in principle be ontologically 'explained', is even more incoherent than that of Dennett. For while, indeed, there are 'emergent properties' to which he compares consciousness, like the hardness of a table arising from the relative speed of molecules, such properties, although observed, are *not* adequately explained in their phenomenality by science, and indeed, only *are* properties for certain kinds of creatures, like us. In this respect, the hardness of the table is just as subjective as the colour red, while, inversely, there is no reason to deny a certain objectivity to 'red', as well as 'hard', if we take it that senses convey to the mind certain 'signs' which allow the mind to reconstitute real *forma* or *logoi* or *eidē* inhering in things themselves. Thus as an 'emergent property' of certain material processes, mind is not 'explicable'. It cannot be compared, as by Searle, to a functional mechanism like the wings on birds which are essential to birds, even though we might imagine that they could be replaced by a kind of motor. This is because the 'common sense' vague definition of consciousness, with which Searle rightly declares we must begin, must be in terms of disclosedness and awareness and these are 'transcendental' attributes in a register that cannot be readily related to functional causality. Thus it *is* to the point that we can imagine a human world of 'Zombies' otherwise the same as our world – except for the presence of human phenomena interpretable as the

exercise of aesthetic and ethical judgement. But this implies *no* 'Cartesian dualism', because for a classical and Christian outlook there are also, *out there in the world,* non-functional, non-efficiently caused realities which are the *forms* or *eidē* of things, 'emergent properties' only to be considered as objectively real and not just 'for us' if we account for them in teleological terms, as existing the way they should and as *intended* to disclose themselves. For the traditional outlook this realm of 'thoughts' (*logoi, eidē)* is out there in the world as well as in us. Thus the 'non-dualism' of this outlook is spiritual as well as material: it is *not* like Searle's material non-dualism which *is* really Cartesian since it thinks of matter as drained of *eidē.* And the disclosedness of things as meaningful forms is *as much* the basis of consciousness as the constitution of our brain as 'mind' able to be aware of this disclosedness. See John Searle, *Minds, Brains and Science* (London: BBC, 1984) and John Searle *et al. The Mystery of Consciousness* (London: Granta, 1997).

37 *On the Soul,* III. i. 4241–426a2 pp. 141–1407.
38 *On the Soul,* II. ix., 421a1–27, pp. 119–21: 'in the other senses [Man] is behind many kinds of animals but in touch he is much more discriminating than the other animals. This is why he is of all creatures the most intelligent. Proof of this lies in the fact that among the human race men are well or poorly endowed with intelligence in proportion to their sense of touch, and no other sense; for men of hard skin are poorly, and men of soft flesh well endowed, with intelligence.'
39 Thomas Aquinas, *A Commentary on Aristotle's* De Anima, trans. Robert Pasnau (New Haven: Yale U.P., 1999), § 54–82, commenting on 421a6–26, p. 250.
40 Op. cit.
41 Op. cit.
42 *On the Soul,* III. x. ii. 434b9–24, p. 192.
43 *On the Soul,* III. x. ii. 426a29–426b7, pp. 149–51.
44 Op. cit.
45 *On the Soul,* III. x. iii. 435a20–25, p. 201.
46 Aquinas, *Commentary* § 85–88, commenting on 421a16–26, p. 251.
47 *On the Soul,* I. x. ii. 403b20–404b28, pp. 19–25.
48 *On the Soul,* III. xiii. 435a20–25, p. 201.
49 Aquinas, *Commentary* 104–14, commenting on 421a16–26, p. 251.
50 Aquinas, *Commentary,* op. cit.
51 Op. cit.
52 On this comparison, see Augustine, *De Libero Arbitrio,* Book Two.
53 See *S.T.* III. Q. 53 a. 6 resp: the resurrected Christ establishes that his body is 'true and solid', 'by offering his body to be handled'; hence he says in the last chapter of Luke (39): '*Handle and see: for a spirit hath not flesh and bones as you see me to have'* (note the poise sustained between touch and vision here). At Q. 55 Aquinas notes, however, that even this sort of proof by touch and sight is still the kind of proof a sensible sign can offer, not an absolute *demonstratio.* At ad. 3 he alludes to the case of the disciple Thomas. And between the angelic Thomas of soft flesh and the doubting Thomas of hardened mind, is there not a certain affinity concerning 'touch'?

4 Truth and language

1 Blaise Pascal, *Pensées,* tr. A. J. Krailsheimer (London: Penguin Books, 1966), § 65.
2 Antoine Arnold and Pierre Nicole, *Logic or the Art of Thinking,* tr. Jill Vance Buroker (Cambridge: Cambridge University Press, 1996), pp. 70–1 and p. 231 re Pascal § 72.

3 Ibid. p. 72; see also G. W. F. Hegel, *Phenomenology of Spirit*, tr. A. V. Miller (Oxford: Oxford University Press, 1977), § 109.

4 Arnold and Nicole, op. cit. p. 231.

5 Ibid. p. 71.

6 Steven Shapin and Simon Schaffer, *Leviathan and the Air-Pump: Hobbes, Boyle, and the Experimental Life* (Princeton, N. J.: Princeton University Press, 1985), pp. 36–7; Steven Shapin, *A Social History of Truth: Civility and Science in Seventeenth-Century England* (Chicago: Chicago University Press, 1995), pp. 194–5; Maurice Mandelbaum, *Philosophy, Science and Sense Perception: Historical and Critical Studies* (Baltimore: The Johns Hopkins Press, 1964), ch. 2; B. J. Shapiro, *Probability and Certainty in Seventeenth-Century England: A Study of the Relationship between Natural Science, Religion, History, Law, and Literature* (Princeton: Princeton University Press, 1983), pp. 61–2; Albert van Helden, 'Annulo Cingitur': The Solution of the Problem of Saturn', *Journal of the History of Astronomy*, 5 (1974), pp. 155–74.

7 Pickstock, *After Writing* (Oxford: Blackwell, 1998), pp. 35–7, 116–18.

8 John D. Caputo, *The Prayers and Tears of Jacques Derrida: Religion Without Religion* (Bloomington and Indianapolis: Indiana University Press, 1997), p. 13.

9 Pickstock, *After Writing*, chapter 3.

10 Jacques Derrida, 'Plato's Pharmacy', in idem., *Dissemination*, tr. Barbara Johnson (London: Athlone Press, 1981), pp. 63–171, pp. 95–6.

11 Pickstock, chapter 3.

12 Henri de Lubac, *Corpus Mysticism: L'Eucharistie et L'Eglise au Moyen-Age* (Paris: Aubier-Montaigne, 1949); Michael de Certeau, *The Mystic Fable*, tr. Michael B. Smith (Chicago: Chicago University Press, 1992); Pickstock, pp. 158–66.

13 de Lubac, *Corpus Mysticum*, pp. 253–4, 266–7.

14 Marion, *God Without Being*, tr. Thomas A. Carlson (Chicago: Chicago University Press, 1991), pp. 161–83.

15 *S.C.G.* IV. 55 (29): 'the universal cause of salvation, . . . must be applied especially to each one, that he may receive the effect of the universal cause', 56 (1): 'it was necessary to show men some remedies in which the benefit of Christ's death could somehow be conjoined to them' (2). Signs are 'like' the 'first and universal cause of human salvation' which is 'the incarnate word'.

16 *S.C.G.* 61 (3).

17 *S.C.G.* 56 (7).

18 *S.C.G.* 58 (4).

19 *S.C.G.* 55 (30).

20 *S.C.G.* 55 (29), (30).

21 *S.T.* III. Q. 48 ab. ad. 2: 'Christ's passion, although corporeal, has yet a spiritual effect from the Godhead united; and therefore it secures its efficacy by spiritual contact – namely by faith and the sacraments of faith, as the Apostle says (Rom. iii. 25); *whom God has proposed to be a propitiation through faith in his blood.*'

22 *S.T.* III. Q. 78 a. 5.

23 *S.T.* III. Q. 75 a. 1; Q. 76 a. 7.

24 *S.T.* III. Q. 80 a. 4.

25 *S.T.* III. Q. 83 a. 4.

26 *S.T.* III. a. 83, a. 4 ad. 8.

27 *S.T.* III. Q. 73 a. 1-a. 2; Q. 74 a. 1; a. 4; a. 5; Q. 75a 8 ad. 1; Q. 76 a. ad. 1; Q 77 a. 6; Q. 79 a. 1.

28 *S.T.* III. Q. 74 a. 3 ad 1; a. 79 a. 2; Q. 81 a. 1 ad. 3; a. 83 a. 5 ad. 2.

29 *S.T.* III. Q. 74a. 8.

30 *S.T.* III. Q. 74a. 6; a. 8; Q. 77 a. 5. For the comparison of priesthood and marriage see *S.C.G.* 58 (6).

31 *S.T.* III. Q. 74 a. 2; a. 3.

32 *S.T.* III. a. 75 a. 8 ad. 4; Q. 77 a. 1; ad. 4; Q. 77a. 3 ad. 2; a. 5.

33 *S.T.* III. Q. 75 a. 8; III. Q. 78a. 2 ad. 2; III Q. 77a. 3; a. 5.

34 *S.T.* III. Q. 77 a. 1, especially ad. 2.

35 P. J. FitzPatrick, *In Breaking of Bread: The Eucharist and Ritual* (Cambridge: Cambridge University Press, 1993), pp. 12–17.

36 See, further, Mark Jordan, 'Theology and Philosophy', in Norman Kretzman and Eleonore Stump (eds) *The Cambridge Companion to Aquinas* (Cambridge: Cambridge University Press, 1993), pp. 232–51; A. N. Williams, 'Mystical Theology Redux: The Pattern of Aquinas's *Summa Theologiae', Modern Theology*, 13.1 (January 1997), pp. 53–74.

37 *S.T.* III. Q. 77 a. 1, esp. ad. 2.

38 *S.T.* III. Q. 77 a. 1 ad. 2.

39 *S.T.* III. Q. 73 a. 1; a. 2; Q. 74 a. 1; a. 4; a. 5; Q. 75 a. 8 ad. 1; Q. 76 a 2 ad. 1; Q. 77 a. 6; Q. 79 a. 1.

40 *S.T.* III. Q. 75a. 8; Q. 78a. 2 ad 2.

41 *S.T.* III. Q. 73 a. 3 ad. 2; Q. 78 a. 3; Q. 79 a. 3; Q. 80 a. 2 ad. 3; aa. 2 ad. 1; a. 9 ad 1.

42 *S.T.* III. Q. 80 a. 4.

43 *S.T.* III. Q. 76 a. 8; Q. 78 a. 1, especially ad. 4; Q. 79 a. 4; a. 5; Q. 80 a. 11; Q. 83 a. 2; Q. 83 a. 4 ad. 1; ad. 6; ad. 7.

44 *S.T.* III. Q. 73 a. 5; Q. 83 a. 2 ad. 3.8

45 *S.T.* III. a. 80 a. 11 ad. 1.

46 *S.T.* III. Q. 75 a. 1.

47 Ronald Hutton, *The Pagan Religions of the Ancient British Isles: Their Nature and Legacy* (Oxford: Blackwell, 1991, 1993), p. 319.

48 Sister Isabel Mary SLG, 'The Knights of God: Citeaux and the Quest of the Holy Grail', in Sister Benedicta Ward SLG, (ed.) *The Influence of Saint Bernard* (Oxford: SLG Press, 1976), pp. 53–88; Andrew Sinclair, *The Discovery of the Grail* (London: Century, 1998), *passim*.

49 *S.T.* III. Q. 76 a. 7.

50 *The Quest of the Holy Grail*, tr. P. M. Matarasso (Harmondsworth: Penguin, 1969), especially p. 230.

Bibliography

Alliez, Eric, '1300: The Capture of Being', in idem., *Capital Times: Tales from the Conquest of Time*, tr. George Van Den Abbeele (Minneapolis: University of Minnesota Press, 1996).

Aquinas, St Thomas, *Opera Omnia*, Roberto Busa (ed.) (Milan: Edizione Elettronica Editel, 1992).

—— *Opera Omnia: Editio Altera Retracta* (Paris: J. Vrin, 1989.).

—— *Summa Theologiae* (Latin and English dual text) (London/New York: Blackfriars/Eyre and Spottiswood/McGraw Hill, 1964–81).

—— *Summa Theologica* (literal English translation) Fathers of the English Dominican Province (tr.) (Westminster, Md: Christian Classics, 1981).

—— *Summa Contra Gentiles*, Anton C. Pegis *et al.* (tr.) (Notre Dame, Ind.: Notre Dame University Press, 1984).

—— *Disputed Questions on Truth*, N. T. Bourke (tr.) (Chicago: Chicago University Press, 1952–4.

—— *On the Power of God*, English Dominican Fathers (tr.) (London: Burns Oates and Washbourne, 1932–4).

—— *Quodlibetal Questions 1 and 2*, Sandra Edwards (tr.) (Toronto: Pontifical Institute of Mediaeval Studies, 1983).

—— *On Being and Essence*, A. Maurer (tr.) (Toronto: Pontifical Institute of Mediaeval Studies, 1968).

—— *A Commentary on Aristotle's De Anima*, Robert Pasnau (tr.) (New Haven: Yale University Press, 1999).

—— *Commentary on the Metaphysics of Aristotle*, John P. Rowan (tr.) (Chicago: H. Regnery Co., 1961).

—— *Commentary on the Book of Causes*, V. A. Guagliardo *et al.* (tr.) (Washington D.C.: Catholic University of America Press, 1996).

—— *Commentary on the Posterior Analytics of Aristotle,* trans. F. R. Larcher O.P. *et al.* (Albany, New York: Magi, 1970).

—— *Faith, Reason and Theology: Questions I–IV of His Commentary* on the *De Trinitate of Boethius* (Toronto: Pontifical Institute, 1987).

—— *The Division and Methods of the Sciences: Questions V and VI of His Commentary on the De Trinitate of Boethius*, A. Maurer (tr.) (Toronto: Pontifical Institute, 1963).

Aristotle, *On the Soul*, tr. W. S. Helt (Cambridge, Mass.: Harvard U.P., Loeb Editions, 1995).

Arnold, Antoine, and Nicole, Pierre, *Logic or the Art of Thinking*, tr. Jill Vance Buroker (Cambridge: Cambridge University Press, 1996).

Augustine, *On the Free Choice of the Will*, Thomas Williams (tr.) (Indiana: Hackett, 1993).

Bauerschmidt, Frederick, *Julian of Norwich and the Mystical Body of Christ* (Notre Dame, Ind.: Notre Dame University Press, 1999).

Beardsley, Monroe C., *Aesthetics from Classical Greece to the Present* (New York and London: Macmillan, 1966).

Beierwaltes, Werner, 'Unity and Trinity in East and West', in *Eriugena* (1994), ed. B. McGinn and W. Olten (Notre Dame, Ind.: Notre Dame University Press, 1994).

—— 'Cusanus and Eriugena', in *Dionysius* XIII (Dec. 1989), pp. 115–52.

Bijou-Duval, D., 'Dieu avec ou sans L'Être', in *Revue Thomiste*, TXCV, no. 1 (Jan.–Mar. 5 1995), pp. 547–66.

Blanchette, Oliva, *The Perfection of the Universe According to Aquinas: A Teleological Cosmology* (Pennsylvania: The Pennsylvania State University Press, 1992).

Blond, Phillip (ed.) *Post-Secular Philosophy* (London: Routledge, 1998).

Boulnois, Olivier, 'Quand Commence L'Ontothéologie? Aristotle, Thomas d'Aquin et Duns Scot', in *Revue Thomiste* TXCV, no. 1 (Jan.–Mar. 1995), pp. 84–108.

—— *Sur la Connaissance de Dieu et l'Univocité de l'Etant* (Paris: P.U.F., 1988).

—— 'Analogie', in J.-Y. Lacoste (ed.) *Dictionnaire Critique de Théologie* (Paris: P.U.F., 1998).

Brentano, Franz, *The True and the Evident,* tr. R. M. Chisholm *et al.* (London: Routledge and Kegan Paul, 1966) 3–25.

Burrell, David, *Analogy and Philosophical Language* (New Haven: Yale University Press, 1973).

—— *Aquinas: God and Action* (Notre Dame, Ind.: Notre Dame University Press, 1979).

—— *Knowing the Unknowable God: Ibn-Sina, Maimonides, Aquinas* (Notre Dame, Ind.: Notre Dame University Press, 1986).

—— *Freedom and Creation in Three Traditions* (Notre Dame, Ind.: Notre Dame University Press, 1993).

Caputo, John D., *The Prayers and Tears of Jacques Derrida: Religion Without Religion* (Bloomington and Indianapolis: Indiana University Press, 1997).

Certeau, Michael de, *The Mystic Fable,* tr. Michael B. Smith (Chicago: Chicago University Press, 1992).

Chenu, Marie-Dominique, *Towards Understanding St Thomas,* tr. A. M. Landry and D. Hughes (Chicago: H. Regnery Co., 1964).

Corbin, Michel, *Le Chemin de la Theologie Chez Thomas d'Aquin* (Paris: Beauchesne, 1972).

—— *L'Inoui de Dieu: Six Études Christologiques* (Paris: Desclée de Brouwer, 1979).

J. F. Courtine, *Suarez et le Système de la Métaphysique* (Paris: P.U.F., 1990), pp. 31–99.

Cross, Richard, 'Aquinas on Nature, Hypostasis and the Metaphysics of the Incarnation', in *The Thomist*, April 1996, vol. 60, no. 1, pp. 171–202.

—— *Duns Scotus* (Oxford: Oxford University Press, 1999).

Cunningham, Conor, 'Language: Wittgenstein after Theology', in *Radical Orthodoxy*, ed. J. Milbank *et al.* (London: Routledge, 1999) pp. 64–9.

Dennett, Daniel C., *Consciousness Explained* (London: Penguin, 1993).

Derrida, Jacques, 'Plato's Pharmacy', in *Dissemination*, tr. Barbara Johnson (London: Athlone Press, 1981), p. 63.

Eckhart, *Parisian Questions and Prologues*, tr. Armand Maurer (Toronto: Pontifical Institute, 1974).

Eco, Umberto, *The Aesthetics of Thomas Aquinas*, tr. Hugh Bredin (London: Radius, 1988).

Elders, Leo J., *The Metaphysics of Being of St Thomas Aquinas in a Historical Perspective* (New York/Leiden: E. J. Brill, 1993).

Emery, Gilles, *La Trinité Creatrice* (Paris: J. Vrin, 1995).

Fabro, Cornelio, *Participation et Causalité selon S. Thomas d'Aquin*, Préface de L. de Raeymaeker (Louvain: Publications universitaires de Louvain, 1961).

Finance, Joseph, *Être et Agir dans la Philosophie de St Thomas* (Rome: Presses de L'Universitaire Gregorienne, 1965).

FitzPatrick P. J., *In Breaking of Bread: The Eucharist and Ritual* (Cambridge: Cambridge University Press, 1993).

Gilson, Etienne, *The Christian Philosophy of St Thomas*, tr. C. K. Shoock (New York: Octagon, 1983).

Gabellieri, Emmanuelle, 'Saint Thomas: une Ontotheologie sans Phenomenologie?' *Revue Thomiste* TXCV, no. 1 (Jan.–Mar., 1995), pp. 150–92.

Hankey, Wayne, 'Denys and Aquinas: Anti-modern Cold and Postmodern Hot', in *Christian Origins*, ed. Lewis Ayres and Gareth Jones (London: Routledge, 1998).

—— 'Stephen Menn's Cartesian Augustine' (review of Stephen Menn, Descartes and Augustine) (Cambridge: Cambridge University Press, 1998) in *Animus* (http://www.mun.ca/animus).

Hegel, G. W. F., *Phenomenology of Spirit*, tr. A. V. Miller (Oxford: Oxford University Press, 1977).

Helden, Albert van, ' "Annulo Cingitur" The Solution of the Problem of Saturn' *Journal of the History of Astronomy*, 5 (1974), pp. 155–74.

Hutton, Ronald, *The Pagan Religions of the Ancient British Isles: Their Nature and Legacy* (Oxford: Blackwell, 1991, 1993).

Inglis, John, 'Philosophical Autonomy and the Historiography of Medieval Philosophy', in *Scottish Journal of the History of Philosophy*, 5.1 (1997), pp. 21–53.

—— *Spheres of Philosophical Inquiry and the Historiography of Mediaeval Philosophy* (Leiden/Boston: E. J. Brill, 1998).

Jenkins, John I., *Knowledge and Faith in Thomas Aquinas* (Cambridge: Cambridge University Press, 1997).

Jones, L. G. and Fowl, S. E. (eds) *Rethinking Metaphysics* (Oxford: Blackwell, 1995).

Jordan, Mark, *Ordering Wisdom: the Hierarchy of Philosophical Discourses in Aquinas* (Notre Dame, Ind.: Notre Dame University Press, 1986).

—— *The Alleged Aristotelianism of Thomas Aquinas* (Toronto: Pontifical Institute of Mediaeval Studies, 1992).

—— 'Theology and Philosophy', in *The Cambridge Companion to Aquinas,* ed. N. Kretzman and E. Stump (1993).

Kretzman, Norman, and Stump, Eleonore (eds) *The Cambridge Companion to Aquinas* (Cambridge: Cambridge University Press, 1993).

Lacoste, J.-Y. (ed.) *Dictionnaire Critique de Théologie* (Paris: Editions du Cerf, 1998).

Lash, Nicholas, 'Ideology, Metaphor and Analogy', in *Theology on the Way to Emmaus* (London: S.C.M., 1986).

—— *Easter in Ordinary: Reflections on Human Experience and the Knowledge of God* (Charlottesville: University Press of Virginia, 1988).

Lonergan, Bernard, *Insight: A Study of Human Understanding* (New York: Harper and Row, 1978).

—— *Verbum: Word and Idea in Aquinas* (Notre Dame, Ind.: Notre Dame University Press, 1967).

Louth, Andrew, *Maximus the Confessor* (London: Routledge, 1996).

Lubac, Henri de, *Corpus Mysticism: L'Eucharistie et L'Eglise au Moyen-Age* (Paris: Aubier-Montaigne, 1949).

—— *The Mystery of the Supernatural*, tr. Rosemary Sheed (London: Geoffrey Chapman, 1962).

McDowell, John, *Mind and World* (Cambridge, Mass.: Harvard University Press, 1994/1996).

Mcginn, B. and Olten, W. (eds) *Eriugena: East and West* (Notre Dame, Ind.: Notre Dame University Press, 1994).

Mandelbaum, Maurice, *Philosophy, Science and Sense Perception: Historical and Critical Studies* (Baltimore: Johns Hopkins Press, 1964).

Marion, Jean-Luc, *God Without Being*, tr. Thomas A. Carlson (Chicago: Chicago University Press, 1991).

—— 'Saint Thomas d'Aquin et L'Onto-théo-logico', in *Revue Thomiste*, TXCV, no. 1 (Jan.–Mar. 1995), pp. 31–66.

—— *Étant donné: Essai d'une phénoménologie de la donation* (Paris: P.U.F., 1997).

Maritain, Jacques *Distinguish to Unite, or the Degrees of Knowledge* (New York: Scribner, 1959).

Marshall, Bruce D., ' "We Shall Bear the Image of the Man of Heaven": Theology and the Concept of Truth', in L. G. Jones and S. E. Fowl (eds) *Rethinking Metaphysics* (Oxford: Blackwell, 1995), pp. 93–117.

—— 'Faith and Reason Reconsidered: Aquinas and Luther on Deciding What is True', *The Thomist*, 63.1 (Jan. 1999), pp. 1–49.

—— *Trinity and Truth* (Cambridge: Cambridge University Press, 2000).

Matarasso, P. M. (tr.) *The Quest of the Holy Grail* (Harmondsworth: Penguin, 1969).

Maurer, Armand I. (ed.) *Thomas Aquinas: The Division and Methods of the Sciences* (Toronto: Toronto Pontifical Institute, 1963).

—— (ed.) *St Thomas Aquinas (1274–1974): Commemorative Studies* (Toronto: Pontifical Institute, 1974).

Mennel, Susan, 'Augustine's "I": The knowing subject and the self', *Journal of Early Christian Studies*, 2.3 (Fall 1994), pp. 261–75.

Milbank, John, *The Religious Dimension in the Thought of Giambattista Vico 1668–1744* (Lewiston: Edwin Mellen, 1991).

—— *The Word Made Strange* (Oxford: Blackwell, 1997).

—— 'Théologie Politique', in J.-Y. Lacoste (ed.) *Dictionnnaire Critique de Théologie* (Paris: Editions du Cerf, 1998).

—— (ed. with Catherine Pickstock and Graham Ward) *Radical Orthodoxy* (London: Routledge, 1999).

Mondin, Battista, *La Cristologia di San Tommaso: Origine, Dottrine, Principali, Attualita* (Rome: Urbanica University Press, 1997).

Montag, John, 'Revelation: The False Legacy of Suarez', in *Radical Orthodoxy*, ed. J. Milbank *et al.* (London: Routledge, 1999).

Moran, Dermot, *Introduction to Phenomenology* (London, Routledge, 2000).

Narcisse, Gilbert, O. P., *Les Raisons de Dieu: Arguments de Convenance et Esthétique Théologie selon St Thomas d'Aquin et Hans Urs von Balthasar* (Fribourg: Editions Universitaires Fribourg Swisse, 1997).

Nicolas, Jean-Hervé, 'Les Rapports entre la Nature et le Surnaturel dans les Débats Contemporaines', *Revue Thomiste*, TXCV, no. 3 (Juillet–Sept. 1995), pp. 399–418.

O'Rourke, Fran, 'Intensive Being in Pseudo-Dionysius and Aquinas', *Dionysius*, XV (Dec. 1991), pp. 31–81.

—— *Pseudo-Dionysius and the Metaphysics of Aquinas* (Leiden: E. J. Brill, 1992).

Pascal, Blaise, *Pensées*, tr. A. J. Krailsheimer (Harmondsworth: Penguin Books, 1966).

Pegis, Anton Charles, *St Thomas and the Problem of the 'Soul' in the Thirteenth Century* (PhD dissertation, Toronto: St Michael's College, 1934).

Pesch, Hermann, *Die Theologie de Rechtfertigung bei Martin Luther and Thomas von Aquin* (Mainz: Malthias Grunewald, 1985).

Pickstock, Catherine, *After Writing; On the Liturgical Consummation of Philosophy* (Oxford: Blackwell, 1998).

—— *A Short Guide to Plato* (New York and Oxford: Oxford University Press, forthcoming).

Pieper, Josef, *The Silence of St Thomas; Three Essays*, tr. John Murray and Daniel O'Connor (Chicago: H. Regnery Co. 1965).
—— *Guide to Thomas Aquinas* (New York: Pantheon, 1962).
Pouivet, Roger, *Âpres Wittgenstein, Saint Thomas* (Paris: P.U.F., 1997).
Poullion, Dom Henri, 'La Beauté, Propriété Transcendentale Chez Les Scolastiques, 1220–1270', *Archives D'Histoire Doctrinale et Littéraire du Moyen Age*, XV (1946), pp. 263–328.
Putallaz, F. X., *Le Sens de la Reflexion chez Thomas d'Aquin* (Paris: J. Vrin, 1991).
Preller, Victor, *Divine Science and the Science of God: A Reformulation of Thomas Aquinas* (Princeton, N.J.: Princeton University Press, 1967).
Priest, Graham, *Beyond the Limits of Thought* (Cambridge: Cambridge University Press, 1995).
Puntel, L. Bruno, *Analogie und Geschichtlichkeit*, I (Freiburg: Herder, 1969).
Rogers, Eugene F., 'Thomas and Barth in Convergence on Romans I', *Modern Theology*, 12:1 (Jan. 1996).
Scotus, John Duns, *Opera Omnia* (Hildesheim: G. Olms, 1968).
Shapin, Steven, and Schaffer, Simon, *Leviathan and the Air-Pump: Hobbes, Boyle, and the Experimental Life* (Princeton, N.J.: Princeton University Press, 1985).
Shapin, Steven, *A Social History of Truth: Civility and Science in Seventeenth-Century England* (Chicago: Chicago University Press, 1995).
Shapiro, B. J., *Probability and Certainty in Seventeenth-Century England: A Study of the Relationship between Natural Science, Religion, History, Law, and Literature* (Princeton, N.J.: Princeton University Press, 1983).
Shaw, Gregory, *Theurgy and the Soul: The Neoplatonism of Iamblichus* (Pennsylvania: Pennsylvania State University Press, 1995).
Schoot, Henk J. M., *Christ the 'Name' of God: Thomas Aquinas on Naming Christ* (Leuven: Peters, 1993).
Sinclair, Andrew, *The Discovery of the Grail* (London: Century, 1998).
Tatawkiewiez, Wladyslaw, *History of Aesthetics* (The Hague: Mouton, 1970).
Te Velde, Rudi A., *Participation and Substantiality in Thomas Aquinas* (London: E. J. Brill, 1995).
Torrell, Jean-Pierre, *St Thomas Aquinas: the Person and his Works*, tr. Robert Royal (Washington D.C.: Catholic University of America Press, 1996).
Ward, Sister Benedicta, *The Influence of Saint Bernard* (Oxford: SLG Press, 1976).
Henry Veatch, 'St Thomas's Doctrine of Subject and Predicate', in *St Thomas Aquinas (1274–1974): Commemorative Studies*, ed. A. J. Maurer (1974).
Vernier, Jean-Marie, *Théologie et Metaphysique de la Creation chez Thomas d'Aquin* (Paris: P. Tequi, 1995).
Williams, A. N., 'Mystical Theology Redux: The Pattern of Aquinas', *Summa Theologiae'*, *Modern Theology*, 13.1 (January 1997), pp. 53–74.
—— *The Ground of Union: Deification in Aquinas and Palamas* (New York: Oxford University Press, 1999).
Williams, Rowan, 'Jesus Christus III, Mittelatter 2 and 3', in *Theologische Realenzyclopaedie*, vol. 16 (1987), pp. 748–53.

Index